Also by Steven Bell

9781785316821

9781785315237

STEVEN BELL

THE EXPLOSIVE LIVES OF
THE BRITISH BULLDOGS

Foreword by Ross Hart
Afterword by Bronwyne Billington

First published by Pitch Publishing, 2022

Pitch Publishing
9 Donnington Park,
85 Birdham Road,
Chichester,
West Sussex,
PO20 7AJ
www.pitchpublishing.co.uk
info@pitchpublishing.co.uk

A CIP catalogue record is available for this book
from the British Library.

ISBN 978-1-80150-080-7

Typesetting and origination by Pitch Publishing
Printed and bound in Great Britain by TJ Books, Padstow

Contents

For my boy, Bruno;
At just two, you already deliver a
mean diving headbutt, and you love
Daddy's running powerslam.

FOREWORD

I MUST ADMIT, when I was first approached by Steven Bell about his desire to write a book about the lives and times of the Dynamite Kid and Davey Boy Smith, I was somewhat sceptical. Many previous accounts about them have been somewhat inaccurate, biased and sensationalised. However, I was so impressed at the considerable research Steven was doing, tracking their entire careers and interviewing different family members as well as credible sources who truly knew them and worked with them, that I knew this book would more than meet my expectations. He has done a tremendous job of narrating a factual, fair and balanced retrospective about them and most importantly the major impact they had on the pro wrestling industry.

Dynamite's arrival here in Calgary in 1978 and Stampede Wrestling would be life-changing for him. His rapid-fire and explosive offence in matches with my brothers Bruce and Bret, as well as other opponents, saved the financially struggling promotion from going under, and soon it was thriving.

Dynamite's success paved the way for Davey Boy to follow his older cousin's career path to Calgary three years later. He certainly couldn't have gotten off to a better start as he was strategically matched in his debut against Dynamite and they had unbelievable chemistry together in the ring. In Tom's eyes, it was a test of how well Davey had learned from their old master Ted Betley – and he passed with flying colours. Britain's two best young stars were shining brightly across the Atlantic. Steven examines their early in-ring and personal relationship as Dynamite continued to challenge Davey's toughness, tolerance and loyalty.

Having the same teacher and early athletic backgrounds, they were able to successfully blend the British and North American styles and keep pace with established stars like the Harts, 'Dr D' David Schultz, Mr Hito, Mr Sakurada, Leo Burke, Jim Neidhart and Bad News Allen, and helped turn Stampede into one of the best promotions in the world.

In a big man's game which was dominated at that time by monster heavyweights like André the Giant, Stan Hansen, Bruiser Brody and Hulk Hogan, Dynamite and Davey did whatever it took to improve their look and add size to their frames. They lifted weights fanatically and, like many of their peers, utilised anabolic steroids and growth hormones to achieve the well-sculpted muscular physiques they developed. In the process, they still maintained their agility and flexibility which was a strong testament to their work ethic and conditioning. Unfortunately, it was their introduction to steroids which later led to an excessive use of painkillers and other prescription drugs and would ultimately take both a physical and mental toll on them.

Steven also takes us through the behind-the-scenes developments resulting in the pair jumping from New Japan to All Japan at the height of the Japanese promotional war in 1984 as Dynamite and Davey became one of the most sought-after attractions in the world.

That leads to the creation of the British Bulldogs and their amazing three-year ride in the WWF. With a rapid rise in the highly competitive tag team division, they became big stars, rivalling Hulk Hogan and 'Macho Man' Randy Savage for popularity and launching a new wave of Britannia not seen since the British invasion of music stars in North America in the 1960s. They had truly achieved their dream of conquering the world and making it to the top. In terms of box office attendance, merchandise sales and the consistent quality of their matches, they are unquestionably one of the greatest tag teams of all time.

Steven considers the humanistic traits and behaviours of Dynamite and Davey, which became emboldened as their profiles grew. There are first-hand accounts of their propensity for mischief and pranks, usually pulled on unassuming wrestlers or fans and often with damaging consequences. This would be encouraged by some people but resented and scorned by others.

We also see their fierce loyalty to friends and allies; the conflicts with those they didn't see eye to eye with; their intense pride and level of competitiveness. Steven analyses Dynamite's role as a leader and Davey's role as a follower; Tom's quick temper and desire to settle scores physically; Davey's protectiveness of others around him, but his impulsive reaction to situations and inclination to be led by Dynamite.

We also come to terms with the tremendous price paid for their high-impact style in the ring as they would each suffer from numerous debilitating injuries. Sadly, this would negatively affect their work-rate and lead to an addiction to painkillers and various stimulants and depressants in order to perform night after night and survive the hellish lifestyle on the road with time spent between shows, hotels, nightclubs, gyms, airports and highways.

Sadly, both Dynamite and Davey succumbed to their ring injuries and deteriorating health caused by years of use of steroids, painkillers, alcoholism, and other lethal substances. The fallout for each led to shattered careers, broken marriages, strained family relations and financial destitution.

Steven assesses the highs and lows of their careers and personal lives through the lens of the pro wrestling eye which clearly shows the transformation from the smaller regional territories to a multi-million-dollar global industry in the 80s and 90s. The British Bulldogs were a major part of this revolution on so many levels, from their remarkable athleticism and incredible matches to their mass global appeal. They influenced so many other wrestlers who carefully studied their matches or were lucky enough to get the opportunity to work with them early in their careers. This long list includes Owen Hart, Chris Benoit, Brian Pillman, Doug Furnas, Phil Lafon, Johnny Smith, Jushin Liger, Mitsuharu Misawa, Toshiaki Kawada, Kenta Kobashi, Eddie Guerrero, Rey Mysterio Jr, Chris Jericho, Lance Storm, Wade Barrett, Drew McIntyre, and Sheamus – all of whom would become major stars.

Davey's son Harry and nephew Tyson Kidd formed 'The Hart Dynasty' and captured the WWE tag team title in 2010. Harry has become a polished technician excelling in mixed martial arts and submission-style grappling.

Niece Natalya (Nattie Neidhart) won the WWE Divas title in the same year and the Smackdown Women's world title in 2017. Nephew Teddy Hart (Annis) is an exceptionally talented yet controversial figure with a somewhat unconventional style.

Dynamite's nephews Thomas and Mark have recently made their ring debut in Britain, fittingly as the Billington Bulldogs as a dedication to their uncle Tom, and show a lot of promise. Dynamite and Davey would both be proud of all of these achievements and we look forward to their bright futures.

Many lessons and insights can be learned from the triumphs and defeats of Dynamite and Davey. Undeniably though, they should be best remembered for how much they contributed to the pro wrestling industry. They made promoters a lot of money, helped establish other stars, entertained fans all over the world and continue to inspire a new generation of young talented superstars. Most importantly, they achieved a standard of excellence in the ring that few others can aspire to. These are reasons why they each deserve to be inducted in every true Hall of Fame both as singles stars and as a team. Indeed, their lasting legacy will continue. This book covers it all, and it is essential for you to read.

Ross Hart

GLOSSARY OF TERMS

The fascinating subculture that is professional wrestling has almost evolved its own language over its century-and-a-half in existence. Rather than continuously interrupt the explosive story to explain each that crops up, here are some of the terminologies and their definitions. The first time each of these appears in the narrative, they will be written in *italics* to remind you to take a look back here for their meaning.

Agent: An experienced backstage handler, used as a point-of-contact for wrestlers, specific matches and events at the behest of the *booker* or promoter. Often referred to as a road agent.

Angle: A fictional storyline.

Babyface: A wrestler who is heroic, who is booked in order to be cheered by fans. Historically called a blue-eye in British wrestling.

Blade/blading: A wrestler intentionally cutting himself or his opponent in order to draw blood for dramatic effect.

Booker: The person in charge of setting up matches and writing *angles*.

Broadway: A match that ends in a time limit draw.

Bump: The skill of landing on the mat or ground in order to *sell* his opponents' offensive move.

Catch-as-catch-can: A submission-based form of grappling that originated in Lancashire.

Curtain jerker: Derogatory term for wrestlers who open the show, often before the audience have even taken their seats.

Enhancement talent: Relatively unknown wrestler(s) competing against established stars with the sole purpose of making their opponents look as strong as possible as they lose displaying little or no offence. Often called jobbers.

Fall: The end of a match, generally obtained by pinball or submission. Matches can be, and mostly were in British wrestling pre-1990, two-out-of-three falls.

Gaijin: Japanese for 'foreigner', gaijin create a third category to the standard *babyface-heel* dynamic in Japanese wrestling, as the patriotic fans cheer their own over the army of invading Westerners.

Gimmick: The character portrayed by a wrestler.

Gorilla position: Named after WWE legend 'Gorilla Monsoon', this is the area behind the curtain just before the stars enter the fray. Used by *agents* and producers to pass on last-minute instructions and communicate with TV commentators at ringside.

Heat: When a wrestler attracts the intended amount, or maybe more, of cheers or boos depending on his *babyface* or *heel* status, he is getting *heat*, and is therefore getting *over*.

Heel: A wrestler who is villainous, who is booked in a manner that will be booed by fans.

House show: An untelevised show where rarely anything meaningful happens. Often the same, or a similar, card can be performed nightly in different towns.

Job: To lose in a wrestling match. Wrestlers who lose the majority of their matches are jobbers.

Juice: Blood, usually spilt intentionally by way of *blading*.

Kayfabe: The presentation of professional wrestling as being entirely legitimate or real. Prior to the mid-1980s, this was universally maintained across all wrestling territories and promotions.

Finish: The series of moves that will bring about the pre-planned ending to a match.

Lumberjack: A wrestler, usually many in number, who stand by the ring in a lumberjack match with the sole task of forcibly returning any competitor to the ring if they attempt to escape.

Over: For a *babyface*, being *over* means loud cheers and universal support of the audience, which inevitably leads to lots of merchandise sales. *Heels* can proudly call themselves *over* when they are booed and jeered or, decades ago, have venues on the verge of a riot.

Pop: A huge positive crowd reaction.

Potato: A strike to the head which makes real contact, usually with intent.

Programme: A scripted *angle* and/or series of matches between feuding wrestlers.

Promo: An in-character interview or monologue aimed at promoting or furthering a current or future *programme*.

Put over: The act of one wrestler helping to boost the status of another, most often by losing a match or by *selling* their opponent as a credible threat.

Puroresu: Japanese professional wrestling.

Push: The conscious effort by promoters and/or *bookers* to raise the profile of a wrestler by giving them airtime, titles and victories.

Receipt: To return a stiff shot, or a *potato*.

Rib: A practical joke.

Royal Rumble: Annual January WWF/E pay-per-view in which the Royal Rumble match, a 30-man over-the-top-rope Battle Royal is the lucrative main event.

Sell: To feign pain and injury in order to make the opponent's offence appear strong and impactful.

Shoot: Any unplanned, unscripted or real-life occurrence within a wrestling event. To shoot wrestle is to fight legitimately.

Smart: Having inside knowledge of the wrestling business. Originally used to refer to those who were aware of the existence of *kayfabe* and the scripted nature of professional wrestling. The act of teaching someone the inner workings of the wrestling business is referred to as *smartening up*.

Spot: A planned move or incident within a match. A *highspot* is a high-flying or more dangerous manoeuvre.

Squash: A short match in which one wrestler quickly annihilates his opponent. Designed to *put over* one wrestler heavily, at the expense of *enhancement talent*.

Stiff: A barometer of how much actual force a wrestler puts into his moves or strikes; stiff wrestlers often put their opponents through more physical punishment in pursuance of realism. *Potatoes* can often be delivered under the guise of *stiff working*.

Turn: A wrestler moving from a *babyface* to a *heel* persona, or vice-versa.

Work: What professional wrestling is – pre-planned with the knowledge of everyone involved.

INTRODUCTION

'IT'S FAKE, Steven,' my dad said to me when I nagged him to turn and face the TV screen as Bret Hart and Roddy Piper beat each other gloriously senseless at *WrestleMania VIII*.

'Maybe sometimes it is dad, but this one isn't. It can't be. Look at all the blood!' I begged him to believe me, because if he believed, he would stop telling me not to believe.

It's my most vivid memory of being a borderline obsessive childhood WWF fan – that of 'Rowdy' Roddy helping a bloodied and battered but victorious 'Hitman' out of the ring after strapping the Intercontinental title belt around his waist following their epic clash. The passion, the emotion, the athleticism, the drama, the crowd, the atmosphere, the spectacle, and of course, the blood; it all served to tell a perfect story. It was real to me.

'It's only red sauce,' he said.

We were both right. By 'fake', he meant they weren't really attempting to maim each other, merely simulating that they were. But I was right too: the passion, the emotion, the athleticism, the drama, the crowd, the atmosphere, the spectacle, and of course, the blood, were all very, very real. It certainly wasn't 'red sauce' (known as tomato ketchup in many parts of the world, but not in the north of England).

Similarly to how I don't remember the exact moment that I realised or found out that Santa Claus wasn't real, I'm not sure that there was any grand dawning that my beloved wrestling was a *work*. My sporting obsession turned towards football and by the time I was beginning high school, I would rather have admitted to believing in Father Christmas than dare to even watch wrestling, so uncool had it become.

The turn of the millennium then blasted unadulterated Attitude into the eyeballs of my brother Martin and me. What more could teenage boys want than The Rock 'laying the smacketh down', Steve Austin opening up cans of whoop-ass, and, well, Trish Stratus?

For the second time in our young lives, we had fallen prey to being Vince McMahon's latest target demographic. Our friend Pete Knee hadn't foolishly sought to be cool during his high school years and had remained a hardened wrestling fan throughout – even curating a large collection of merchandise, including almost all of the WWF pay-per-view events on VHS tape. We brought them home by the sackful and watched them nightly, beginning with the first ever *WrestleMania* from 1985.

I had remembered the British Bulldog well from my adolescence, and so when the 'British Bulldogs', a tag team, appeared in most of the opening tapes, I assumed they had just dragged in the first English wrestler they could find to be Davey Boy's tag partner; he was the star, after all. Right?

The first indication that I had misled myself in believing that the Dynamite Kid was a sidekick soon arrived when, at 16, I read Mick Foley's wonderful first book, *Have A Nice Day*, in which he wrote of Tom Billington's mid-80s brilliance.

A decade or so further on, I read *Hitman*, and with that I was forced to (sorry Mick) award my championship belt for the greatest sports book of all time to Bret Hart. It also served to truly lay bare to me the explosive careers and lives of the Bulldogs, and now being geographically and socially aware, it dawned on me how closely I shared a heritage with them. An ongoing interest developed into what would become the genesis of my research for this book.

When I later decided to follow my passion and embark on a second career as an author, and after my second book, a biography of professional wrestling's first British superstar Douglas Clark received national praise and attention, I dared to dream that I may be the author to bring wrestling's most needed and elusive book to fruition.

Just 60 miles separate my hometown of Featherstone and Golborne, where Tom and Davey were raised. Like all such towns, they are eerily similar: red brick buildings line the pothole-ravaged roads; a series of run-down public houses provide the local landmarks; and a semi-permanent greyness hangs over them – a combination of the bleak northern weather and centuries of local industry.

My dad, Chris, was born in the very same year as Tom: 1958. My grandfather was a foreman down the pit, my grandmother worked part-time in the local fish-and-chip shop and they had five boys. Three of the five followed their dad down the pit before the heart was ripped out of the community when the coal mines were closed by the Conservative government. Those that were trained as electricians or mechanics down the mine could transfer their skills and get decent alternative employment, but the hardworking shift labourers struggled to find anything that would provide the same level of camaraderie, satisfaction or reasonably healthy pay.

I grew up hearing my dad's tales of his own hard childhood: at Christmas the five of them would fight over the solitary wireless radio they were supposedly to share, although they did get a whole juicy orange each to themselves. Mealtimes were pandemonium, as the bowl of deep-fried chips was devoured on a first-come-first-served basis, the slowest to the table often having to spread a single chip onto a slice of bread to form his 'butty'.

A couple of weeks per year at one of the local seaside towns such as Bridlington or Blackpool was all that could be expected as a holiday, with foreign travel reserved for those belonging to a far-removed societal class.

A strong community spirit has always existed, as lifelong friendships are formed as babies through passed-down generational family kinships. This transcends into a form of brotherhood with a firm sense of loyalty; but strangers and outsiders can often be treated with suspicion and trepidation.

Those that were lucky enough to serve a full career down the pit would often retire hard of hearing or walking with a limp, borne either from wear-and-tear or as the result of an underground accident. But alternative employment options for the strong, breadwinning alpha-male types of the north were scarce between the end of World War Two and the persecution of the mining industry in the 1980s. These were rugged, hearty, family men; many of whom prided themselves on their toughness. Those that were born to a father with a reputation for being a 'hard-case' were largely expected to continue that lineage.

The state education system was poor, and people from the northern towns simply weren't given the tools or opportunities to go to university and become doctors or lawyers or architects.

There was one possibility for a small fraction of the young men though: top-level sport. These communities are sporting crazy, with small boys wanting little else than to kick or throw a ball of any shape or size.

Every town regales of its historical sporting heroes, those that have played at Wembley in either football or rugby, or the local boxer that once took a future champion the distance.

In the neighbouring Lancashire towns of Wigan and Warrington, which Golborne sits in between, another sport had evolved as a very real option: professional wrestling.

Wrestling, in its innumerable raw and natural forms, goes back to the dawn of time. Seemingly every country and region worldwide had developed a competitive sport that required no special equipment or apparel – just two consenting competitors.

During the 1800s, as people finally found ways to travel to other parts of the world and immerse themselves in new cultures, the full plethora of wrestling types began to merge. By the turn of the 20th century, there were only three main umbrella types under which the smaller, regional forms could fall, therefore allowing the wrestlers to enter bigger competitions across different territories and even around the world. Those three types were Graeco-Roman, Japanese jiu-jitsu and *Catch-as-catch-can.*

America became the home of these new global versions of the historic sport and the 'prize ring' was born for freestyle wrestling.

Wrestlers from around the world began to flock to the popular territories such as New York and Chicago. The diversity of the competitors, their cultures and their styles made it a hit and huge audiences formed to watch live cards in all kinds of auditoriums, theatres, and community centres.

A problem emerged when the grappling itself got underway though, as many contests would merely involve two equally matched men who the crowd had no affinity or connection with, clinched together on the ground as minute piled upon minute. It was often tedious for the paying customer. In the 'Russian Lion' Georg Hackenschmidt there was a dominant champion who made easy and unentertaining work of anyone who was put in front of him.

At the turn of the 20th century, he was asked by promoter Charles B. Cochran to put on a show for the audience, to play to the crowd. This tactic had been used by tricksters and conmen at carnivals for years, as grapplers hustled the crowds into parting with their cash.

But now this seed had been sown professionally and other promoters and wrestlers were asked to *work* the crowd; to put on an exhibition; to make it entertaining. They would be recompensed for putting the quality of the show ahead of their own natural instincts to go all out for the victory.

Major personalities emerged from the elite wrestlers of this pre-World War One boom, and when any two of them met, the local press and sporting fraternity would come to a standstill. Amongst the most notable stars were Hackenschmidt, Frank Gotch of the USA, the Polish Zbyszko brothers (Stanislaus and Wladek), and the 'Terrible Turk' Ahmed Madrali.

With many being natives of Europe, these exponents were soon travelling the globe and by the 1920s most of the wrestling world was aware and even complicit in skulduggery. A pact formed between the wrestlers, that they would do all possible to protect one another in the ring and ensure that both came away uninjured. This way, unlike in any other sport, they could perform every night of the week, should they wish. Way before the internet and with newspapers mostly regional, they could roll in and out of different areas, putting on exactly the same show under the guise of it being new and exclusive. With no cameras present and the wrestlers so well-versed in legitimate mat skills, no one present would suspect anything amiss – especially when one of the competitors might *blade* to the delight of the bloodthirsty customers.

It was a revelation and the wrestlers and promoters made fortunes. American promoters set about globalising this new regime. In 1930, 'All-In' professional wrestling was born in the United Kingdom. When former international rugby hero Douglas Clark won the British heavyweight championship and remained undefeated for the whole decade, he became the face of the UK wrestling scene.

Based in Huddersfield, Clark would pack out arenas nightly. With Leeds-based former Olympic champion George de Relwyskow as his manager and promoter, and his son George Jr the popular lightweight champion, the north of England became a wrestling hot-bed.

The sport went underground during World War Two. A young lad from Warrington, Ted Betley, served his country in the Royal Air Force, but Ted had been drawn to wrestling by its northern revolution, especially by all-conquering middleweight Billy Riley, who was from nearby Wigan. Following Riley's retirement from in-ring action in 1947, he opened a gym dedicated to training the next generation of working-class grapplers.

Like most of his generation, Ted Betley had first started wrestling as an amateur in the catch-as-catch-can style. These were legitimate sporting contests pitting the toughest men around against one other in a battle of strength and mat-wrestling technique. In a pro wrestling world dominated by worked contests, legitimate styles later became known as *shoot* wrestling, and its participants *shooters*.

Old-timers like Ted believed shooting and working went hand-in-hand, and that the best wrestlers should easily be able to compete in both disciplines. This would retain the realism in a predetermined product that wrestlers without genuine mat skills and an innate toughness simply could not provide.

Television station ITV launched in 1955 and was looking to fill its schedule with fresh new content. Professional wrestling would now air live on prime-time national TV on Saturday afternoon's *World of Sport* programme.

Joint Promotions had formed and was providing a monopoly on the UK wrestling scene, bringing one regional promotion from each area of the country under its umbrella. ITV and Joint agreed the daytime TV product should be less violent and more family-friendly than wrestling had previously been.

As the years went by, more emphasis continued to be put on giant behemoths with outlandish *gimmicks* providing slapstick entertainment over any sporting spectacle.

By the 1970s, Ted Betley was coaching youngsters in what was slowly becoming a lost art, but he knew that genuine wrestling fans still recognised and appreciated the skill and storytelling craft of the genuine workers of the business.

* * *

This story is based upon extensive research and on the documented accounts of others (chapter-by-chapter referenced sources are printed in the back). Where sources contradicted each other, the author has decided, based on the overall picture his research has brought him, how to narrate.

Some minor details and dialogue are imagined.

PROLOGUE

CHAMPIONS OF THE WORLD

'While a cage match with Hulk Hogan vs King Kong Bundy,
a Battle Royal involving several NFL football stars and a
boxing match with Roddy Piper vs. Mr T took centre stage
in the build-up, there was little doubt the best match of the
second *WrestleMania* on April 7, 1986 in Chicago at the
Horizon was the Bulldogs winning the tag team titles from
the Dream Team, Greg Valentine and Brutus Beefcake.'

Dave Meltzer

'Rule, Britannia. Britannia, Rule The Waves'

The iconic opening notes of the patriotic classical anthem erupted
into the arena and were immediately met with a chorus of loud cheers.
This was the main event of the evening for the 9,000-strong crowd
in attendance at the Rosemont Horizon – just one of three venues in
which the greatest wrestling extravaganza of all time was taking place.
The opening hour had gone down in New York, with a boxing match
between Hollywood star Mr T and wrestling loudmouth 'Rowdy'
Roddy Piper headlining that part of the groundbreaking show.

Following the upcoming tag team championship match, the pay-
per-view TV audience would be taken to Los Angeles for the final
instalment – which would climax with all-American hero Hulk Hogan
defending his WWF heavyweight title against the dastardly giant King
Kong Bundy in the violent confines of a steel cage.

The tag team champions, stocky blond veteran Greg 'The Hammer'
Valentine and the obnoxious Brutus Beefcake – who arrogantly called

23

themselves the 'Dream Team' – were already waiting in the ring. Despite being the champions, they had been introduced to the audience first, and with little fanfare. The crowd were desperate to see their new British heroes take the gold – and strongly suspected they were about to do so.

With the rousing music echoing around them, the audience swung their heads towards the narrow walkway down which the wrestlers made their way to the ring. A whole entourage emerged. Leading the way was the team manager, 'Captain' Lou Albano – an intense, unkempt mainstay of the American wrestling world. To his left, wearing a garish peach coloured suit, with flashed blond shoulder length hair, was former Black Sabbath frontman and heavy metal superstar Ozzy Osbourne. Security guards flanked them either side as the frantic crowd tried to lean over the railings to get closer to the world champions elect. In the middle of the posse were the British Bulldogs themselves – the Dynamite Kid and Davey Boy Smith. They wore short, royal blue baseball-style jackets atop their sky-blue wrestling tights.

Once in the ring, the dynamic pair ripped off their jackets to reveal huge, sculptured physiques as the unlikely duo of Albano and Osbourne whipped up the audience to fever-pitch.

At just 5ft 8in tall, Tom Billington was a few inches shorter and a few years older than his real-life cousin David, who was just 23. They both sported slicked-back dark hair and strong jawbones.

After the bell rang and the match got underway, the young partners dominated. They were stronger, fitter, faster and more aggressive than the champions, whose offensive flurries were short and irregular. Dynamite suplexed, clotheslined and performed his signature high-flying, high-impact manoeuvres. Davey Boy grappled, power-slammed and body-pressed the unfortunate pair high over his head. The crowd gasped in amazement at the physical feats they were witnessing.

Out of desperation, Greg Valentine ascended to the top turnbuckle in an attempt to gain the high ground, but Dynamite caught him up there and launched him high into the air, forcing him to crash heavily in the centre of the ring. Dynamite immediately went for the pin, only for Beefcake to run in and intervene. Davey Boy ejected the illegal man from the ring and the Bulldogs sensed an opportunity – with

Valentine still felled, Davey Boy pressed his own partner at full arm's length above his head and prepared to launch him headfirst towards Valentine, in a reckless but extraordinary variation of Dynamite's patented flying headbutt. Sensing danger, the wily veteran rolled out of the ring. Dynamite gave chase, rolling his opponent back under the bottom rope, but as he re-entered the ring himself, Valentine had sprung to his feet and was able to ambush Tom.

'The pendulum has shifted, here,' said commentator Gorilla Monsoon, as Valentine then put a sustained period of punishment on Davey after Dynamite had made the tag. A vicious shoulder breaker may have been enough for the champions, but Valentine – not feeling he had inflicted sufficient physical retribution for the opening ten-minute battering – pulled out of the pinning position and began taunting the crowd, who had now fallen silent. Dynamite climbed to the second rope and leant over, calling for Davey Boy to get to his feet – which Davey dutifully did and caught Valentine off-guard. He powerfully rammed him toward his perched partner, who sacrificed himself by headbutting the onrushing veteran. Dynamite flew wildly off-screen for the pay-per-view audience, crashing heavily into the steel barriers and then on to the concrete floor as Valentine collapsed to the canvas, where Davey Boy laid atop him for a pin. One. Two. Three.

The audience erupted with joy. Captain Lou Albano and Ozzy Osbourne grabbed a championship belt each and jumped around the ring in celebration as 'Rule Britannia' once again filled the arena.

'Fantastic, man! The British Bulldogs forever!' an electrified Ozzy screamed into 'Mean' Gene Okerlund's microphone. Tom, with thick blood suddenly dripping from his head and pooling on the blue mats, stayed on the outside – the truth was, he didn't care so much for the love and adoration of the fans.

Davey Boy clambered into the ring. 'Thank you very much, Mean Gene,' he began in his thick Lancastrian accent after receiving the congratulations of the interviewer. 'As we told all the people in the United States of America, if we became the world tag team champions, we would *stay* in the United States of America! This is where we're gonna stay!'

The crowd cheered with delight once again. But the truth is, neither Bulldog stayed in the USA for nearly as long as the fans may have wished. The more horrifying truth is, by their respective 40th birthdays, one was in a wheelchair and the other one was dead; and they hadn't spoken to one another for more than a decade.

Just where did it all go wrong, for the British Bulldogs with the world seemingly at their metaphorical paws?

PART 1

THE DYNAMITE KID

'I've often been asked what made Dynamite so special. Well, first, he was a phenomenal athlete, remarkably adaptable to virtually any style or format – be it British, North American, or Japanese. What really set him apart was his timing: he seemed to have this innate ability to know precisely when to do things. Beyond that, like all the truly great workers, he was capable of making damn near anyone he worked with look good – in many cases, better than they ever dreamed of looking – myself included.'

Bruce Hart

1

DOCTOR DEATH

'The Dynamite Kid was the one, a great wrestler. He was an
introvert, but the minute he got in the ring he changed.'

Max Crabtree

Warrington, England. 1971

Ted Betley walked out of his front door; the low morning sun peeking
above the houses opposite forced him to squint. He was having
the house heavily renovated; it was effectively a building site. Ted's
weathered face cracked into wrinkles as he smiled at what made him
realise it was Saturday morning. It was the fact that Billy Billington, the
builder in charge of the work, was walking towards him accompanied
by his 13-year-old son, Thomas – who would've been at school on any
other of the six days per week that Billy came to work.

Ted watched on as Billy pointed between the dumper truck parked
up nearby, the large pile of rubble and the skip on the roadside. Thomas
glanced between the objects and then looked back to his dad, who
threw him the keys to the truck before proceeding towards his client.

'Energetic young lad you've got there, Bill,' teased Ted, watching
Thomas sprinting away and then jumping into the driver's seat.

'Aye, he's training to be a boxer – just hope he gets better at it than
I ever 'ave! All I ever got out of it is a few quid every couple o'month
and a thick head every time for the trouble.'

'He looks a handy lad, like,' said Ted, looking on as Tom leapt down
from the driver's seat to the floor, then threw the straggling bricks that
had escaped his dumper bucket into the skip. 'Does he wrestle?'

'No,' replied Billy dismissively, 'just boxing for now.'

'I can't recommend wrestling highly enough for an active lad like him, you know. It's a profession for 'em, not a hobby. They can wrestle as many nights of the week as they want, 'cos they so rarely get hurt, you see. Them that get on the telly earn decent money and travel all over.'

'Well, that's sorta thing I want for him, ya know. Not like me; all them years down t'pit didn't get me anywhere. Now I'm mixing cement for the rest of my days and getting my head punched in every now and again to be able to afford the odd treat.'

Billy and his wife Edna had three children to support; their eldest Julie was a year older than Thomas, with Carol five years younger.

With the pile of bricks gone and the dumper parked back where he had found it, skinny little Thomas strolled back over to his dad, patting the dust from his hands on to his faded blue jeans.

'Hello son,' Ted introduced himself to fair-haired Thomas. 'I was just asking your old man here – have you ever fancied trying wrestling?'

'Nah. Fake, innit. I wanna fight for real.'

Ted laughed in an all-knowing sort of way, before flicking his head towards the open front door. 'Come on in. I'll put kettle on.'

After putting tea and biscuits on the table, Ted left the kitchen and went up the stairs. He returned with an ancient-looking wooden box. He put the box on the table alongside the tray of refreshments and sat down before sweeping a thick layer of dust from the top of it. Thomas looked on curiously as his host lifted off the lid.

Ted began to show young Thomas a series of photographs and old wrestling programmes. On each photograph, there was a large wrestler wearing a black mask, and on each programme appeared the name 'Dr Death'.

'That's me,' Ted said, proudly tapping a particular photograph, in which he was also wearing a floor-length black cloak and the huge crowd surrounding him appeared to be yelling and gesticulating in his direction.

'That's you?' gasped Thomas, passing the pictures to his dad.

'Aye. I spent 20 years wrestling after the war. Then opened the gym when I retired. Got some good young lads down there that I train. You're more than welcome to come and give it a go.'

'They don't seem to like you very much?' Tom scoffed, taking back hold of the photo.

'That lad,' he said, 'is 'cos I was good.'

* * *

Born and raised in the village of Golborne, young tearaway Thomas Billington hated school. He was one of the smallest in his age group, but this didn't stop him playing pranks and getting into fights and he could regularly be found in the headmaster's office with a cane being whipped across his wrist. At home, his dad was also quite a strict disciplinarian. Billy's father, also called Thomas, had too been a strict, fighting man; a bare-knuckle boxer, he had bribed Billy with a crisp ten-pound note to continue the 'Thomas Billington' family name if the baby was a boy. Thomas junior was born into a family of tough, fighting men. He excelled in sports, playing both rugby league and football for Wigan Town and had natural athleticism, coordination and agility. In his physical education classes at school, he loved to show himself off as an extraordinary acrobat, laughing and joking whilst accomplishing highly complex routines in gymnastics.

He had emerged a teenager with a cocky and streetwise attitude and was keen to take up a combat sport as a hobby. The invitation from Ted Betley, even if it was into 'fake' wrestling, was great timing.

When he first arrived at the gym with his dad, Tom (as he was most commonly known) thought they had walked into an abandoned army barracks rather than the wrestling establishment he had expected. He heard crashing and groaning and looked in to see two boys, both older and bigger than him, practising their moves on one another in the ring. Ted greeted them and got Tom kitted up as best he could, but his tiny, skinny frame barely filled any of the apparel on offer.

As was his way with all newcomers to his gym, Ted wanted to test Tom's fortitude and willingness to fight. He told Tom to get in the ring and replace the younger lad in there – leaving Tom with the biggest, oldest boy. With no tuition at all, Ted told them to wrestle – 'no punching or kicking'. Within minutes, Ted knew he may have a special talent on his hands as Tom never took a backward step and matched his bigger, stronger, more experienced opponent with tenacity, aggression and a low centre of gravity.

'Make sure you bring him back tomorrow,' Ted told Billy, who then continued to take Tom to the gym every single day after school, and Saturdays too, for the next three years. In this acrobatic form of fighting, Tom had found a discipline within which all his natural skills and passions combined perfectly.

The gritty style taught by the master coupled with the aggression and determination of the apprentice was an ideal formula. The pair bonded and Ted became a second father figure to Tom, and soon his advice went beyond the world of wrestling.

'Tommy,' Ted began one day, 'no matter what you have to face in life, no matter how scared you are, don't ever take a step back. Always take a step forward. It doesn't matter how good you are, or how many people you beat, there'll always be somebody who will beat you.' Tom listened intently to the advice.

Hoping to add even more intensity and realism to Tom's wrestling, Ted took him to Billy Riley's infamous gym in Wigan. Riley had trained world-renowned shooters-turned-workers like Billy Robinson and Karl Gotch. Despite appearing to be little more than a shed from the outside, it was a legendary place in the world of shoot wrestling. It earned the name the 'Snake Pit' amongst the Japanese wrestling royalty, after Gotch in particular had spent much of his career there, becoming known as *Kamisama* – 'God of Wrestling' – and being a trainer and promoter there into the 1980s.

Here, Tom entered the ring opposite grown men who were entering the sport with the aim of legitimately hurting people, and who looked down upon the 'fake' profession. They threw him around and put holds on him until he screamed – even when he did, they didn't let go.

Ted's teachings were bringing a flock of talented and competitive youngsters to the fore at his gym. Steve Wright, from Warrington, was five years older than Tom and already a major part of the Joint Promotions circuit and a regular on TV. He would stretch and hurt Tom, who would struggle back in vain and never back down.

'Whatever they do to you, Tommy, don't give up; never submit,' Ted would enforce.

Ted then began taking Tom to Billy Chambers' gym as he used every bit of the local artistry available to progress his protégé. Chambers was yet another old-time shooter and would stretch Tom to strengthen him; to test him. By going back twice every week for more, Tom passed the test. He was growing in reputation and stature.

He was introduced to his first live audience as 'Tommy Billington', as he made his pro wrestling debut in Warrington on 11 March 1975 against a Ted Betley stablemate in Bernie Wright – the younger brother of Steve. Tom's first bouts were non-advertised extra matches at the beginning or end of the billed shows of local promoter Jack Atherton. Soon, the punters were staying in their seats to watch the exciting bonus bout with this unknown acrobatic daredevil.

When asked about his young prodigy, Ted would say, 'Oh, he's dynamite, this kid,' and so when asked what name to bill Tom as when he was finally added to the main card, the 'Dynamite Kid' was born.

Dynamite quickly became a firm fan favourite, with his never-say-die attitude enabling him to claim victories against the established *heels*. He had grown to the 5ft 8in tall at which he would stay and had to work hard and aggressively to truly convince the audience that a lad of his emaciated-looking frame could even compete, let alone win. A professional career surely beckoned, and the family really needed Tom to support himself following the arrival of his new baby brother, Mark.

Tom recorded his first *World of Sport* TV bout on 30 June 1976 against Yorkshire veteran 'Strongman' Alan Dennison. It was strength versus speed and Tom's acrobatics wowed not just the crowd, but Dennison too. Supposedly frustrated by the youngster's consistent ability to handstand out of any predicament and land on his feet, Dennison began launching Dynamite across the ring whilst locking his hands behind his back, only for Tom to repeatedly spring off the canvas with his head and land on his feet anyway, bringing gasps of amazement from all around. The match was ended when the Dynamite Kid missed with a high-flying offensive dive and crashed into the ropes erratically and 'injured' himself so badly he was unable to continue. Dennison grabbed the microphone and asked that the match be declared a no-contest, telling the live audience and those watching on TV that, at just 17, the Dynamite Kid was a unique and sensational talent whose performance didn't deserve to end with a technical defeat.

That match didn't air until 30 October, by which time a second recorded match had been aired on *World of Sport* on the 9th, in which

Dynamite defeated Pete Meredith by two *falls* to one in the dingy town of Castleford.

By 1976, three brothers from Halifax, West Yorkshire, were effectively running Joint Promotions. They had been on the wrestling scene since before the ITV-led reboot of the mid-50s. They all had blond hair, two were average sized, but one, ironically named Shirley, was a huge man standing 6ft 7in tall and with a 64-inch chest – something that would later see him enter the *Guinness Book of World Records*. Shirley had begun weight training and body building in the late 1940s and was spotted as a potential professional wrestler due to his good looks, physique and great strength. His two athletic brothers, Max and Brian Crabtree, had gone along into the business with him and all three were soon active on the circuit.

Shirley had gained momentum and popularity by the end of the 50s and was being considered as the future face of the industry. But it just seemed like it would never quite happen for him and he became a journeyman, flitting between unsuccessful gimmicks such as the 'Blond Adonis', 'Mr Universe' and the 'Battling Guardsman'.

Both Brian and Max's in-ring careers were cut short by injury. Brian became a referee and eventually the Joint Promotions main compere and MC – an instantly recognisable figure in the ring with his garish, bright-coloured, sequinned suits.

Max, the sharpest of the trio, had earned himself a stellar reputation as a wrestling promoter and *booker* – and Joint Promotions had given him the northern area to run in 1975. He chose to give Shirley a *push* for the twilight of his brother's career and booked him as the new monster heel, 'Big Daddy Crabtree', and soon he was tag-teaming with a man who dwarfed even him in Martin Ruane, aka 'Giant Haystacks'. With Shirley over 25 stone and Haystacks close to the 7ft mark and 45 stone in weight, the audience were awestruck as the pair obliterated their opposition. In truth, they lacked mobility and agility, and the matches were over in seconds – but the audiences just loved to lay eyes on the gargantuan pair.

Shirley was now middle-aged but with his blond hair and clean-cut appearance, he made for a rather cuddly and friendly figure to the new family audience – especially when on the screen with Haystacks, who appeared in scruffy, ripped denim, with straggly, unkempt hair emanating from both his head and face. His teeth were shades of brown and he angrily yelled at members of the audience, with saliva launching toward them as he did – much of it getting caught up in his beard.

Max saw the opportunity to *turn* his brother and make him a TV favourite and the face of British wrestling. Daddy and Haystacks began a decade-long rivalry – the most lucrative in the history of British professional wrestling. Daddy's singlet evolved into brighter shades and was suddenly emblazoned with a Union Jack; he would appear with a glittery top-hat upon his head, smiling from ear to-ear, waving at the packed-out crowds and hugging kids in the front rows. He became a national icon of the era and launched the popularity of wrestling once again. The ITV *World of Sport* ratings rose to unprecedented levels. Max got the credit, and eventually total control of Joint Promotions.

The problem was, the ageing Shirley was now around the 25-stone mark and could only manage a few minutes of genuine in-ring action. Max therefore needed a fit lad to team with his obese brother in tag team matches at the top of the bill. The younger and skinnier the better, as the formula was clear: a pair of heels in one corner dominate and bully the brave kid whilst Big Daddy waits eagerly for the tag; the audience would will the game youngster to make a fightback and eventually, tag in their rotund hero, who would belly-butt both the bad guys into oblivion for the victory and the glory.

Dynamite was an ideal Kid for the job.

Regular national TV exposure followed, but Tom much preferred his singles matches, which would be against some of the smaller men in the middle of the bill. In these matches he faced some of the most respected workers around, such as Mark 'Rollerball' Rocco, Marty Jones, Jim Breaks, Johnny Saint, Tony Scarlo and the legendary Mick McManus – who was almost old enough to be his grandad. These bouts were presented as respectful, legitimate sporting contests, beginning and ending with a handshake between the competitors and displaying a series of holds and counter-holds that would create the story of a gutsy young boy acrobatically holding his own and even upsetting the established stronger stars. They were generally best-of-three-falls matches split into boxing-style rounds in the traditional British wrestling manner.

Tom was studying his veteran opponents and learning and improving all the time, determined to be the best. Having left school, he trained with Ted by day, and wrestled professionally in the evening – earning just £8 per show from Max Crabtree's notoriously shallow pockets.

Tom's dynamic action, high-flying agility, realistic work and authentic bravery meant that, regardless of his position on the card, the Dynamite Kid was the name on the lips of the punters as they left the venues. Whether the crowd was made up of hundreds in the countless smoky town halls and civic centres the length and breadth of the country, or several thousand in iconic arenas such as the Royal Albert Hall or Manchester's legendary Belle Vue – the paying customer was never short-changed when this youngster was on the card.

At just 18, he was the best lightweight in the country, and was rewarded for his outstanding performances by being made the youngest ever British lightweight champion, winning the title from Bradford's veteran heel Jim Breaks.

He later won the European welterweight title from Jean Corné, nearly lifting the roof from the De Montford Hall in Leicester. He was voted 'Wrestler of the Year' by the readers of *TV Stars Wrestling* magazine as he turned 19, relegating former tag team partner Big Daddy, the top star and top earner, to third place. Having been told a small guy like him could never topple the heavyweight stars, he was already proving them wrong.

'Tommy, the world is your oyster now,' Ted Betley would tell his star pupil, 'if you want it, you take it.'

The first person to be inspired by young Tommy Billington was his own younger cousin, David Smith. David's mum Joyce was the older sister of Tom's dad Billy.

Shortly after having David, his parents Sid and Joyce emigrated to Australia with him and his older brother Terrence. They returned to Golborne when David was five, and the family grew when sisters Tracey and Joanne were born.

David was struck down by a severe eye infection during his childhood, which left his sight badly damaged. But he was a good enough and dedicated enough athlete to overcome that deficiency, enjoying and excelling at cricket, football and Olympic diving. But he hated wearing the glasses he needed to be able to get the most out of his education. Already shy, the self-conscious youngster lacked confidence and fell behind at school. Worried what his son's future held, Sid sought to find David a passion he could concentrate on to keep himself on a positive path throughout his formative years.

Apparently, Sid approached his brother-in-law Billy regarding connecting 13-year-old David with Ted for him to begin his own wrestling training in the wake of Tom doing so well. But Billy seemed cold and dismissive of the idea, and so Sid went directly to Ted himself. Ted was thrilled to take David, who was the same age and just as athletic as Tom when he had first stepped into his gym, but slightly taller.

With Tom on the road, Davey became Ted's new star pupil. But having left school, he had to earn his training by carrying out chores for Ted. As a by-product, this helped with his fitness, as he spent several hours each day delivering fruit and vegetables on a bicycle and climbing giant trees to prune the large branches with a hacksaw.

David's early training went very differently to Tom's, though. David's impaired eyesight meant many of his moves had to be carried out on instinct following hours and hours spent practising the perfect timing; he was also much quieter and more reserved than his cousin and less likely to challenge the more senior apprentices in the gym. Ted soon knew he had another potential star on his hands; what he didn't know was that the first wrestling-related wedge had been forced between the Smiths and the Billingtons. Tom was a unique and brilliant star that had always shone alone. It appears that both he and Billy believed he was one-of-one, not one-of-two as it would inevitably be perceived if and when David turned pro, so Tom made a conscious decision to maintain daylight between him and his cousin in the eyes of the wrestling world.

STAMPEDE

'The Dynamite Kid went out and put on one of the most awe-inspiring performances I've ever seen.'

Bruce Hart

Cleethorpes, North Lincolnshire. 13 November 1977

As the queue of fans slowly disappeared into the Pier Pavilion, they dropped scraps from their early fish and chip suppers. Ravenous seagulls swooped in as the low sun set, leaving only a bitterly cold evening behind for the traditional seaside town – the latest to welcome the Joint Promotions roadshow. There was a discernible excitement in the air though, as all of the household names were in town, including Big Daddy, Giant Haystacks and Rollerball Rocco.

Inside, Tom sat in the changing room alongside Ted Betley as he prepared for his match against Rocco. Ted was there not only to support Tom, but also to meet the wrestler who was currently sat opposite them, lacing up his cowboy boots with a Stetson perched on his head.

'I believe you must be Bruce?' Ted introduced himself, holding out his hand.

'Sure am,' replied Bruce Hart, peering at Ted from underneath the rim of his hat.

'My name is Ted, and I believe we have a mutual friend in John Foley.'

'Yeah, most of you guys around here seem to know John,' replied Bruce in his Canadian drawl, his shoulder-length blond hair emerging from under the oversized hat.

Ted chuckled. 'Yeah. But this lot know him by reputation. I helped to train him many years ago. That's the difference.'

Bruce remained mostly preoccupied by the complicated lacing arrangement of the new boots he'd just acquired to keep up the cowboy gimmick Max Crabtree had given him for his tour. Bruce was one of the many sons of Stu Hart, owner of Canada's biggest promotion, Stampede Wrestling. Many Brits had successfully wrestled in the territory in the past, including Billy Robinson, Danny Lynch, Black Angus Campbell, King Kong Kirk, Les Thornton, Geoff Portz and Kendo Nagasaki. North America was still regarded as a land of riches and opportunity when compared with Max's penny-pinching wages and the glass ceiling that was formed by his brother Shirley being seen as the one-and-only man that could headline the big shows and arenas. But Bruce knew differently regarding the Calgary-based Stampede territory, which was haemorrhaging so much money that it was threatening to bankrupt the family. As a result, his dad was secretly in the process of selling up to a group of local businessmen.

Bruce, at 27 years old and having been around the industry his whole life, had seen the writing on the wall; he had returned to college and got his high-school teaching qualifications and was prepared for a career outside the family business as soon as the Calgary Board of Education began hiring in the new year. In the meantime, he had decided to take his final chance to travel to England, planning to return home to his large family of 12 siblings for Christmas.

John Foley was a grizzled veteran wrestler from Wigan and a graduate of Billy Riley's Snake Pit, who had found a friend in Stu Hart and a home in Calgary after a life on the road. When Bruce had told Foley of his intention to have an extended vacation in his homeland, Foley said he would contact his old pal Max Crabtree so that Bruce could turn it into a working holiday and experience the booming British wrestling scene and the travelling roadshow of athletes and misfits. Both Bruce and Max loved the idea. Max's memory of Billy Two Rivers, a native-American import who had been hugely popular with the British audience, led to him suggesting that Bruce don the cowboy outfit and go by the name of 'Bronco' Bruce Hart.

'See that lad over there, Bruce?' Ted nodded towards Tom. 'Well, he's the Dynamite Kid and he is already the best in the country. He's the finest talent to ever come out of my gym, and I trained "Wonderboy" Steve Wright!'

Many wrestlers had approached Bruce over the previous few weeks whilst he had been touring England, selling themselves and inquiring about a possible position on the Stampede roster. He didn't want to tell them he was quitting himself or that the promotion was struggling so badly, as it would have made him and his family appear weak, at a time Max was pushing him strong. Instead, he chose to give them the line that Stampede was not looking for talent at the moment, but he would be sure to watch them perform anyway.

'Watch Dynamite against Rocco tonight. I believe he is ready to prove himself overseas; I think you'll agree. And good luck with your own match, Bruce,' Ted smiled the smile of the gentle old man he now was – outside of his gym, anyway.

A man of his word, Bruce finished up getting ready and found a viewing spot for the match – despite believing Ted was little more than a used-car salesman. But his scepticism turned to amazement as Dynamite and Rollerball electrified the crowd with a series of innovative moves and original counters; it was realistic, *stiff,* beautiful and intense. Bruce couldn't take his eyes off the action as Tom's high-octane offence took over and ignited an already thrilled crowd. He showed supreme ring psychology to tell his story and sailed around the ring with speed and agility. When Dynamite had his arm raised in victory over the already internationally established Rocco, Bruce knew that this was no fluke performance. Ted Betley was being nothing but honest – the Dynamite Kid was the real deal.

Bruce couldn't get over the irony. He may well have discovered a once-in-a-generation talent who wanted to come to Calgary, but for the first time in 30 years, his family was no longer going to have a promotion to bring him to.

When Ted and Tom approached Bruce after the show to get his opinion – knowing there was only one possible opinion to have – Bruce acted casual and down-played his thoughts, describing the performance as 'not bad' and ruefully reiterating that Stampede wasn't looking for talent at the time.

Bruce returned to Calgary in time for Christmas as planned. His trip had been a huge success and had reinvigorated his love for the wrestling business – with the Dynamite Kid at the forefront of his thoughts. Being a smaller wrestler too, he could see in his mind's eye how his own career could take off if he was to share a ring with that kid, who, as well as electrifying offence, was unselfish in the ring and bounced around and sold on behalf of his opponent to make them look almost as supreme as himself.

Therefore, Bruce was secretly delighted when his father Stu told him during their reunion that the businessmen who were buying them out had reneged on the deal – Stampede would be staying with the Hart family. Bruce immediately set about selling Dynamite to his dad, but met resistance due to the fact that Stu, like most old-time wrestling promoters, believed only heavyweights could draw big money. But when the new year came and the promotion continued through desperate times, Bruce urged his dad to reconsider and fly Tom out to Canada.

He even lied to his own dad, exaggerating Tom's size as 'about 180', knowing all too well he was closer to the 150-pound mark. With nothing left to lose, contact was made with Ted Betley through John Foley and an offer was made to the teenage sensation, who was currently being paid just £12 per show by Max Crabtree. The offer was for an initial six-week tour and was worth $400 per week plus an apartment and a car on hire. Tom accepted and pulled Max to one side at the next show to inform him.

'Listen, Kiddo,' a suited Max began the charm offensive. 'You're the champ! If you go, you can't just come back under the same circumstances.'

'What ya talkin' about, Max?'

'You'll have to forfeit the belt before you go.'

'But I'll only be gone six weeks!' pleaded Tom in disbelief – he'd seen champions be out injured longer than that and return without any issue at all.

'It doesn't matter. If you go, you'll be losing on the way out, and then you'll have to start again from the bottom when you get back. Anyway, those Canadian bastards will murder you – they don't know what to do with you high-flying whippersnappers! I'll tell you what, if you stay, those belts will be yours for the foreseeable future, and I'll give you a pay rise.'

With Max's words hanging heavy, Tom reversed his decision and the message was passed to Stu, who cancelled the plane ticket. After the following show in Leicester, Max handed Tom his pay packet. Tom opened it to see just how much the unconfirmed value of the pay rise was. He found £13. Just £1 extra. Max knew Tom was young and naïve and had already cancelled his trip without formalising the new deal.

'I'm not being funny Max, but what is this?' Tom opened his hand to display the measly amount of money he had emptied from the envelope.

'Oh, you're only a young lad, Kid. That's a lot of money for you.'

With that, Max turned and walked away. He left Tom bitter and angry, and feeling manipulated. The moment he got home he called Ted and asked him to get in touch with John Foley or Stu Hart and see if the deal could be reignited. He swore no one would try to take advantage of him like that again.

Tom soon received a one-way flight ticket to Calgary in the post. It was still only the same short-term deal, but Tom no longer felt any loyalty toward Max, and was determined to prove him wrong about being buried and wasted in Canada.

The Dynamite Kid wrestled for Joint Promotions right up to the day of his flight and left without losing his belts – vacating them with dignity instead.

When Tom climbed out of the passenger seat of Billy's car at the airport, he casually said goodbye to his dad and told him he would see him in June. He had just £20 stuffed in the back pocket of his jeans.

Tom arrived in Calgary late on Thursday 27 April and made his debut there the following night. It was then, in the locker room, he met Stu Hart for the first time, and the Hart patriarch's opening words would stick with Tom forever: 'Hey, errr, you're a skinny little bastard, aren't ya?'

3

HART HOUSE

'All I ever wanted was to be the best wrestler I could be.
I wasn't interested in gimmicks or being a great talker; I
wanted to be remembered for my ability in the ring. That was
my ambition.'

Tom Billington

May 1978. Regina, Saskatchewan, Canada

'Keith, you promised me I'd be working with Paddy,' 20-year-old
Bret Hart moaned to his older brother in the locker room before a
Stampede show.

After a few years flirting with the idea of pursuing alternative
career choices, Bret had succumbed and joined the family business. His
amateur wrestling achievements and natural ability for the professional
game – almost learnt via osmosis being brought up as a Hart – had
lured him to help out his father's struggling promotion. He had learned
how to execute a simple match with a similar standard of grappler –
Paddy Ryan was such an opponent.

Keith, acting as booker for the evening, had told Bret he would
be working with Paddy, but Steve Novak – a slow, 260-pound slob
of a wrestler – had refused to *put over* this scrawny young newcomer
the Dynamite Kid and stormed out when told there was no room for
discussion on the matter. So, Bret had been promoted to be Dynamite's
fall guy for the show.

Dynamite was lacing up his boots, listening to Bret's woes. Tom
was still only 19 and very slender, yet this brooding kid from England

cut an intimidating figure. Bruce had already been proven correct by Tom's ability in the opening week of his run and Stu was suddenly very enthusiastic for his new star to be pushed. They knew he was special and hoped to keep him happy, in the desire he would stay with Stampede long-term and help the promotion flourish once again. They needed to push Tom, and that meant him winning in the plucky underdog *babyface* role he knew so well. But in an industry dominated by large men whose careers depended on them appearing strong and masculine to the crowds that ultimately paid the money they relied on to feed their families, losing to a teenager a fraction of their size was not something they were climbing over each other to do. The 'Cuban Assassin' (loyal Stampede stalwart Ángel Acevedo) was fine with it though, and Tom had already spent his opening week wowing the crowds by defeating him with his unique flurry of stiff strikes and high-octane offence. The Cuban Assassin was a consummate professional and the perfect foil for Tom to look his supreme best and announce his arrival in the territory. Fans and wrestlers alike had taken note of the dynamic youngster in their midst.

Lancastrian comrade John Foley, familiar with the British style in which Tom excelled, was also keen to oblige, and the two quickly began a friendship built on their almost identical heritage, separated only by a generation.

But Tom needed a new opponent and Steve Novak had been chosen, but like many others, he had refused to do the *job* once he had set eyes on Tom. Therefore, Bret had been told by Keith that he was going up against Dynamite, who was now in a typically foul mood. Not only did Tom find the attitude and work ethic of his potential opponents extremely unprofessional and disrespectful – something Tom had been told by his father and by Ted never to take lightly – he had also been disappointed with the failure of Bruce, as yet, to deliver on the financial package he had promised. The Calgary apartment was so far a room in Wayne Hart's own apartment, the car hadn't materialised, and his first week's pay-packet was $50 short of the $400 agreed upon.

'Maybe you should wrestle Dynamite,' Bret said to Keith. Bret's resistance to wrestling Tom was in no way disrespectful – quite the opposite. Bret had been watching Tom in awe and simply didn't believe he was capable of doing him justice. He wanted to watch him and learn from him, and to improve enough so that when they did meet in the ring, they could set Stampede alight.

With a shake of the head from Keith – his boss for the night – Bret trudged over and sat next to a silent and moody Tom. Whilst he tied up his bright red boots, Bret began describing his own limitations, almost apologetically. He talked through what he could do well, and tentatively suggested some *spots* for the match. Tom didn't say a word; he just stood up and walked away.

From the moment the bell rang, Bret – taller and physically thicker than Tom – was helpless to stop an onslaught of stiff, heavy blows raining down on him. This piqued with an elbow smash to the face that crushed Bret's nose and sent thick, dark blood pouring down his face and chest. The blood may have been the only thing that kept the crowd's attention, as the display in front of them was effectively a one-sided shoot that ended early and contained none of the spots the humiliated and beaten-up Bret had suggested.

Tom's electrifying talent was being noticed, and ticket sales rose in parallel with his reputation and position on the Stampede card, but his unmistakeable angst was a concern for the Harts.

Stu welcomed all the Stampede wrestlers – be they resident or on a short-term tour – into the family mansion, known as 'Hart House'. Situated atop a hill in a leafy suburb on the outskirts of Calgary, Hart House was a 24-room red brick behemoth, complete with Stu's collection of old Cadillacs strewn across its 30-acre yard.

Stu had been an undefeated amateur wrestling champion, when the Second World War came along and ruined his wonderful chances of gaining rare Olympic glory for Canada as the 1940 edition of the Games was cancelled, followed by the 1944 Games. He quickly found himself representing his country in a Navy uniform rather than his wrestling attire.

After the war, Toots Mondt hired him for his New York-based promotion and introduced him to professional wrestling. It was in the Big Apple that he met Helen and they married on New Year's Eve 1947. She toured the United States alongside Stu, who became one of the country's finest pro wrestlers. In 1951 they used their money to move to Calgary and bought the biggest house they could find for the huge family they intended to rear.

Stu was hugely respected and used his wrestling knowledge and contacts to establish his own promotion, which would later become Stampede Wrestling.

The 24 rooms were soon filled. The couple already had three young sons when they finally moved to Calgary: Smith, Bruce and Keith. In Canada, two more boys followed in Wayne and Dean, before two girls arrived, Ellie and Georgia. Bret was born in the summer of 1957. Alison, Ross and Diana came next before the eternal baby of the bunch, Owen, arrived in the spring of 1965.

As well as mum, dad and 12 children, there were dogs, cats and a revolving door of wrestlers of all shapes, sizes, colours and creeds. They would call at Hart House to collect payment, to socialise, to talk business, or to train in the underground wrestling gym, which would later be sinisterly nicknamed 'the dungeon'.

Before the 1980s, *kayfabe* was absolute in the wrestling world. Only those within the business knew of its inner workings. The majority of fans believed that the explosive sporting drama being played out in front of their very eyes was nothing but legitimate. It was this belief – or as a minimum, the ability to achieve a definite suspension of disbelief – on which the wrestling business was built. 'Protecting the business' was a serious point-of-order taught on initiation. Therefore, the younger Hart kids believed the men strolling around their home, many of whom they saw on the weekly Stampede TV show as snarling, evil, violent villains, were genuinely snarling, evil, violent villains. Couple this with blood-curdling screams emanating from the basement as their dad tried out prospective talents by putting them in agonising submission holds to test their pain threshold and their commitment to the job under the guise of teaching them, and it is little wonder that the creaking wooden door to the cellar became a menacing presence in their childhood.

Two of the most menacing and intimidating sights were those of Archie 'The Stomper' Gouldie, a muscular, shaven-headed heavyweight, and Abdullah the Butcher, a 300lb-plus monster with deep crevices on his head from all the butchery he had performed on himself. Both were Canadian (although Abdullah was billed as being from Sudan to add extra faux horror; his real name was actually Larry Shreve). Stu liked to have at least one of these two men working for

Stampede all of the time, as audience figures and revenue was so much improved with them featured. They would perform as the fearsome heel at the top of the card for the terrified and transfixed crowd. A local lad would be offered up as the brave underdog, and more often than not, that lad's surname would be Hart, as Stu's boys were *smartened up* one by one and invited into the dungeon for their initiation.

Tom was encouraged to spend even more time at Hart House than most. With Archie and Abdullah's time with the promotion decreasing due to the fact that far more money was on offer in New York, Japan and parts of Europe, Stu was keen for a new star attraction and finally accepted that the unique dynamism of the Dynamite Kid might be just what they needed. They lavished Tom with their company, their food and their drink (although clean-living Tom was teetotal and dedicated to his profession) in a bid to make him enjoy his time in Canada and potentially stay longer. Beyond that, they had quickly sanctioned the new British Commonwealth mid-heavyweight championship belt and claimed the young star was the holder of the title from his homeland and had brought it to Calgary with him.

On Sunday afternoons, the boys would run off their giant family dinner with a game of touch-football. Within minutes of being introduced to the game for the first time, the speedy and slippery Tom rolled back to his rugby youth and was soon running rings around the Hart boys who had grown up playing the sport.

The first time Tom truly felt at home in Canada was when he walked down the industrial metal-grated steps to the dungeon: the stench of stale sweat and the blood soaked into the wrestling mat; the welded, homemade weight machines and the dumbbells stacked around the perimeter; the ceiling polka-dotted with holes from wrestlers' flailing boots and skulls, all reminded Tom of the gritty gyms he had trained in back home in Lancashire. A wash of steely determination flooded over him; he knew he could be the best in the world, and maybe he had found the place to help him realise that potential. He began working out obsessively and maniacally down there, became leaner and quicker, but not thicker and bulkier like he knew he needed to be to break through the glass ceiling his stature burdened him with.

Ángel Acevedo wanted his Fidel Castro-like 'Cuban Assassin' character to embark on a longer *programme* with Dynamite, as even in defeat he looked better than he had ever believed he could whilst in the ring with Tom. But the Harts booked grizzly Australian heel Norman Frederick Charles III into the sought-after spot as challenger to Tom's British Commonwealth title.

The Stampede crowd had quickly come to adore the Dynamite Kid. Tom was playing the role he had all of his young career: the plucky babyface against the naturally bigger and intimidating bad guys. His fast-paced, high-flying, gymnastic style was revolutionary and some of the most exciting wrestling they had ever seen.

* * *

Stampede Wrestling was named after the annual ten-day summer rodeo that Calgary was most famous for. For decades, Stu had used the festival – dubbed the 'Greatest Outside Show on Earth' – as the premier week to his wrestling year, as the biggest stars in the wrestling world would come and take advantage of the large crowds on offer. The Hart family and their roster of giants and midgets and everything in between would ride the parade on dedicated heel and babyface convertibles to promote the live show that same evening. A ring would be pulled along by a large truck.

The Stampede Corral, the original home of the Calgary Flames professional hockey club, would host the traditional super show climax with a guaranteed full house of 6,000 fans. But for the rest of the year, it was the Victoria Pavilion that Stampede would call its home. Here they would perform to a couple of thousand regulars every Friday night and film the one-hour weekly TV taping. It was small, raw, and intimate – just two feet of concrete floor separated the ring apron from the feet of those in the front row.

Outside of Calgary the Stampede vans would tour far and wide, travelling hundreds of miles in the Canadian snowstorms as the National Wrestling Alliance's official promotion of the Calgary 'territory' (in reality, it covered the whole of western Canada and even Montana, stateside of the US border).

The National Wrestling Alliance (NWA) was the USA's equivalent to the UK's Joint Promotions, acting as the national governing body overseeing the regionalised promotions that were affiliated to it, mainly across North America and Canada, but promotions in Mexico,

Australia, New Zealand and Japan were also part of the union. They had a friendly rivalry with the American Wrestling Association (AWA), which controlled some other regions and promotions.

Each territory had its own champions and resident talent, but promoters would trade wrestlers to keep their product fresh. The NWA world champions (heavyweight, junior-heavyweight, women's) were promoted above their home region and made up the main events of the NWA roadshow, touring the territories across the country and beyond, allowing the local talent to challenge for the titles and get the opportunity to show the wrestling world what they were capable of. In Calgary, this was aligned with the July rodeo and became known as 'Stampede Week' in the NWA calendar. It gave Stu a guaranteed lucrative spell in the middle of the year and, if done well, would ensure the weeks that followed would be fruitful, as new rivalries, storylines and stars were introduced to the large crowds. He spared no expense on this annual kick-start for his business. As well as showcasing the NWA champions, he would bring in independent stars such as André the Giant, and even non-wrestling celebrities such as champion boxers Rocky Marciano, Jack Dempsey and Joe Louis as guest referees. It was a festival that buzzed with excitement.

NWA champions were the glitterati of professional wrestling. They were the money drawers, the entertainers, the merchandise sellers. The heavyweight champion was simply *the man*. These champions would reign for long periods, with a single man dominating for several years, as he would attract money for the NWA and for each promotion he toured during his era. In the 1950s, that man was all-American hero Lou Thesz, an amateur prodigy who became a deity-like champion. After three separate reigns – with a combined length of over ten years – Thesz passed on the torch in 1966. By then, however, the tide had swept into muddier waters. Five years earlier, 'Nature Boy' Buddy Rogers, representing the New York territory (which actually covered most of the north east), had become champion. Rogers was brash and cocky – both in and out of the ring. He was the antithesis of what the NWA and Thesz had previously stood for and represented, but he was good-looking, talented, unique, and supremely hated by the fans.

It was felt that Rogers wasn't giving fair distribution across the country, spending a disproportionate amount of his time in his own north east cities. The New York territory was run by Capitol Promotions, whose bosses were the legendary Toots Mondt and his latest business partner, Vincent J. McMahon.

In 1963 the NWA board, which was mostly made up of the territory promoters, decided to remove the title belt from Rogers. This was not a popular decision with Mondt and McMahon; New York was the largest and most powerful area geographically, financially, and also in terms of fanbase within the NWA, and they felt their opinions and votes should be proportionally the most powerful in respect of that.

Thesz was chosen by the board to regain the title for the first time in six years, largely because even at 47, he was still the toughest and most legitimately well-respected shooter around; there would be no attempts to subvert orders with Lou Thesz in the ring, but it was feared Rogers may be under separate instructions from Mondt and McMahon, beyond those given to him by the board. Subsequently, Thesz felt the need to warn his adversary before the match: 'We can do this the easy way, or the hard way.'

Disgruntled, Mondt and McMahon pulled their Capitol Promotions and the New York territory out of the NWA. To make it appear more global than territorial, they renamed their organisation the World Wide Wrestling Federation (WWWF). They installed Rogers as their champion and openly disputed the NWA title-change (pre-internet and with no national TV syndication, it was commonplace for wrestling results to be disputed, changed, invented or even just wiped from history). The WWWF became another rival of the NWA, alongside Verne Gagne's AWA, although all three understood and respected the age-old agreement not to infringe the territorial boundaries.

The WWWF then made a superstar out of local Italian immigrant and working-class hero Bruno Sammartino. They were regularly filling Madison Square Garden with raucous and passionate fans. In response, the NWA felt they needed their own blue-collar idol, and Harley Race was the perfect answer.

In 1960, at just 18 years of age, Race had got married and his bride Vivian was pregnant. Handsome and athletic, he was viewed as a rising star in the wrestling business, but a terrible car crash crushed his leg and, far worse, killed his new wife and unborn child. With only wrestling left in his life, 'Over my dead body,' he told the doctors who planned to amputate his leg. Despite being told he may never walk again, Race took the long and hard road to rehabilitate his leg and get back in the ring.

Already a tough kid, the whole ordeal made Harley a no-nonsense, gun-carrying, legitimate hard-man. By the 1970s, he was feared but universally respected by everyone in the wrestling business. At over 6ft tall and naturally thick-set, Harley was certainly a heavyweight, but he wasn't of the athletic, muscle-bound build of Thesz or Sammartino. Whilst those champions would be working out, Harley could undoubtedly be found in the local watering hole, knocking back beer upon beer and chain-smoking cigarettes. He had fair, curly hair and faded tattoos on his forearms, and certainly gave the appearance of a barroom brawler rather than a mat technician. He backed up that differentiation with his tough, simple, but effective in-ring style. He would pummel and slam his opponents hard into the mat, before climbing up on to a second turnbuckle and dropping a flying headbutt onto his stricken foe for the *finish* – an impressive but rare sight for a heavyweight in that era.

A FIRST TIME FOR EVERYTHING

'I knew I'd reached a point where other wrestlers would
definitely think twice before trying it on with me.'

Tom Billington

July 1978. Stampede Week, Calgary

As Stampede's premier non-heavyweight, the Dynamite Kid had
been chosen to wrestle the NWA world junior-heavyweight champion
Nelson Royal for shows during the week, which began at the regular
venue of the Pavilion. It would then take in a typical 'Stampede
loop' – covering over 2,000 miles of mostly dirt and gravel road – of
Edmonton, Regina, Saskatoon, Medicine Hat and Yellowknife, before
the final night back in Calgary for the glorious climax at the Corral.

Nelson Royal was a 42-year-old highly respected veteran. He was
a lean and slick mat technician, and Dynamite – 23 years his junior
– was looking forward to putting on a wrestling clinic and thrilling
the crowd. Harley Race would defend his heavyweight crown against
Dory Funk Jr in the main event – the only match to follow Dynamite
and Royal on the card. But the main event certainly couldn't follow
its predecessor in terms of match quality and excitement, as the roof
was torn off the Pavilion by a battered and bloodied Tom, who, after
bumping all around the venue and making Nelson Royal look 22 rather
than 42, lost just before the one-hour time limit expired, despite a
heroic effort.

The bar was lifted again the following night in Edmonton in front of a sell-out crowd. Invigorated and uplifted, the gracious hosts opened the complimentary crates of beer to their tourists. Always first to the beer was Harley Race – who, as the heavyweight champion, had been given one of Stu's Cadillacs for the week rather than having to clamber in and out of the smelly old vans with the rest of the locker room. He was joined by fellow champion Nelson Royal and they were to take a couple of the locals in the back to act as their hosts and navigators, with Tom and Keith Hart getting the nod for the trip to Saskatoon. As the clock struck midnight, Keith Hart and Tom attempted to make Harley aware that the Calgary Stock Ale Stu had provided was 8.8% proof and wasn't really designed for a man about to negotiate a four-hour drive. Harley, who had also successfully defended his title, cast Royal a smug glance as he knocked the cap from another bottle, 'I could drink as much as André and I'd still be driving that Caddy,' he said. 'In fact, I might just do that!'

Tom was still teetotal and Keith, knowing it was the most crucial week of the year for the family business, was also keeping his alcohol intake low.

As the drunken Harley sped east on Yellowhead Highway, the dark of night obstructed the scenic views of the rolling hills and lakes. When Keith noticed Harley bite the cap from yet another bottle, he reiterated his concern and suggested they swap places, with Tom quick to second the motion.

Harley squinted in his rear-view mirror. 'Ya know, Nelson, I can't understand a fucking word that Limey bastard says!' Harley rasped.

'That's okay, Yank, 'cos I can fuckin' understand you, which means I must be cleverer than you, eh?' Tom responded. Harley's eyes narrowed and he took another long drink.

When the driving became more erratic, Keith spoke up firmly, insisting Harley pull over and let him take over. As the car screeched to a halt beside the roadside ditch, Keith and Tom breathed a sigh of relief.

'You wanna drive boy, you'll have to fight me for it!' Harley said as he swung open his door and walked towards the ditch.

Both being brought up in fighting families, Tom and Keith begrudgingly obliged. As they walked towards him, Harley grabbed both of them by their hair and attempted a comedic pro wrestling spot by banging their heads together . Keith quickly tripped Harley and they fell into the ditch, with the younger, smaller, sober lad gaining the high ground and there was only going to be one winner of the scuffle. With this, an equally inebriated Nelson Royal stumbled out of the passenger seat and rushed towards the action, brandishing his cowboy boot, but Tom stopped him in his tracks firmly and proceeded to play peacekeeper.

Harley climbed out of the ditch and as he dusted himself down, he handed the Cadillac keys to Keith and the two world champions relegated themselves to the back seat, humbled by Stampede's junior-heavyweights.

Tom and Keith had gained the respect of NWA champion Harley Race. Tom became enamoured with Harley's attitude and the respect it gained him in the locker room and within the wider business; he naturally shared the same no-bullshit agenda and believed himself to be a legitimate tough guy in and out of the ring, and should demand those same levels of respect from his peers.

Tom would wrestle classic after classic against Nelson Royal the whole week to absorbed and electrified crowds. Bret Hart, who was not yet deemed up to 'Stampede Week' standard, watched their final match wide-eyed and slack-jawed, seeing first-hand the kind of match he dreamt of putting on one day.

But, for the huge finale back home in Calgary at the Corral, Dynamite was relegated a place on the card and wrestled his regular opponent Norman Frederick Charles III. Tom was disgruntled his spot against Royal had been given to Keith, who he saw as lesser-skilled, for the biggest event of the week in front of the biggest crowd. Not only that, Keith was given the honour of wrestling a one-hour *broadway* against the champion, whereas Tom had been booked to narrowly or controversially lose in all of his own title challenges. But his show-stealing performances had certainly been good enough to raise the eyebrows of the world's talent-spotting promoters in attendance. German Edmund Schober was the first to approach Tom and offered him a place in the lucrative six-week tournament his promotion, Catch Schober, put on each year in Hanover to coincide with German festival *Oktoberfest*. The deal had to be ratified and agreed with Stu as Tom was under contract with Stampede.

On completion of the talks, suddenly Bruce and Smith would be accompanying Tom in Germany too.

Tom was now spending most of his time either training or socialising at Hart House. He became very friendly with Helen, who would regularly invite him for the huge Sunday family lunch they hosted. Tom's uncle Eric lived in Edmonton, having emigrated there when Tom was a child, and Stu would happily lend him one of his many Cadillacs for the journey should he want to visit during a rare break from wrestling.

Bruce and Keith invited Tom skiing with them one sunny day. When they got to the local resort at Banff, the temperature was below zero. Tom was wearing his typical T-shirt and jeans. Not wanting to give them the satisfaction of seeing him cry off, Tom continued with his maiden attempt to ski. Bruce and Keith each strapped one boot over the legs of Tom's faded blue jeans.

One ski boot came off almost instantly when Tom began his first descent. With no experience on the slopes and now with only one ski, even Tom's gymnast-quality balance and agility was not enough to save him from a cold and painful tumble down the mountain. When the Hart brothers proudly walked into the resort café following their own enjoyable descents, they found a shivering Dynamite Kid nursing a steaming cup of coffee. Tom laughed along with them at his own plight, but seethed internally, and swore to himself he would have the last laugh.

Soon after, following a typically tough training session down in the dungeon, Tom and Bruce were washing off in the adjoining shower room. One set of taps controlled the notoriously sensitive water temperature for the full set of shower heads, which were positioned all around the perimeter. As Bruce lathered himself, Tom turned off the cold tap. Almost instantly, the water turned searingly hot and scalded Bruce, whose scalp and shoulders later came out in blisters.

Many months later, Tom couldn't resist when an opportunity for revenge on Keith presented itself in the ring.

'Don't move,' Dynamite whispered surreptitiously in Keith's ear after slamming him hard in the centre of the mat. Keith lay motionless as Tom climbed to the top turnbuckle and the crowd held their breath. Tom launched himself high into the air, guiding a pointed knee into the face of his opponent. Keith didn't need to *sell* this one; his pained reaction was nothing but genuine as blood gushed from his mouth. Tom hadn't pulled out on impact.

'What the hell was that supposed to be, Tom?' Keith asked angrily in the locker room, whilst grimacing and dabbing blood from his face with a towel.

'Just a minute 'ere, lad,' Tom responded, feigning innocence. 'I did tell you not to move. I had it all weighed up perfectly. You must've flinched.'

Keith Hart wore a gumshield in almost every match for the rest of his career.

* * *

In Germany, Tom met Sylvester Ritter, who wrestled as 'Big Daddy Ritter' but would be best known as 'Junkyard Dog' a decade later; his wrestling talent was limited, but he was big and charismatic and could put on a good show for the crowd. Playing to his strengths to ensure the work kept coming in, Ritter was one of the many wrestlers now taking steroids in a bid to further improve their physiques despite having little time between shows and travelling to actually work out and maintain the kind of diet and lifestyle that would otherwise be required. Steroids were legal in the United States and most of the world at this time but had been banned by the International Olympic Committee as a performance enhancing drug in 1975. Whilst not as well-known as they are today, the negative side effects on the minds and hearts of users were known. Most sports were following suit in banning their use, but wrestling, by definition, didn't have the concern that drug cheats would gain an unfair advantage in an otherwise fair sporting contest, as the result, of course, was predetermined. Promoters also had a natural conflict of interest: if they enforced any ban or introduced drug testing, wrestlers might avoid their territory and work for their rivals instead.

Whilst steroid use in other sports declined in the late 1970s, it rose just as quickly in wrestling. This was largely due to the success of 'Superstar' Billy Graham – the WWWF heavyweight champion who had been originally trained by Stu Hart in the dungeon. Graham had gigantic muscles, which shone up nicely on his artificially bronzed and oiled skin; his champion status was generally seen as being more due to his look and charisma than his grappling ability, and so others were inspired to concentrate on these traits ahead of mastering the art of wrestling.

After hitting it off whilst spending time in the bars together during the *Oktoberfest* tour, Ritter sold the benefits of steroid use to Tom – a bigger, more muscular frame possibly being the final ingredient the Dynamite Kid needed to make him a global star. Tom still felt his lack of height and his slender frame were unfairly holding him back. Ritter gave Tom some dianabol pills, and his life changed forever.

Tom showed almost as much pride in his abilities as a prankster as he did as a trailblazing wrestler. Axel Dieter was the German champion, a wily old veteran who was the locker-room leader, the unofficial booker and the local crowd favourite. He liked to ensure newcomers to the region knew he was in charge by gloating about what a great shooter he was. One night early in the *Oktoberfest* tournament he wrestled Afa Anoa'i (who was also a member of the tag team the 'Wild Samoans' with his brother Sika). Afa was quiet and mild-mannered and Axel clearly thought he was a good choice of victim to stiff and prove to the rest of the North American and British contingent that he was firmly in charge. But Afa was a very legitimate tough guy who didn't take kindly to bullies and proceeded to prove to Axel and his adoring fans that he wasn't so tough.

In the changing room after, a humiliated and irate Axel pulled a revolver out of his bag and cut a deranged figure as he warned all the other newcomers not to try anything like that with him ever again. Afa was very well respected and popular on the North American circuit and the boys rallied together in support of him, which made for a frosty atmosphere for the next five weeks as the local wrestlers pulled in line with Axel.

Part of the tradition at the *Oktoberfest* tournament is that fans bring along gifts for their favourite wrestler, from cards and cash to alcohol or baked goods. When November arrived and the tournament neared its close, Axel proudly walked away every evening with his large collection of gifts. But Tom, Bruce and Smith struggled to hold back their laughter as they saw him and his posse feasting on a homemade dog food pie and wine into which Tom had injected liquid laxative through the cork.

After three months away, Stu Hart welcomed his star attraction back to Calgary – as well as his two sons. He excitedly informed Tom that Bret was the new British Commonwealth mid-heavyweight champion, having beaten Norman Frederick Charles III, who Tom had dropped the belt to before leaving. Stu said he saw great things in a long-term programme between the Dynamite Kid and Bret Hart. Assuming this was another example of nepotism in Stampede, Tom's natural reaction was one of frustration that he would once again have to carry a series of matches against what he saw as a mediocre Hart; little did he know that Bret had made dramatic improvements and had himself been the one wowing the Pavilion in their absence.

5

SHOOTING UP

'To tell you the truth, I preferred being the villain. If I could get the crowd riled to near riot level, I'd do it. Because angry or not, those people definitely got their money's worth, and a match they could talk about for a long time.'

Tom Billington

December 1978. The Victoria Pavilion, Calgary

The audience was at fever pitch. Cheers turned to jeers; screams turned to gasps. Stu Hart, now 63 years old, stormed toward the ring. His gait was slow following half a century of wrestling, his face grimaced with legitimate frustration. When he reached the ring, he banged both of his giant hands on the mat and screamed through the ropes to his two young stars: 'We need eight more minutes for TV, goddammit!'

Bret and Tom were beating each other into bloody messes in the ring. It was the end of the second week of their planned three-week programme working together, which would end just in time for them to lick their wounds over Christmas. December had started with Dynamite stiffing Bret in their matches. He was proving he didn't care about the Hart dynasty and the Stampede hierarchy – he was the star.

As the days and weeks went by, Bret retaliated more and more. He stopped trying in vain to perform his predetermined spots and he began to fight back instead.

The idea of the programme had been that of two young babyfaces grappling with honour and dignity for the title and the glory. Now, on a TV taping no less, the climax to the non-kayfabe feud that had descended into violent chaos was happening in the ring. The match hadn't started too recklessly as they cautiously eased into the action. Bret knew Tom wanted to hurt him and Tom was now aware that Bret was, when required, willing to give his own share of *potatoes* back. This gave the fans a rare feeling of ultra-realism, as the ever-merging grey area between 'real' and 'fake' within pro wrestling swirled towards a dark intensity before their very eyes. They had come to expect blood from the pair's match-ups, and both of the young men were prepared to provide it. On this occasion, it was Bret's turn to slice open his hairline with the blade concealed in his wrist tape. Bent over on all fours, feigning agony, Bret ran his hand through his hair, with the blade pressed purposely against his scalp. According to Bret in his book, Tom took this opportunity to kick him in the head like he was kicking a soccer ball. That was the final straw for Bret, who leapt to his feet and the pair began having an all-out brawl in the blood-soaked ring. Wayne Hart was the referee but couldn't regain control as the fans' excitement spilled over with the drama that they were witnessing. That was when Stu came storming down to the ring in an attempt to retrieve the situation.

Once Stu had given them the signal that they could finally wrap up the carnage, they trudged back to the locker room.

Panting heavily, they sat and stared at each other with the blood drying dark around their faces, each waiting for the other one to make the first lunge. Wrestlers stood between them, as the tension sizzled.

By ringside, host Ed Whalen was wrapping up the TV taping by saying sorry for his lack of commentary during the main event. 'I am going to apologise to you right here and now,' he said, staring into the camera. 'I have been sitting here for 48 minutes with my mouth open, watching one of the finest fights I have ever seen. I do not exaggerate.'

The New Year brought about changes in Stampede. They now had the talent, but the Bret Hart–Dynamite Kid programme notwithstanding, the booking was failing to deliver the audience reactions intended from it, and TV ratings and ticket sales hadn't improved as much as they needed to.

Smith Hart had an old friend from his time working in Puerto Rico, a booker whose talents he raved about so much that he convinced Stu to hire him. Dick Steinborn arrived and set about putting his mark on the ailing promotion when he started work on New Year's Day 1979. The first thing he saw was too many babyfaces, with all the Hart brothers having the undying loyalty of the fans. Meanwhile, he had the Dynamite Kid, who was still embroiled in a programme in which he was enjoying beating the shit out of a Hart boy.

On 6 January in Edmonton, Dynamite ended his month-long babyface feud with Bret by regaining his title. A week later in Calgary, Bruce and Tom were tag team partners in a seemingly easy match against John Foley and Bob Boucher. But with the wily pair rule-breaking and double-teaming Bruce, the crowd willed him to get to the corner and tag in Dynamite, who leant over the ropes with his arm outstretched, desperate to get in the ring and save his friend. Frustration built as time after time Bruce would narrowly fail to make the tag before being dragged back into the middle of the ring.

When Bruce finally made his heroic dash to the corner, his attempted tag found nothing but fresh air as his partner was suddenly distracted – busy fastening his bootlaces. The crowd were livid as Bruce was slammed to the mat and beaten down once again, and the match was lost.

Foley was continuing the beatdown when Dynamite finally dashed into the ring, but rather than making the save, he joined in the assault. Security had to escort Tom out of the arena, such was the vitriol. Fans threw cups and coins at him, they spat at him and tried to climb over the guard rail to confront him.

To complete the heel transition, Steinborn felt Tom needed an on-screen manager, someone to do his talking and help him lie, cheat and steal his way to victories and titles. He had the perfect man in the wily old John Foley. With *Dallas*'s J.R. Ewing the most hated baddie on TV at the time, Foley unveiled himself as sharply dressed money-bags manager, J.R. Foley, who had apparently inherited a fortune and subsequently retired from wrestling to manage a stable of champions to oppose his nemesis Stu Hart's brood of sons, who he referred to as the 'Hart Mafia'. His first recruit and the leader of his pack would be the Dynamite Kid.

'Money talks, Ed,' a cowboy-hat-and-suit-wearing Foley would rasp into a furious Ed Whalen's microphone after buying the loyalties of yet another member of the roster for his army, whilst clutching a wad of notes in his fist.

Foley's presence, as a fellow Wigan native and Snake Pit graduate and one of the final shooters to come from that famous conveyor that Billy Riley produced, had already been a source of home comfort for Tom. Foley was younger than Billy Robinson and Karl Gotch, and his smaller stature prevented him from having their level of legend, but he had been a notoriously hard man on the wrestling circuit during the 60s and 70s and spent most of his time in that final decade touring the North American NWA circuit. Alongside former rugby league player and Yorkshireman Ted Heath, Foley had formed the notorious tag team, the 'British Bulldogs'.

Over those years, he had built up a good relationship with Stu and liked Calgary, and following an incident in a southern territory, Foley decided to settle down and make roots in the remote safety of western Canada. He had taken more and more to the bottle as the years had gone on, and as the wrestling business moved away from the shooter-turned-worker and to a world in which being legitimately tough mattered far less, a drunken Foley had come to resent many up-and-comers, and was getting a reputation as a bully. At one show in the States he had taken liberties with a pair of second-generation brothers under the guise of stiff working. The brothers were Randy and Lanny Poffo, sons of the highly respected Angelo, who was in the arena backstage. Angelo took offence to Foley's bullying and stormed the ring, and the three Poffos gave Foley a sound beating – a very real one. Randy Poffo would go on to become 'Macho Man' Randy Savage.

Foley remained a drunk, but an extremely jolly one; he told jokes and he sang songs. Popular at Hart House and within Stampede, Stu hired him as a part-time veteran wrestler and as a mentor to many youngsters. J.R. Foley's alcohol-fuelled charisma and microphone abilities came to the fore as he took the role of the rich, dictating manager willing to buy wrestlers' and referees' loyalties. He became a resident and entertaining figure on Stampede TV, with his wrinkled face, beer belly and quick, barbed wit. With the addition of a small Hitler-style moustache, his venomous tongue was aimed in the direction of any babyface that crossed his or Dynamite's path. Stampede Wrestling had created a pioneering duo the people of Calgary and beyond could truly despise.

Foley saw much of himself in Tom, and a strong friendship grew, as they exchanged nostalgic stories of the Lancashire wrestling community they had left behind. They tended to do this over a beer or two as Tom's previously stubborn, straight-edge attitude was derailed further under the drunken charm of John Foley.

Over the coming months some fans got more than their money's worth from the Dynamite Kid. Tom felt liberated by being a cocky and arrogant antagonist; he could be his natural self with no more of the faux smiling and politeness. He would swear and snarl at the crowd that now hated him, and when he or Foley wound them up beyond breaking point, he would happily wade into the baying crowd swinging fists regardless of the size of the individual or the horde.

With some alcohol in his system, Tom's temper would snap easily. Proud but insecure about his thick accent, any wisecracks in bars about this or his lack of size for a wrestler would often result in the local drunk being launched into the air or picking up his teeth from the beer-soaked floor.

The bond between Tom and John Foley grew quickly. Tom felt liberated and comfortable around John; they shared the same wicked sense of humour and Tom knew any pranks on John would be laughed off. They roomed together and were perennially the final two in the bar. When they would stumble back to their hotel, Foley would fall instantly into a loud and deep sleep. For his own sanity and entertainment, Tom would often carry Foley – mattress or even bed and all, with the help of Bruce or Marty Jones – out of the room. Cleaners and maids would regularly get a shock as they opened an elevator or linen closet door to find a snoring J.R. Foley slumped only in his stained underwear.

Tom's most notorious rib whilst rooming with his manager came in Saskatoon. After noticing cigarette butts floating in the toilet after Foley had spent a while in there, Tom figured Foley obviously finished his smoke whilst sat on the throne and popped the butt between his legs. So, Tom doused the porcelain with lighter fluid and waited for the inevitable flash and scream. The plan was successful, and a shocked Foley emerged with singed privates.

Tom had sourced himself a regular supply of steroids from a doctor of the Boxing and Wrestling Commission in Edmonton and they were really beginning to show their effect. He was now a popular part of the furniture at Hart House and siblings Dean, Ross, Ellie and Bruce invited him to join them on a mid-winter vacation to Hawaii.

One night, whilst walking back late to their hotel from a bar, Tom, Ross and Bruce heard a girl screaming hysterically for help from down a dark alley. The boys dashed down to assist her and found her being assaulted. The real-life heel whipped out a blade and told them to mind their own business, blissfully unaware of the speed and ferocity of the Dynamite Kid. In a flash, the assailant was disarmed and grounded, with boots getting laid into him from all angles. But the girl began to fight against them, squealing at them to stop. When Tom turned around and saw her wild hair, dilated pupils and choice of attire, he realised she was a prostitute and they were beating up her pimp. 'Make up your fucking mind!' he snarled at her, before they left the scene.

Tom returned from Hawaii almost unrecognisable from when he had originally landed in Calgary, as his new thicker and more defined physique also sported a deep tan. With his manager J.R. Foley doing much of his microphone work for him, there was a feeling that at just 20 years of age, the Dynamite Kid was the finished article, and promotions from around the world were circling like vultures hoping to pluck him from the otherwise fallow landscape of Stampede.

* * *

'Now, when you start seeing the spots,' Stu began calmly in his unique raspy tone, 'that means your brain is being deprived of the oxygen it needs to properly function.' The squirming and terrified new trainee was Jim Neidhart. Jim was a Californian in his early 20s and had pinned his professional hopes on making it into the NFL following all-American standard school years in both shot-put and football. But having narrowly missed the cut for the Dallas Cowboys squad selection, his career options were in tatters. Therefore, he had turned up at Hart House with just a small bag of belongings and a scrap of paper containing Stu Hart's details. Moments later, his deep, gravelly voice was the latest to fill the air around the house with blood-curdling screams.

'From there, errr, within a matter of moments, you'll lose consciousness,' Stu continued, 'you might also lose control of your, errr, bowels. So, errr, when you see those spots, you make sure you give my arm a squeeze, hey?'

Stu had a passion for converting athletes into wrestlers, and when he set eyes on the 6ft barrel-chested and muscular red-headed Neidhart, he knew he could make him a Stampede star. Jim got himself an apartment in Calgary and committed to becoming a pro wrestler, but much like Tom, he didn't know anyone so took advantage of the wonderful hospitality the Hart family offered and spent most of his time there – even when not being trained and tortured in the basement. But unlike Tom, Jim had arrived already with a taste for alcohol, and had a wild edge to him once he was a few beers deep. As the weeks wore on, it became clear Jim had an extra reason for spending so much time at the mansion: he had hopes of winning the affections of the most wild-tempered of the Hart siblings in eldest daughter Ellie, and the two soon began dating.

There were more new faces in the territory. One of Dynamite's mentors Marty Jones arrived for a short tour from England and had a series of scintillating matches with the ever-learning and improving Bret. Following a particularly spectacular match at the Pavilion, they were congratulated backstage in a mysteriously slow and deep voice, which had a strong southern accent.

'Unbelievable. Y'all had a helluva match out there. Solid as hell,' said this tall, long-haired and moustachioed smooth-talker. His name was Jake Roberts. He and Bret hit it off and Bret invited Jake to stay in the spare room of his house during his upcoming stint with Stampede.

Big Daddy Ritter had arrived and quickly become North American champion and was put on a collision course with Jake, whose intense and sinister promos on the mic had audiences hypnotised and eagerly awaiting the next instalment of his psychological saga.

Despite an initial boost, Dick Steinborn's booking concepts weren't bearing fruit and Stu let him go early in the spring. Brothers Bruce and Bret joined forces behind the scenes as the new booking team and in the ring as a tag team, battling comrades Marty Jones and Dynamite in a series of electrifying tag and singles matches across the territory. During this period, Tom finally realised and accepted that Bret was genuinely very talented and was now more than capable of carrying the less able stars to the kind of realistic and dramatic fight he would be proud to work himself.

On Friday 23 March, the Pavilion had its first sell-out crowd of 1979. It was the culmination of the tensely built rivalry for the North American championship between sinister anti-hero Jake Roberts and the bully persona of Sylvester Ritter.

Dynamite and Bret put the main event under ample pressure by delivering a match of supremely tight and absorbing work with the British Commonwealth title on the line. In the locker room afterwards, Tom approached Bret, unable to conceal his delight. He held out his hand and thanked Bret for the perfect execution of their match. Bret had finally cracked the stony exterior of Tom Billington. Tom's acceptance of someone as a friend came with a fierce loyalty. In the year he had been in Calgary, only a very select few had extinguished the ever-lit fuse of the Dynamite Kid.

To round off a fantastic night for the crowd and the promotion, Jake won the title to a huge pop. Unfortunately, it was a limping Jake that emerged backstage; he'd severely injured his knee and it looked like he would be out of action for some time. The programme between Jake and Ritter was proving to be a winner with the fans, and with both men able to continue the rivalry using entertaining and unique promos, it was decided Jake would stay in Calgary longer than initially planned. As the title-holder yet to defend his belt, he could sensationally return to the ring at Stampede Week after a couple of months of psychological warfare with his foe. With this in mind, he moved out of Bret's house and into one of his own – which just happened to be in the same block as Tom's.

Newcomers and rookies were always inducted into the herd via a relentless series of ribs, and the size and strength of Jim Neidhart wasn't going to make any of the boys go easy on him. In the van on a long ride to the small town of Drumheller, they had spent hours convincing Jim that, back home, they had made Stu believe that he had been sodomising Hart House's beloved pet cat Heathcliffe. Stu was apparently going to rip Jim's limbs off during their next training session in the dungeon, and Ellie would undoubtedly be dumping him. As they approached their destination, Jake digressed from the topic slightly to tell Jim that Stu had actually been born in Drumheller and was such an iconic hero that there was a 30ft statue of him in the town centre.

'No way?' Jim replied, sensing this was just a continuation of the relentless teasing. But Jake, through the art of his transfixing promos, had trained himself to be captivating and convincing, and as the van rounded the corner to where Jake had him believing the statue stood, Jim had his cheek pressed hard against the van window, desperate for his first sight of it – whilst the rest of the gang struggled to contain their giggles.

'You fuckers!' Jim yelled ruefully as hysterical laughter finally bellowed out at the site of Drumheller's famous giant Tyrannosaurus Rex statue (the town is known for the amount of dinosaur remains dug up there over the years). This rib would become a staple torment for many rookies on their first arduous loop of the giant territory.

* * *

'You know, we're going to have to carry things while Jake recovers,' Tom said to Bret as they prepared to headline a show in Regina on 1 June, 'so let's show 'em that we can be the main event.'

Tom and Bret worked intensely in the dungeon to perfect their bumps, their highspots, their chemistry, their dynamism. They even practised the facial expressions that would best portray their personas to the crowd. Over the next few weeks, they set new standards of dramatic storytelling inside a Stampede ring. There was no repetition, just original finishes and a realism that left even the most sceptical of fans questioning if what they were seeing could possibly be a shoot.

When the time came to switch the title back following a five-week reign by Bret, the young pair thought up yet another original match to keep the crowd's attention piqued – they would use Tom's heritage as an excuse to install the traditional English rules: best-two-out-of-three-falls and with the match split into five-minute rounds. Before the final round, with the score tied at one fall apiece, Dynamite looked fatigued and spent, slumped on his stool in his corner with J.R. Foley shouting encouragement frantically into his face. Meanwhile, an energised Bret prowled, eagerly awaiting the restart. Desperate for a revival, Foley threw a full bucket of water over Tom's head and face, also covering that corner of the mat.

When summoned to resume the match, Dynamite stumbled to his feet in the corner as the crowd urged Bret to dash in and finish him off. An elbow smash lifted Dynamite clean off his feet and the fans popped, knowing the end was nigh. Bret whipped Tom to the far corner and Tom's back cracked hard against the turnbuckle; Bret repeated the punishing move and sent Tom back to his own corner, sprinting after him. Tom cunningly leapt up and out of the way as a dashing Bret slipped on the wet canvas and crunched the small of his back around the bottom of the ring post. The crowd gasped as Bret screamed. Tom pounced, dragging his stricken enemy to the centre of the ring, before twisting and contorting him into an excruciating-looking one-legged Boston crab. Bret squealed and submitted instantly. Backroom staff and security came to the ring – even *they* were unsure whether or not what they had seen was a legitimate accident. Bret crawled to the corner of the ring, where a worried 14-year-old Owen greeted him on the outside of the ring. 'You okay, Bret?' Owen whispered.

'Yeah! How'd it look?' Bret replied with his forearm concealing his mouth.

'It looked like he killed you.'

NEW JAPAN

'Despite his size, the Dynamite Kid was being touted as the
next big sensation in wrestling.'

Bret Hart

July 1979. Calgary

When the Canadian snow finally thawed and the summer sun arrived,
it felt like a bright dawn for Stampede Wrestling, too. Jake Roberts was
on track to return from injury and face arch-rival Big Daddy Ritter and
the eyes of the wrestling world were once again on the Calgary territory
for Stampede Week, as NWA champions and stars including Harley
Race, Nelson Royal, André the Giant and Dory Funk Jr arrived in town.

The Dynamite Kid was to resume his challenge for the NWA world
junior-heavyweight title with evergreen champion Nelson Royal, in the
main event of the week's curtain-raiser at the Pavilion.

On the day of the match, Tom paced up and down the living room
of Jake's apartment, restless with nervous energy. 'I want to show 'em
all what I am like these days, Jake,' Tom said, referring to his new heel
persona and his powerful, steroid-enhanced body.

'How long are you wrestling for, tonight?' asked Jake, who lay
horizontal on the sofa.

'As long as possible.' Tom continued to pace.

Jake slowly rose and walked across the room. He rummaged in
a drawer before turning and handing Tom a tiny clear bag with one
solitary pill in it. 'Here's some help,' he said, taking a long drag of his
cigarette. 'Take it. Only thing with that is, it will make your mouth dry.'

It was a 'Yellow Jacket'. Amphetamine. Speed.

That night Tom wrestled for a whole hour at full pace and intensity. The crowd and the promoters in attendance were blown away.

In truth, Oklahoma-based NWA booker Leroy McGuirk had been so impressed with Tom as a heel that he saw him as their next champion and had informed Stu of his plans to sanction a title change, but Nelson had refused to drop the belt to Tom. Neither Tom nor Stu protested too much to McGuirk, because if Tom had taken that mantle, he would've effectively had to join the NWA tour full-time, just as he was helping to turn Stampede around – in addition, Tom didn't yet have a US working visa.

Dynamite ended the match getting disqualified; he retained the look of an almost unbeatable heel that truly belonged at world level, but Royal kept his belt.

Stu and Stampede knew they had their own stars and matches that could steal the show. They were desperate for Tom and Bret to display their unique chemistry, so for the final couple of shows of the week, that rivalry was resumed. In Edmonton the following night, Jake would defeat Big Daddy Ritter for the NWA world heavyweight championship number one contendership and go on to face Harley in the main event of the week's finale. Dynamite and Bret had had another violent barnstormer the previous day, and once again Tom and Jake chatted in Jake's apartment. Tom's eye was bruised, swollen, and cut following a potato from Bret's fist.

'Bret's gonna get his *receipt* for this tonight, Jake,' Tom told him, pointing with one hand and a beer in the other, as the pair mixed uppers and downers in a bid to wrestle at the peak of their abilities every night for a week, but also be able to rest in between.

'Yeah, I understand why you gotta do that,' replied the once-again horizontal Jake.

'So how should I do it?'

'What ya mean?'

'A knee, an elbow, or a punch?'

Jake sat up, looking uncomfortable.

'C'mon, tell me which one,' pressured Tom.

'Gee, I dunno ...'

'Then I'll do all three.'

'Oh, okay, an elbow. Jeez,' Jake finally answered, laying back down.

'Okay. And what should I split?' Dynamite continued the interrogation. Jake sat up once again, looking at Tom with both concern and confusion. 'C'mon. Should I split his eye, his nose, or his chin?'

'Argh c'mon Dynamite, don't put that on me!'

'Fine. Then I'll do all thr...'

'Okay, okay, do his eye! Jesus!'

'Okay well you better be watching Jake. Or else I'll do both his eyes!'

The glorious, sunny afternoon and carnival atmosphere arrived, and the fans had a stacked card to look forward to back in Calgary: André the Giant would surely win amongst the carnage of the annual Battle Royal (he always did), two of the most popular wrestlers in the NWA in Harley Race and Jake Roberts would battle it out for the heavyweight championship. Sandwiched between was the small matter of yet another British Commonwealth title match between Bret and Tom.

The local fans in attendance knew what would happen, but the new faces and those watching on the TV tapings did not. Bret and Tom brought their full repertoire to the fore; every bump and every highspot that they'd perfected was executed with hard-hitting and intense realism. They stole the show before the main eventers had even laced up their boots. Even Bret's split open eye couldn't ruin their elation at the performance.

André the Giant congratulated Tom and Bret on their match, his huge hands engulfing their comparatively child-like ones. André had been born with acromegaly, often known as 'gigantism'. It had remained undiagnosed well into his adulthood and his legendary career. It is treatable with a risky operation, something André surprisingly opted against when it was finally diagnosed, despite knowing he would ultimately die prematurely with the condition. He loved the wrestling business and knew nothing else; it is theorised that he was concerned that the operation may affect his unique size and appearance or leave him unfit to wrestle. He chose a short life in wrestling over the possibility of a long life without it. André was a hugely popular and respected gentleman on the wrestling circuit worldwide, and addressed everyone as 'Boss' – a moniker that everyone returned to him in kind.

The other wrestlers all then found a viewing spot for the main event. The huge crowd was invested in every move as the drama swung backwards and forwards, but there was a sense of inevitability as Harley Race took control and the match neared its conclusion. Tom was transfixed by the way Harley carried himself with an aura that seemingly formed a bubble around him; fans, wrestlers and staff alike showed him immediate and total respect.

With Jake stricken in the centre of the ring, Harley lined up his traditional finishing manoeuvre when he hopped up on to the middle rope of a corner turnbuckle, and with his arms outstretched for balance, dropped a diving headbutt into the face of Jake. It was over. One. Two. Three.

When Harley got backstage, he too made a beeline for Tom and Bret. 'You two had a great match,' he enthused. 'But I'm telling ya, if you go on taking all those bumps, you'll both end up in wheelchairs!' Harley smirked as the locker room, as always, hung on his every word.

'You're one to talk, y'old fuck!' Tom instantly replied with a laugh. Once again, Harley chuckled at Tom's cheek, shook his head and tousled Tom's hair affectionately. The enormous respect was becoming mutual.

The Dynamite Kid's performances brought about a sudden offer from Japan in the form of the International Wrestling Enterprise (IWE). He was offered $1,000 for the ten-day tour. Eager to see the world and especially be involved in the unique buzz that existed about Japanese pro wrestling, Tom accepted and was soon on the long-haul flight. Naïve Tom hadn't realised IWE was just Japan's third-biggest promotion.

In Japan, *puroresu* had been founded in 1953 with the formation of the Japan Pro Wrestling Alliance (JWA) by Korean former sumo wrestler Kim Sin-Rak, more commonly known as Rikidōzan. The sport quickly became a cult phenomenon and the promotion a huge success; Rikidōzan became a wealthy and powerful celebrity. Money and success almost inevitably attract Yakuza (organised crime) involvement in Tokyo, and in 1963, Rikidōzan was assassinated in a nightclub by the urine-soaked blade of a Yakuza member.

IWE was established in 1966 to challenge the weakened JWA, whose two top stars were still young, having been Rikidōzan's two teenage prodigies: Shohei Baba and Kanji Inoki – respectively known as

Giant Baba and Antonio Inoki in the wrestling world. They had been friends, training partners and tag team champions, but their extreme individual ambition forced them apart and split the company in two. Inoki formed New Japan Pro Wrestling and Baba established All Japan Pro Wrestling. The rivalry was fierce and meant that both companies had to keep their product high in quality. Whilst most professional wrestling in the world slowly became less realistic and violent in a bid to lend itself to a TV audience, in Japan – an island often insulated from outside influences – wrestling got even more gritty and hard-hitting. The fans craved realism and were keen to be involved in it, and the live spectacles often became tense, raucous and uniquely atmospheric.

Tom couldn't speak a word of Japanese, he didn't know anyone on the tour and didn't understand the currency. He wrestled a series of explosive matches against IWE's junior-heavyweight champion Ashura Hara, but as he sat in Narita Airport awaiting his flight home to Calgary, he was in no great rush to ever return to Japan. As always, his exciting performances had raised eyebrows and blood pressures alike. In homage to Harley Race, Tom too had begun finishing his matches with a diving headbutt; but in true Dynamite Kid style, he went right to the top rope and he leapt high into the air, where he hung majestically like a stalled missile before beginning his descent, which would end with enormous impact, and the match would be over.

Scheduled to return in January 1980, Tom had signed an ongoing deal with IWE for his exclusivity in Japan. What Tom didn't know was that New Japan was expanding further and had signed up to a partnership with Vincent J. McMahon's World Wrestling Federation (who had recently dropped 'Wide' from the title for a slicker-sounding name), which would help both promotions expand globally.

In January 1978, Tatsumi 'Dragon' Fujinami had defeated Carlos José Estrada in New York to win the WWF junior-heavyweight championship. With the Japanese style and roster more suited to a junior-heavyweight division, the title was taken east by its new lean, muscular and hard-hitting babyface champion.

New Japan organised a North American tour in conjunction with the NWA and the WWF and wanted Fujinami to defend his belt relentlessly on the tour, to enhance his growing global reputation. With this match being outside Japan and not a New Japan exclusive show, the Dynamite Kid was still eligible to be Fujinami's challenger as the tour went through Calgary.

17 August 1979
Victoria Pavilion
Calgary, Alberta, Canada
WWF Junior-Heavyweight Championship Match
The Dynamite Kid v Tatsumi 'Dragon' Fujinami
Approximate attendance: 2,000

When the Dynamite Kid climbed into the ring, it no longer felt like anyone was viewing a young sensation with potential – before their eyes was very much the real deal. He snarled at the audience while J.R. Foley, wearing a garish peach-coloured ruffled shirt and oversized black bow tie, paraded him to the jeering crowd as the ring announcer introduced him. His pectoral and abdominal muscles were defined, his shock of thick hair was now down to his shoulder blades and his once skinny and frail-looking legs were now muscular, and over them he wore mustard-coloured tights and boots.

Fujinami was bigger still and was greeted with joyous delight as he bounced in his corner of the ring. The audience hoped this celebrated stranger from another land was going to come into the Dynamite Kid's back yard and teach him and his arrogant manager the lesson no local challenger seemingly could.

The fight started at a frantic pace, with Dynamite raining down blows with any limb available to him. The crowd popped when Fujinami burst back with any offence of his own, and Dynamite bumped hard and realistically; he screamed in agony and begged for mercy. Foley taunted the fans as he paced up and down the narrow gap between them and the ring apron. The frenetic intensity continued for the entire 20-minute contest which swung back and forth. Blood gushed down Tom's face from his nose (to add even more reality, rather than cutting his forehead when the impact being sold was to the face, Tom had taken to ramming a thumb up a nostril with such force it caused an horrendous nosebleed).

The match ended when Dynamite climbed to the top rope and sent himself airborne for his diving headbutt, only for his seemingly stricken Japanese foe to emerge dynamically from the mat and meet Tom's advancing torso with a perfectly timed dropkick. Dynamite sold the impact like it was a gunshot wound and rolled outside the ring to the feet of the delirious crowd. An energised Fujinami dove through the ropes and continued the assault on the outside; neither man would make it back into the ring before the count of ten. A double count-out. A wild success. As Tom Billington battled at people's feet, he had the wrestling world falling at his own.

Global superstars Stan Hansen and Antonio Inoki wrestled the final match, but the crowd had already seen their main event.

When the New Japan office saw tapes of the Fujinami–Dynamite Kid match, they were in further awe of Tom Billington. As the year was coming to a close and Tom's IWE January tour approached, New Japan made an offer to him through Stu. They were offering almost double the weekly rate and a lucrative five-week tour rather than the three weeks Tom was booked for with IWE. Stu educated Tom on the size of the respective promotions and the extra exposure and more regular tours available to him with New Japan. Tom took Stu's advice and reneged on his IWE deal and signed with New Japan.

IWE continued to advertise the Dynamite Kid for their tour and even began legal proceedings for the damages incurred to their business. New Japan took care of the legal battle as the Dynamite Kid continued to become one of wrestling's hottest and most sought-after talents. His style was, at the time, unique and sensational. His moves were fresh and ground-breaking – he was snap-suplexing his opponents before the snap-suplex was even recognised, and a perfectly executed 'nip-up' from a down-and-out position wasn't a highspot in a Dynamite Kid match, it was merely a standard part of the routine. Every match would feature new acrobatics and brutal intensity.

Tom knew the New Japan tour was going to be a completely different experience the moment his feet touched the ground at Narita. He was whisked immediately into the first-class section of the *shinkansen* – the famous bullet train – and was checked into a five-star hotel when he reached Tokyo.

He wrestled Fujinami in singles matches, or sometimes tag matches at the top of the bill with the likes of Hansen and Inoki in packed-out arenas, night after night. The wrestling was how Tom liked it: stiff and hard-hitting. The volatile and vociferous fans demanded sweat and blood and a tangible sense of legitimacy. Ironically, the 'Wigan-style', as it was called in Japan, was laced into the fabric of their *puroresu*, as it had been so heavily influenced by Billy Robinson and Karl Gotch in its formative years. Obsessive and knowledgeable on their wrestling, this connection wasn't lost on the fans, who saw the Dynamite Kid as possibly the next *Kamisam* – Gotch's 'God of Wrestling' sobriquet. Gotch trained New Japan's young talent – known as the 'Young Boys' – in their dojo in Tokyo, and those same prodigies would tour with the stars, carrying their bags and learning from them. They worshipped Tom, who felt he was finally getting the treatment and recognition he deserved.

Foreign wrestlers, known as *gaijin*, were heels by default as the local support was passionate and patriotic; even André the Giant, adored as the smiling gentle giant across the rest of the world, was a snarling monstrous invader whilst in Japan. This suited Tom perfectly, as he loved his heel persona; he embraced it so much that while in Japan he shaved his head right down to the scalp, exposing the cuts and scars on his hairline. He was encouraged by the New Japan promoters to confront and even fight with any fans that lost control of their animosity towards him, to further perpetuate his evil character.

Tom grew a little goatee, and his skin had reverted back to its natural ashen tone. So committed to his art, he developed a chameleon-like ability to transform and bury himself into his character. His body and muscles were growing rapidly. He was becoming immersed in the wrestling business and its associated lifestyle, which included steroids, alcohol, drugs and painkillers.

In style and heritage there was something magical and perfect in the new relationship forming between the Dynamite Kid and *puroresu*; a tangible sense of destiny.

A global stir was caused by the matches between the Dynamite Kid and Fujinami, and with New Japan in coalition with the WWF, it was only a matter of time before they were booked for a New York show. When the booking was made for that December, it wasn't just any New York territory show: they were to headline at the iconic Madison Square Garden for the WWF junior-heavyweight championship. Tragically for Tom, his US working visa didn't clear in time and just one day before the biggest event of his career – which remarkably was still only four years old – he had to be withdrawn. Bret had been touring the Georgia territory and was on his way home to Calgary when he got the call to divert to New York and take Tom's place. He was thrilled at the huge opportunity.

When Bret arrived in New York, his friend and colleague Mr Hito, who was there representing Stampede, met him in the hotel lobby looking sullen.

'Who's died?' asked Bret.

'You off,' said Japan native Hito, giving Bret the bad news quickly, like ripping off a plaster. 'No work Fujinami. Vince McMahon says you no big name to work Madison Square Garden. Me sorry.'

Heartbroken Bret returned to Calgary with Mr Hito, resenting the decision he believed had been made by Vincent James McMahon.

A decade earlier, Toots Mondt had retired and given up his share of the WWWF promotion, leaving his partner McMahon in sole charge of the WWF. McMahon had given his son, Vincent Kennedy McMahon, a job as a ring announcer. As the 1970s had worn on, McMahon Sr was aging, and the wrestling world was changing. McMahon Jr had become more influential in the company and was a booker as well as an announcer by 1979. It had actually been Vince McMahon Jr that had turned away Bret Hart for not being a big enough name for his show at the Garden.

With their division of smaller wrestlers thriving, Stampede commissioned a new title belt: the world mid-heavyweight championship. They immediately awarded it to Dynamite, who had supposedly won it by way of being victorious in a Rio de Janeiro tournament. He subsequently dropped the British Commonwealth title to Bret and his worldly travels were now, in storyline, him defending his 'world title' – which would increase in value and prestige each time he returned with his reign intact.

YOUNG DAVID

'I was so skinny. The guys used to tease me all the time. I was thin, but really fit. I could wrestle for two hours straight, no problem. But the teasing used to upset me.'

Davey Boy Smith

3 December 1979
Aylesbury Civic Centre
Buckinghamshire, England
Young David v Jim Breaks
Approximate attendance: 1,000

There was a curious feeling of déjà vu happening as 'Young David' was introduced to the crowd at a televised match against veteran heel and European lightweight and British welterweight champion Jim Breaks – the same man Tom had beaten to capture his first major professional title. Tom's younger cousin David Smith had followed in his footsteps: training hard with Ted Betley and at the Snake Pit with Billy Riley and graduating with the same honours in the art of realistic and gymnastic grappling.

He had made his professional debut in May 1978 at the age of 15 against stablemate Bernie Wright. His *World of Sport* TV debut came just four months later and he left school early to follow his wrestling dreams. This also gave him time to improve his physical strength and conditioning, and he added daily weight-training sessions with local professional bodybuilder Walter O'Malley to his regime; Walter would turn into a close friend and mentor.

In his early bouts, David was simply booked as 'Dave Smith', which became 'Dave Boy Smith', and then Max Crabtree decided to double down on David's youth and boyish good looks by giving him the moniker 'Young David'.

Max correctly saw David as the second coming of the Dynamite Kid, and soon booked him into the same role as the fall guy in tag matches alongside his immobile superstar babyface brother Big Daddy. David had done excellently in the unenviable position of constantly taking all of the huge bumps handed out by behemoths like Giant Haystacks and King Kong Kirk. The fans had once again fallen in love with the plucky underdog youngster and just one month after his 17th birthday, David stood opposite Breaks at the beginning of his own singles career.

He had grown a few inches taller than Tom to 5ft 11in but remained very skinny despite his weightlifting. He wore a blue singlet to cover the pale and frail frame that would've made the audience question the legitimacy of his ability to go toe-to-toe with the likes of the vastly experienced, much honoured and stocky Breaks.

David looked nervous as he smiled broadly, revealing huge dimples on his literal babyface, and waved at the supportive crowd as the ring announcer introduced him as a 'wonder boy'. The announcer stopped to fill in the crowd on an updated stipulation for the match. Embarrassed to be facing such an inadequate-appearing junior in this non-title, two-out-of-three-falls contest, Breaks was patronisingly giving Young David a one-fall head start and also putting a £100 wager on the line, so confident was he that David could not score a fall against him. The crowd booed the arrogance of the bully, and further cheered the brave teenager.

'He's got a lot to learn yet, of course, but the more we see him the more we realise that this boy has got it,' said legendary commentator and host Ken Walton as the match got underway. 'But I still can't see him securing the second fall he needs against this man, Jim Breaks, who just has too much experience.'

It started as a tame affair, the men entering into tie-ups in which Breaks appeared to have the upper hand with his extra strength and experience. But on each occasion, David would perform an outstanding and original reversal, including cartwheels and headstands into his own hold or arm-drag to the delight of the crowd. With each counter, Breaks grew more frustrated and angry; he began to lash out with punches and kicks as the pace of the match, and the vociferous support for Young David, picked up.

As the match wore on, David's reversals got fewer and Breaks's attacks and submission holds became more relentless. David fought valiantly, consistently refusing to submit as the tension grew. In between holds, Breaks was throwing David from ring post to ring post and slamming him hard into the mat, often sending him somersaulting through the air. Breaks concentrated on the left arm and worked it constantly, and in round three, in an impossible position, with his arm contorted and lifted clear from the ground, David finally gave the nod to the referee and submitted to level up the match, which had swung heavily in the direction of the veteran.

The fourth round of the scheduled eight continued in the same vein, but as Breaks dashed at the midriff of his young foe for yet another takedown, David caught him, raised him up into a powerbomb position, showing his own surprising strength, before slamming him to the mat and beautifully rolling over him and into a bridged position with so much leverage Breaks wouldn't have kicked out for a count of ten. One. Two. Three. As the referee's hand struck the mat for the third time the audience erupted with joy and shrieks of delight. It was a sensational and dramatic ending.

'How about that for a turn up!?' called Walton. 'Breaks can't believe it and I must admit I can't believe it; I would've bet anything against that.'

David grimaced with pain and sold his left arm injury as his right arm was raised and he was awarded his cash prize.

Jim Breaks, so often the gatekeeper between domestic dominance and dutifully putting over international stars or those destined to be so, had done the job for Young David just as he had the Dynamite Kid years earlier. It was a brilliant match and a story wonderfully told, but the story wasn't over yet, as Breaks complained that he still hadn't lost, and it was actually a 1-1 draw. A rematch was quickly scheduled and aired on national TV on 29 December; this time there would be no head start for David, but the result was the same: a two-falls-to-one victory. This was confirmation that Young David was here to stay. But

Breaks complained still, this time that he had been distracted for the deciding fall by fellow veteran Alan Dennison, who was in the corner of the youngster for support.

They had a longer break to really build up the tension and the storyline before the third and final instalment of the trilogy. It finally aired on 23 February 1980 and took place in Southend as part of British wrestling's regular touring of the traditional seaside towns. This time, the British title would be on the line. It was more of the same gripping action but scheduled for 12 rounds. With the gold hanging in the balance, there was a more epic feel. The wrestlers delivered on this, maintaining the pace and intensity for almost the full scheduled hour. Sporting an elbow brace in a continuation of the angle that Breaks would target the weakened limb, David was one fall down for most of the match, as the crowd willed him on to find the equaliser. With just seconds left until the final bell, having put up with Breaks's typically frustrating tactics and unsporting behaviour, David gave him a taste of his own medicine as he feigned injury and lured Breaks to come in for the kill. As he did, David quickly executed a perfect roll-up for a three-count and equalising fall. Dennison jumped into the ring as jubilation erupted in the audience. It finished a draw and Breaks retained the title and his standing within the roster. This led directly to another feud with Dennison, and the veteran duo rolled back the years as they entertained crowds far and wide – with Dennison finally taking the title from Breaks.

For Young David, it was the making of a superstar. But was this shy teenager – so different to the cousin that had preceded him – ready for such stardom?

* * *

The Dynamite Kid was now a global phenomenon and was wrestling wherever and whenever he wanted. He was splitting his time between New Japan and Calgary. He would occasionally work a trip home to England into his travelling schedule to see his family and, being completely addicted to the buzz of wrestling, work some shows for Max Crabtree and Joint Promotions against some of his old friends and colleagues, such as Rollerball Rocco and Marty Jones. Invariably, these matches would be TV sensations and really serve to show the British fans what they were missing, as their own domestic main events were still dominated by embarrassingly slow and obese novelty acts – with ticket sales and TV audience figures beginning to wane as a result.

Tom was both a blessing and a curse for Stampede and the Hart family. He was their star attraction; he was *the man*. But he was only spending half of his time there. Bret was doing his best to fill the holes left by his absence. Jim Neidhart had trained on well and was being groomed as a super strongman character, but an opportunity had arisen for him to resume his first-choice sporting profession with the Oakland Raiders. His and Ellie's romance had become a whirlwind love affair and they were already man and wife despite both having fierce tempers and often turning the air within Hart House blue.

Bruce Hart was tasked with bringing in some fresh talent. This led to 'Wonderboy' Steve Wright agreeing to spend some time in Calgary. Tom told the Harts that he had trained with Wright as a youngster, but not that Wright had bullied him back then. They thought this could be a goldmine for the promotion – both the storyline and the in-ring action would surely do great business.

Tom also pulled off a coup whilst back in Britain when he tapped up Giant Haystacks for a spell in Canada. Haystacks – real name Martin Ruane – was a slow and stagnant hairy beast of a man, difficult for wrestlers to work with and equally difficult for the viewers to watch, but he was such an ugly behemoth that he was easy to sell as a monster heel, and guaranteed to fill seats at the Pavilion and beyond.

Bret was taking his first official turn as booker, and when Haystacks arrived Bret billed him as 'Loch Ness Monster'. They began having him *squash* opponents whilst doing his routine of snarling and spitting at the crowd.

Tom was having trouble with his knee ligaments. Part of his routine was performing painful-looking knee-drops on to the head and face of his felled opponent which appeared so real and authentic the audience would often audibly wince. He would do two or three of these per night – usually including a flying one from the top rope. The impact was minimal on his opponent in reality, but that was because Tom was soaking up all of the impact on to the knee he planted into the solid mat. He was also innovatively performing a tombstone piledriver on opponents long before the Undertaker had left Death Valley high school, but Dynamite's version saw him leap high into the air and land down hard, once again soaking up the impact that looked like it may have killed his opponent with his knees. He was taking painkillers every day to enable him to wrestle every evening, but one knee finally gave up and blew out whilst he was in Japan, so he returned home to Calgary early to recuperate.

The combination of painkillers and steroids enabled Tom to return to the ring after a minimal period of physiotherapy, just his usual and regimented hard work in the gym. In truth, he was addicted to the high that performing gave him more than any other drug. Bret was naturally thrilled at the prospect of having his shining star available and booked him immediately into a long-planned programme with Steve Wright, who had arrived from his new base in Germany. A frostiness had been apparent between the two since Tom had returned from Japan. Steve, even more so than Tom, wore the Wigan-shooter tag with pride and it soon came to light that he had been one of the older boys that had taken great delight in stretching, hurting and testing schoolboy-aged Tom at Ted Betley's gym. Seven years on, Tom was the bigger star and enjoyed having the fearsome reputation of a tough guy and a shooter himself. The programme had to be binned after the disastrous opening encounter on 29 February confirmed the suspicions that had arisen: not only did they not like each other; they didn't trust each other. The match descended into a shoot as they grappled close and refused to give away leverage, which was eventually gained by the bigger man in Wright, who began to enjoy legitimately hurting Tom in the ring. When he applied a surfboard submission hold and writhed at Tom's wrists and, worse still, his knees, Tom grimaced in pain and the wrestlers and staff watching on from the back grew concerned. Overlord Stu eventually stormed down to the ring once again and banged his huge hands on the mat below the bottom rope, shouting 'I'm paying you to work, not to shoot, damn it!'

Steve Wright's time in Calgary was not to be an extended one. He, his wife and his young son Alex had not acclimatised to the colder and dryer climate of Calgary's winter. Steve also did not socialise much with the brash and talkative Canadian and American wrestlers on the Stampede circuit and never felt comfortable in such an environment. He gave his notice to Stu to finish and would return to Germany. In a rematch with Tom, the two set aside their long-standing differences and had an incredible back-and-forth English-style match with Tom winning decisively with his tombstone piledriver.

The Loch Ness Monster, however, was proving a huge success. He was over with the audience as a real-life monster and was vaporising multiple opponents at a time and never looking hurt or weakened in any way – that was until Jim Neidhart returned following his unsuccessful foray back in the NFL and lifted the giant from his feet and sent him crashing to the mat with a huge bang, the impact and reaction to which had the Pavilion physically rumbling. Giant Haystacks's willingness to fall in this segment made Jim a fan favourite and promoted him up the roster – he would no longer need an NFL career.

Business was up. Dynamite had been in town but wouldn't be for long, and with just two weeks remaining of Loch Ness's time in Calgary, it was decided to capitalise. As the promotion's current top two heels, they had worked as tag team partners in main events and so it was decided to put them in a short programme with Bret and Keith – the current tag champions.

In the first match and with the belts on the line, Dynamite delivered his missile-like diving headbutt to Bret whilst the referee was distracted, before legal man Loch Ness crumbled down on top of him. One. Two. Three. The gold straps were presented to the Dynamite Kid and the Loch Ness Monster as J.R. Foley cackled with glee.

The former champions immediately called for their rematch, which was booked for the following week's TV taping at the Pavilion. It was a packed house as the fans sensed the crescendo of the recent weeks' fantastic shows was upon them. They cheered every move the valiant Hart boys made against the British duo. Their desire to cheer on their local underdogs against a legitimate and unbeatable foreign force had been reignited. When they sensed the match nearing its end, they willed their boys to take control.

Keith and Dynamite were the legal competitors but were in opposite corners of the ring, battling it out with Loch Ness and Bret respectively. Keith was predictably beaten down, releasing the Monster to charge towards Bret and Tom as they traded blows, with Tom squashed into the turnbuckle. Tom's timing was perfect as ever, as he whispered to Bret, telling him the exact moment to move out of the way of the oncoming runaway train. Tom was squashed like a fly and Loch Ness reeled back towards the middle of the ring from the impact. Keith recovered and dragged himself into a kneeling position behind the unsteady giant. The crowd were on their feet, sensing the impossible was becoming possible. Loch Ness's arms flailed as he struggled to maintain his balance as Bret performed two perfect dropkicks to his chest. When his boots met the kneeling body of Keith, Loch Ness tumbled like a felled tree and the roof was blown from the Pavilion as Bret scrambled on top of him. One. Two. Three. The Loch Ness Monster was vanquished.

This perfectly executed storytelling instigated jubilation in the dressing room; even Tom allowed himself to hug and congratulate his colleagues on a job very well done.

Tom's influence in and out of the ring was saving Stampede. He was on fire. He strutted and posed like a catwalk model and cut arrogant and brutal yet humorous promos beside his friend John Foley. He was having fun expressing himself and being given the freedom and the platform to do so. He'd raised the performance levels of the wrestlers individually and collectively, acting as a standard-bearer and insisting his opponents keep up the pace when in the ring with him, and he wasn't afraid to mete out physical punishment on those who slacked.

During this period of recruitment, Smith Hart had brought in Charles Buffong – a muscular black Antiguan wrestler – and hoped to build him into a star, despite the fact he lacked mobility and coordination. One night, Tom got so frustrated in the ring with the new recruit's lack of ability that he punted him in the face whilst he was down on the mat. Buffong's proposed push was over as he would spend several weeks allowing his surgically-repaired jaw to heal.

The sight of the Dynamite Kid brawling with irate fans was becoming more commonplace. But business boomed so much when he was in town that he was immune from the otherwise strict discipline of Stu Hart. Despite only spending half of his time in Calgary, Tom was the locker-room leader and their talisman. He would always be carrying gold – sometimes holding more than one of Stampede's titles simultaneously.

An underlying rivalry ran throughout the Stampede programming between Tom and Bret. Even when they were feuding with other wrestlers, they would tear into each other in tag matches and regularly that would evolve into another one-on-one storyline between them.

Their matches continued to pull in the punters and left them in awe, without fail. Every time they went through Edmonton, one particular small boy was so entranced by what he saw that he fell in love with professional wrestling and immediately embarked on his own journey into the sport. At just 12 he had begun setting up and putting away the fold-out chairs for the events and getting to know the staff. By the age of 13 in 1980, he had begun working out every day in the basement of his family home using the weight set he had begged his father to buy him for Christmas. Following yet another electrifying performance by the Dynamite Kid, the boy engineered himself a backstage meeting with his hero. The boy was Chris Benoit.

'When I'm older, I want to be a wrestler, exactly like you,' young Chris said to Tom.

'Okay, very good,' Tom replied, not thinking much of it. Chris became part of the furniture at all the Edmonton shows, getting tips and training from the established stars, then as a teenager he began travelling to the Calgary shows. A few years later he would be invited to formally begin his wrestling training in the dungeon with Bruce.

* * *

Bret had been dating a girl from Regina called Julie; the relationship had slowly evolved but had become serious enough that Julie moved to Calgary to be with him. But Bret was so old-school he still hadn't smartened Julie up – she still believed wrestling was legitimate fighting and as such, worried every day as her new boyfriend left her to go and battle seemingly the biggest and nastiest men on the planet.

As the Stampede van readied itself for a nine-hour drive to Billings one evening, Julie was there to see off her man. Bret was conscious of the fact that the van was loaded with both babyfaces and heels – as it could often be for the longer journeys – and ensured she was facing away from the bus as he looked towards it. As she leant in and gave him a loving kiss goodbye, his heart sank when he saw the eyes of Tom looking on through a van window. He climbed aboard and shuffled into the only seat remaining, which happened to be next to Tom.

'What's with that?' Tom asked sternly.

'I like her a lot, Tom,' replied Bret as he braced himself for the inevitable barbed comments.

Instead, Tom spoke quietly, 'I know what you mean, Bret. I wish I could find a girl like that.'

Little did Bret know just how 'like that' the girl Tom would find would be.

Julie had been a mother-figure to her 17-year-old younger sister Michelle, who followed her to Calgary and got a job waitressing in a local diner. In the autumn of 1980, Wayne Hart had bought a bungalow in Calgary with a converted basement. He agreed to move into the basement and rent the whole ground level to Tom, who was now earning good money as an in-demand star. The house was close to the diner that Michelle worked at and Wayne and Tom took to eating there regularly.

Michelle would also go along to the Stampede shows with Julie, where she would watch her handsome regular customer with the English accent fly around the ring like a ping-pong ball, thrilling the crowd and inevitably having his hand raised in victory. He would stop and chat with Michelle while the other matches played out.

Tom and Michelle began to see each other but agreed to keep it quiet from Bret and Julie – Tom knew that whilst he and Bret were friends, he probably wouldn't give him a glowing reference as a boyfriend to his girlfriend's little sister. Even if he wanted to, he would first have to smarten up Julie due to the babyface–heel divide that separated them. So, Tom and Michelle would take long romantic walks around the snowy, lamp-lit streets of Calgary, wrapped up in warm clothes, disguising the evil Dynamite Kid from plain sight, Tom allowing his charming side to make a rare appearance as they chatted and laughed for hours.

One evening, however, when they decided to have an evening indoors, Wayne let slip to Bret that he was giving his own house a wide berth as Tom had Michelle round. Bret immediately warned Michelle to stay away from his in-ring nemesis; 'Tom will hang you up like he does his wrestling boots,' he told her, 'and you're better than that.'

But when Bret confronted Tom regarding his intentions, he was left satisfied by the answers he received and eventually gave them his blessing. Julie and Michelle were invited into wrestling's inner workings and the quartet became surreptitiously inseparable – even travelling to events together with one of Bret or Tom having to hide under coats on the back seat as they got close to the venue so that fans didn't see them arriving together.

Tom was due to return home to England for six weeks over Christmas, and after just weeks of dating Michelle, he told her that she should join him. Billy had to pick up a double bed to replace the single one in Tom's room with just two days' notice as the Billingtons welcomed her into their home.

Tom naturally picked up some work at the top of the bill for Max Crabtree. A serendipitous moment came a when he main-evented on 17 December at the iconic Royal Albert Hall. It was a tag team match which lasted only ten minutes but was packed with high-octane and sensational action rarely seen in a British ring. Dynamite and his partner, 'Sammy Lee', beat Rollerball Rocco and Tally Ho Kaye that evening by two falls to nil. For once in his career, it wasn't Tom that most wowed everyone in attendance; it was his partner.

Through Karl Gotch, Max had brought in Sammy Lee – real name Satoru Sayama – from New Japan. Sayama had trained intensely with Gotch as well as Antonio Inoki in their infamous dojo and his martial arts expertise made him resemble Bruce Lee (hence Max's ring name choice for him) as he spun around the ring on the tips of his toes, seeming to levitate whilst swinging venomous roundhouse kicks. But he could also grapple, flip, roll and counter with beautiful agility and rhythm. He had become a cult hero in his short time in England and even Tom, standing in the corner watching Sayama that night, vowed to one day work one-on-one with him, knowing what they could produce together.

Perhaps even more serendipitous, just three days later Tom would appear on the same show as his cousin, Young David. Unfortunately, David's name would be at the opposite end of the card. Having just turned 18, his career in 1980 hadn't quite followed the same trajectory as 1979. His inability, despite training hard, to add much muscle to his slender frame meant that he wasn't being taken seriously as a contender – his appearance had been beneficial in his role as the perennial underdog in tag matches alongside Big Daddy and against veteran heels such as Jim Breaks in singles. But now he was established himself and was expected to win, the story was wearing a little thin. He also suffered in the UK the same way Dynamite had to begin with in Canada, as many wrestlers refused to sell for him or put him over in fear it made them look weak. Worse still, they might be overly stiff and take liberties with him in the ring. He didn't yet have Tom's belief in himself as a leg54rritimate,tough guy, or the confidence to answer back and put down his seniors with a barbed comment when required to stick up for himself. Meanwhile, David had seen his muscle-bound, shaven-headed bad-ass of an older cousin return a comparative superstar and lift the roof off the Victoria Hall in Hanley, challenging Marty Jones for the British light-heavyweight title.

Heel Jones was particularly despised in Hanley, but with Tom's stint back in Britain only being a pitstop, Jones had to retain his title. To send the punters home happy, an impromptu tag match was called to wrap up the evening, and the competitors from the opening contest were called back out. With that, Tom and David joined forces for the very first time, and their dominant two falls to nil victory over Marty Jones and John Naylor was an early sign of what was to come when the cousins were deployed as a dynamic tag team.

* * *

Sandy Scott was a lanky Stampede referee from Scotland; he was one of the boys and drove the bus and drank and smoked heavily. Throughout 1980 they had pushed him as a heel character – a referee in the pocket and on the payroll of J.R. Foley that gleefully did his bidding in the ring. He played the role perfectly and was getting so much heat antagonising the babyfaces that he was on the verge of becoming the top bad guy in the company.

On the road, Sandy had a reputation as a womaniser, which had earned him the nickname 'Chopper'. He boasted of having a girl in every town. One such lucky lady was a rotund married 'ring rat' in her fifties who the boys nicknamed the 'White Tornado'. She would invite herself into the locker rooms or even on to the bus to the next town, where unsuspecting wrestlers would find themselves being pleasured.

Tom was now proficient in the art of spiking drinks, with his favourite and least harmful being a handy dose of the laxative ExLax.

When the White Tornado and Sandy were suddenly struck down by violent bouts of diarrhoea straight after a gathering at Sandy's, they assumed they had become the latest victims of the Dynamite Kid's patented prank. Sandy had become a key part of the show, so Stu was angered when Sandy called Hart House to confirm he was sick and wouldn't be able to make the next couple of shows. Sandy explained what he believed had happened and Tom finally got a ticking off from Stu.

With his intestinal performance back to normality a week later, Sandy met the van at his usual meeting place of the Mohawk gas station on Calgary's Edmonton Trail. The moment he turned towards the seats, he was suddenly reeling backwards once again after Tom had punched him in the mouth, sending his false teeth flying. Shocked and embarrassed more than in physical pain, Sandy looked emotional as he picked up his teeth and his bag, turned around and walked away from the bus and headed home.

Tom would no doubt have been brought up to believe that being a 'grass' was worse than being the actual perpetrator, and to be grassed on for a crime he hadn't even committed had left him furious.

Tom had actually come off worse from the altercation physically, with his right hand swelling like a football. When they got to the venue in Red Deer that night, Tom knocked back yet more pain pills in the locker room whilst 'Dr D' David Schultz held court, boisterously defeating all challengers at arm wrestling. The wrestlers were gathered around in various states of undress as Schultz surprisingly even beat the notorious strongmen, such as Jim Neidhart. John Foley had been acting as referee and Tom had been watching on from a bench, nursing his right hand and smoking a cigarette with his left. With all other challengers vanquished, shirtless Tom got to his feet, flicked the lit cigarette across the room and said, 'I'll try ya, David, but it'll have to be left-handed.'

Schultz shifted his body around and perched his left elbow on the makeshift grappling platform. Tom took a seat opposite, looking confident.

The tension grew and more tights-wearing brutes gathered around as Foley attempted to get the two alpha males satisfied that they weren't giving away any advantage from the starting position.

'Go!' Foley shouted, growing impatient.

The faces of both competitors were soon moving through different shades of purple and red. Their arms vibrated, but neither moved downward. Tom's huge muscles twitched and pulsed and the veins in his neck and forehead protruded from the skin's surface.

Schultz was slowly broken down as the relentless pressure from Tom's powerful body took over. Leverage was gained and Dave Schultz felt the back of his left hand touch the table.

'It's down!' Foley pointed towards the point of contact, almost reverting to his J.R. character as he chaperoned winner Tom.

Mortified Schultz begged for a rematch as the watching crowd gasped and laughed. Tom leant back and looked smug. There would be no rematch.

Smith Hart would later admit to spiking Sandy and the White Tornado with the ExLax. Some weeks later, Tom went and knocked on Sandy's door in an attempt to shake his hand and let bygones be bygones, but Sandy refused to speak to him.

8

CLIMBING THE LADDER

'People forever ask me what my greatest match was. It may
well have been the night of the ladder match in Regina,
Saskatchewan, in 1981.'

Bret Hart

February 1981. Regina, Saskatchewan

A brown canvas bag hung from the rafters and swung ominously above
the ring. The zip couldn't quite be fully closed due to the supposed
$5,000 in cash that was crammed inside. The 'cash' had been put on
the line by J.R. Foley as the latest exhilarating programme between
the Dynamite Kid and Bret Hart reached its apex.

The object of the match was to beat your opponent down to the
extent you had the time to set up, position and climb a ladder to unhook
the bag – then keep the cash.

With Bret already in the ring, the loud and brash sound of the
classical 'Pomp and Circumstance' boomed out around the arena, as
the Dynamite Kid became one of the first stars in North America to be
given entrance music to enhance his persona. Led by Foley, Dynamite
paraded out to the ring and the match got underway.

After a few minutes of frenzied blow-trading, it was clear that
weaponry would be required to break the deadlock as the brawl
continued on the floor outside the ring. When Bret slammed Tom's
head into a steel chair, Tom sprang back to sell the impact, but Bret
hadn't moved out of the way and the back of Dynamite's head crashed
into Bret's face. Bret felt his nose and his little finger sank fully into a

gaping wound. Blood poured out of a split on the crown of Tom's head. No blades would be required on this occasion.

Bret rolled the stricken Dynamite Kid into the ring and by the time he got back in himself Dynamite was on his feet – albeit unsteady. Bret rained down more blows with his fists as Tom grasped his opponent around the waist in a bid for a reprieve. The realism was astounding, and the crowd were going wild as blood stained the torsos of both men and the mat alike.

When their heads came close enough, Bret asked Tom how bad his nose was. 'Oh fuck, it's bad!' came the predictably honest response.

The match swung back and forth, each man performing impromptu highspots. With Bret down, Dynamite ran across the ring, jumped and grabbed the standing ladder as he passed it and slammed its top step into Bret's head. The crowd gasped as Bret, who in reality had hardly felt a thing, such was Tom's immaculate judgement and coordination, rolled around in faux agony. Calling the next spot, Tom crawled to Bret and said, 'Just barely touch the ladder, I'll control how I go over.'

The Dynamite Kid climbed the ladder as the fans urged Bret to recover. As Tom approached the top and reached for the bag, Bret sprung to his feet and performed a textbook dropkick, with his toes just brushing the ladder. His timing as perfect as ever, Tom leant the ladder over one way, making it look as though the impact of Bret's kick had caused it. He wobbled the unbalanced ladder left and then right and the tense audience willed it to fall; just before it did, Tom leapt from it, straddled the top rope with his crotch and bounced up and down with the face of a man who has just caught himself in his jeans zipper. As Bret climbed the ladder, Foley prepared to enter the ring to stop him, but Tom flopped from the ropes to the outside of the ring and on top of his manager. The deafening noise from the crowd was only stunted by the fact some of them were losing their voices from screaming so hard for so long, but they found them again to cheer their local hero as he grabbed the bag and returned down with his nose shattered, his body bloodied, but his career rocketing skywards.

The concept of the ladder match had been devised in Stampede almost a decade earlier by Dan Kroffat, who suggested it for his 1972 match against Tor Kamata. It was a box office smash and the iconic Kendo Nagasaki – touring Stampede from Joint Promotions at the time – was so inspired he took the idea home to Britain, where he had multiple ladder matches himself in the mid- to late-70s. But the 1981 encounter between Bret Hart and the Dynamite Kid redefined the ladder match into what it would later become, which subsequently gave birth to the TLC match and the 'Money in the Bank' ladder matches – and rarely will one go by to this day without one of the heel competitors being 'crotched' on the top rope to the delight of the fans.

Bret drove them to Pasqua Hospital with one eye swelled shut. Tom was in the passenger seat while Julie and Michelle dozed in the back. Tom and Bret barely spoke so that they didn't wake the girls, but every now and again they would glance at each other's twisted faces and broken noses through the dried blood that was crusting and flaking. They nodded in mutual appreciation, knowing they had both just worked the greatest match of their careers so far.

Tom's body was approaching broken, but he had no time for it to be, as he was heading back to Japan for his most lucrative tour yet, which was for the whole month of April.

When Tom stumbled into Hart House the day after the ladder match, wearing sunglasses to cover his blackened eyes, Bruce greeted him in the kitchen with the news that his uncle Sid had written to Stu about the possibility of his son David coming over to the territory.

'Like fuck he's coming 'ere,' was the surprising response from Tom.

'What?'

'One of the reasons I came 'ere was to get away from that little fucker hanging 'round me all the time. It's family shit Bruce, but I'm telling ya, if he comes, he'll be replacing me, 'cos I'll leave.' Tom snarled and left the kitchen.

Bruce had a dilemma. He had it on great authority that David could be as good as Dynamite, and Stampede needed talent, especially with Tom, and now Bret, in such high demand elsewhere. But he couldn't risk losing the notorious Dynamite Kid, who was the principal reason people were flocking through the turnstiles.

Bruce put it to Tom that David would come over on a six-week deal, and Tom would be in Japan for the majority of it anyway – he would hardly have to see his little cousin. A shrug of Tom's artificially enhanced shoulders gave Bruce the green light he needed.

Bruce was keen to drop the 'Young David' gimmick, as was David himself. They considered returning him to his previous 'Dave Boy Smith', but wanted something that would suit the young heart-throb babyface he was going be, and thus, 'Davey Boy Smith' was born.

Davey didn't come alone from England; Bruce also brought over veteran Adrian Street and Frank 'Chic' Cullen – who he gave the gimmick of 'Robbie Stewart' due to Cullen's uncanny likeness to rock superstar Rod Stewart. It wasn't going to be easy for Davey Boy to make his mark in Stampede, as the talent roster was now expansive and the slots near the top of the card were precious and highly competitive.

LOVE IS ALL AROUND

'We put him in right away with Dynamite. They had
awesome matches. The fans immediately loved Davey because
Tom made him look fantastic. But Davey could keep up with
him. We had a classic British rivalry. His work was superior
to everyone except Dynamite in those days.'

Ross Hart

Tokyo. 23 April 1981

An irate Dynamite Kid picked up the flowers and petals left from the
opening ceremony – which sees local girls present the wrestlers with
decorative flowers – and angrily threw them at booing members of the
audience. He kicked the bottom rope and he snarled out towards them.
Their jeers suddenly turned to cheers though when their new hero
'Tiger Mask' was introduced to them. Full of energy and enthusiasm,
he jumped in the ring and waved at them, as they began to chant, 'SAY
– YAM – HA; SAY – YAM – HA.'

Even though the diminutive wrestler was wearing a mask – that of
a tiger's face – they knew who was behind it: Satoru Sayama. Just four
months after being amazed by tag partner 'Sammy Lee' in Britain,
Tom was now getting his wish to go one-on-one with Sayama. Having
proven himself a star in England and Mexico, Sayama had been
welcomed back to New Japan, who had ingeniously bought the image
rights to cult anime and comic book hero Tiger Mask – who wore blue
tights, went bare-chested and donned a lifelike mask that contained fur
and whiskers – to perfectly complement Sayama's lightning-fast skills.

Antonio Inoki and the New Japan bookers had handpicked Dynamite to debut opposite their new phenomenon. The match was even better than they could have dreamt, as flip followed roll and never-before-seen offence was disrupted only by innovative counters. The chemistry was instant and the language barrier inconsequential – they were speaking a language in which seemingly only the two of them were fluent.

Tom's cocktail of drugs meant that he staved off excruciating pain for just long enough to perform but had enough adrenaline and testosterone coursing through him to always be at his explosive best.

* * *

With his cousin in Japan taking strides towards legendary status at the age of just 22, David Smith had left the family home in Golborne and Davey Boy Smith had arrived in Calgary – but he arrived a few weeks later than originally planned and he and Tom landed in Calgary almost simultaneously at the end of April. Davey had been broke and his grandma had promised to pay for his one-way ticket to Calgary. But then he was given the opportunity of wrestling a tour of South Africa with Adrian Street and Steve Peacock, so he delayed his departure for Canada in order to go and earn some extra money to help get him there. It was eye-opening for Davey, still just 18 and being based in Soweto. He was bitten on the arm by a large mosquito and by the time he landed back in England for a brief couple of days before getting his flight to Canada, the bite had become infected.

Seventeen-year-old Diana Hart whiled away many hours leafing through the filing cabinet that contained the profiles of the wrestlers in the office at Hart House. She was amused by the pictures of handsome brutes and glamorous women; giants and dwarves. Whilst Davey was almost 10,000 miles away in South Africa, Diana dragged his picture out of the box and instantly fell in love. The picture was paperclipped to a handwritten letter signed at the bottom by a Mr Sid Smith. Written in a beautiful scrawl and polite language, the letter was about Sid's wrestling son David, who had accomplished so much by 18 that he wanted to come and join his cousin, Thomas Billington, in Stampede Wrestling. Diana kept her ears open around Hart House so that she knew when to expect the arrival of dreamy young David.

Davey was quickly whisked to Hart House on arrival in Calgary. As he sat in the living room shyly waiting for Stu, Diana was conveniently in there too. 'Hey, errm, what's that on your arm?' she asked, to break the ice.

'Oh, yeah, could you get me a plaster please?' Davey said slightly embarrassed, as he realised his infected arm was weeping.

'Sure,' said Diana as she dashed out of the kitchen, up the stairs and into the office, where Helen was working.

'Mom, that new English wrestler is here and he asked if I have a "plaster"?'

Helen explained that he needed a Band-Aid, which Diana then proudly produced.

'Oh, errm, do you have any cotton wool?'

'Sure,' Diana said confidently as she dashed up the stairs once again.

'Mom, now he wants some "cotton wool"?'

Finally armed with all she needed, Diana helped Davey clean and dress his arm.

It had been arranged for Davey to move into Wayne's and Tom's house, to see how he settled before arranging anything more permanent.

Upon setting eyes on Davey's style and his attributes in the dungeon, the Harts knew they wanted the cousins in the ring against each other, and that they could be sensational. Immediately matching up against Tom would also help Davey acclimatise style-wise to Stampede, as both were cut from the same cloth.

Tom was cock-of-the-walk when he returned from Japan. Suddenly, his old stone-washed denim was replaced by crisp brand-new Levi's and leather jackets; a new olive-green Eldorado was soon parked outside the house and Michelle was flaunting a new fur coat. It was supply and demand, and what the Dynamite Kid could supply was in huge demand. Another short tour of Hawaii was worked into his schedule. His price per show and his addiction to the high of lifting the roof off an arena meant that time off to recover was simply not an option he ever considered.

Davey was naïve and innocent enough to expect Tom to treat him like the teenage family member in a strange land that he was. Instead, Tom treated him like any other wrestler in the locker room and Davey soon found himself with regular and sudden bouts of diarrhoea. As

Davey was going to be a babyface and Dynamite the top heel, they had to hide Davey from plain sight as they both lived in the same house. 'Davey, get in the fuckin' closet!' Tom would call out whenever he saw fit.

Out of concern for Davey, who was the same age as her, Michelle confided in Bret as to what had been happening in the house; Davey had grown wise and stopped accepting any food or drink from Tom. Under the guise of them wanting to protect kayfabe and the legitimacy of the upcoming rivalry between Dynamite and Davey, Bret told Davey to pack his bags and move in with him – Stu apparently had insisted.

But Bret too couldn't help but tease Davey, telling him that there was a cat pound in Calgary and that a van would round up all the cats that weren't indoors. Davey was soon climbing trees and ushering strays into Bret's place to save them from the fictitious van.

* * *

'It's just like rounders, Bax,' Tom said as a nervous Davey Boy readied himself to take part in a charity baseball game that the extended Hart family had been roped into. He'd taken to calling Davey 'Bax', short for 'Baxter', in reference to a simple-natured character featured in futuristic children's show *The Great Space Coaster*.

Tom casually strolled up to the plate and knocked the ball around the park like a well-seasoned veteran, making his way around the bases and back home each time whilst flicking his cigarette butts around the field. Davey, on the other hand, swung wildly and missed every single time. But there was something magnetic and infectious about Davey's kind-hearted face, and the crowd watching on cheered his failed efforts more than Tom's successful ones. The loudest cheers for each of Davey's attempts came from Diana.

When Davey glanced nervously back towards Diana after another big swing found nothing but air, it became clear to the Harts that filled the dugout that he wanted to impress her.

The bats laid out in front of the dugout just happened to have been separated into two piles.

'Here, Davey,' shouted Bruce, hopping from the dugout to the pile of bats furthest away, 'why don't you try one of these left-handed bats.'

The sniggering from all around didn't stop Davey believing this may well be the antidote he needed.

He returned to the plate, pushed out his chest and smashed the next pitch out of the park. He jumped for joy and spun around towards the cheering crowd. 'It wa' the fuckin' bat the whole time!' he shouted.

* * *

With a few carefully targeted questions around Hart House, Diana found out when Davey's next day off was.

Confident that Davey would be there alone, Diana called around to Bret's house and gave him the opportunity to break his boredom by accompanying her to the cinema.

'Yeah, okay.' Davey jumped to his feet and got ready for his first date with Diana Hart, even though he had no idea that was what it was.

Despite Tom warning Davey that the Hart girls were out of bounds and he would be sent straight back to Golborne if Stu found out, the seeds of friendship between Diana and Davey quickly grew into a teenage romance.

The time soon arrived for Tom and Davey to begin their programme working against one another.

Bruce opted to start this by having them wrestle in a singles match in which the crowd and TV audience would assume Dynamite would roll over the young rookie with ease, but Davey – so adept and skilled at playing the underdog babyface role – would give the arrogant Dynamite Kid the fright of his life with a dazzling array of offence and a never-say-die attitude.

However, Tom's attitude towards Davey had now raised concerns about how the plan might unfold – Tom might just shoot on Davey and annihilate him; the programme would then be over before it started and Davey would be forced to see out the rest of his time in the territory doing jobs before returning to England with his career in tatters. Tom knew this too.

On 1 May 1981, the Dynamite Kid and Davey Boy Smith stood in a wrestling ring opposite each other for the first time, for the traditional Friday night show at the Pavilion. When the match got underway, Bruce's nerves began to settle as he was relieved to see Tom working well with Davey. His relief turned to joy as time went on and the audience began to go crazy for the match and the story that they were being told in a bumping masterclass from the Dynamite Kid. Tom wasn't only being professional; he was going the extra mile to make his cousin look a million dollars. Every beautiful flip and roll and counter from Davey was met with impassioned cheers as the fans tried to will the slender youngster – still wearing a singlet to cover his skinny torso – on to a famous victory over the venomous Dynamite Kid.

The exhilarating brawl descended into chaos outside of the ring, leading to a double count-out and a sensational draw for the newcomer over the established headliner.

The rematch was set for the following week, when the relentless action continued. This time, Davey Boy snatched a shock pinfall victory to the sheer delight of the crowd, but when the referee turned his back Dynamite dropkicked him in the back. When he came to and turned round, the referee was conned by Dynamite into believing the attack had come from an overzealous Davey and reversed the decision, disqualifying Davey to the indignation of Ed Whalen and the crowd, who turned into a baying mob wanting the blood of the Dynamite Kid.

Despite moving out of Tom and Wayne's place to maintain kayfabe, Davey was still sneaking around to excitedly discuss their matches as the programme reached its climax. Davey was still self-conscious about his size and weight, and when he saw the vials and various types of steroids lined up in Tom's fridge, he anxiously suggested that he should start on them too.

'Yep. You're gonna need to get on 'roids, I'm afraid, Bax,' Tom told him.

Davey looked resigned to it. 'But I don't know anybody to get them off, Tommy.'

'I'll give you a couple of shots right now if you want. Just to get you started, then we'll take it from there.'

'Okay then Tommy, if you're sure. Thanks.'

'What's family for, eh? Now get y'arse cheeks out, there'll be one goin' in each of 'em'.

Davey turned and lowered his slacks while Tom went to the fridge.

'This is Winstrol V, a water-based steroid. I'm giving you two CCs in each cheek,' Tom commentated.

It was over in a second, and Davey Boy Smith's own steroid use had started – or so he thought.

The following morning, most of the boys were already sat in the van, which had the engine running, waiting to get on the road for the familiar three-hour drive to Edmonton. Dynamite dashed aboard excitedly, knowing Davey hadn't arrived yet. 'Listen to this, boys, last night that dipshit Baxter came round to mine wanting some steroids, so I injected some milk in each of 'is arse cheeks!' Tom giggled, as did most on the van.

Davey sat quietly on the journey as usual, only speaking when spoken to. Some of the wrestlers began making moo and meow noises in his direction, which would instigate a round of laughter. Davey was confused and after a couple of hours of this, had become paranoid. Jim Neidhart finally put him out of his misery when he shouted out, 'Bax, ya daft bastard, he injected you with milk!'

Davey did continue his dedicated quest to become bigger and more muscular, working-out tirelessly. No matter what pranks Tom played on him or what form his mild bullying took, he retained Davey's trust.

Everyone had taken to calling Davey 'Bax' or 'Baxter', but when Diana used the reference on a date with Davey, he looked solemn and asked her not to call him that. He explained the origin of the nickname and that it made him feel like everyone thought he was stupid.

On the next loop and back in Regina, Tom snuck into babyface Bret and Davey's tiny hotel room to discuss the evening's show, which he and Davey were headlining once again.

'Ya know what we need to do to get you over even more, tonight, don't ya Bax?'

'What's that Tommy?' Davey replied, enthusiastic to take the next step on the journey his cousin was guiding him through.

'It's time to get you some *juice*.'

Davey shuffled nervously. 'But I've never done it before, Tommy,' he said.

'Fuck, it's nothing, I'll do it for ya. You'll not feel a thing, just a pin prick,' Tom said as he got up and walked to the bathroom.

Bret shuffled towards Davey and said in a hushed tone, 'Never let anyone cut you, ever. Do it yourself, or don't do it at all. This business is all about trust, and you can't trust him.'

When Tom returned, they all began getting ready to leave for the show and Davey said to him, 'You won't hurt me, will you?'

Bret watched the match from his regular viewing spot behind the curtain as Dynamite and Davey put on a thrilling masterclass of high impact moves and death-defying bumping and flying. The crowd were transfixed, as was Bret himself. In the ring, Davey was delivering the performance of his career so far. The pace of the match quickened, and the pair bounced to and from the ropes and the turnbuckles, jumped over and slid under one another until Dynamite stopped a full-speed Davey in his tracks with a firm knee to the stomach, bringing about a round of angry jeers. He then tossed Davey to the outside of the ring before running him headfirst into the back wall of the building, close by where Bret was looking on in horror as Dynamite reached into his tights and his hand re-emerged with a short scalpel blade. Scalpels had recently been brought into wrestling by some as a preferred tool for blading over the traditional shard of razor. Under the guise of a choke hold, Dynamite dug the blade deep into the top of Davey's forehead. Thick, dark blood immediately began to gush down Davey's face, and when he understandably panicked and squirmed, the blade went even deeper and cut across his scalp. The claret engulfed his whole face like he was a slasher-movie victim. Bret leapt out and ushered Dynamite to the side, causing confusion in the audience, but Bret believed Davey may bleed to death if he didn't get him to the hospital as soon as possible.

'What the hell has happened this time?' asked the same doctor at Pasqua Hospital that Bret and Dynamite had seen on multiple occasions for his stitching-up services. Delirious Davey, taught to always maintain kayfabe, began clumsily telling a nonsensical story that involved his opponent using knuckle-dusters. Recognising the potential severity of the situation, Bret cut the worked story off and shot, 'The wrestler he worked with took a razor blade and tried to cut the top of his head off!'

Davey's head was patched up with 22 stitches. The act was seen by Tom as a form of initiation; by not complaining and acting like nothing had happened, Davey had passed the test. Tom's frostiness toward his cousin was thawing as Davey continued to prove himself at every turn.

Davey Boy was left disappointed that his momentum wasn't followed through into Stampede Week, where he was booked amongst the *curtain jerkers*.

Dynamite would only be wrestling regular opponent Bruce Hart, too. This was largely because the long-term NWA champions Harley Race and Nelson Royal had been dethroned in favour of 'American Dream' Dusty Rhodes and veteran Les Thornton, who had been one of the initial British trailblazers to come to Stampede in the early 70s before touring the rest of the NWA territories. The NWA bosses had called Stu at the end of May to say that Rhodes couldn't work Stampede Week into his busy schedule. Instead, Stu had called in a favour with rival organisation the AWA and booked their heel world heavyweight champion, Nick Bockwinkel. NWA royalty Lou Thesz had promised he would make a special appearance, and so to get the best from a bad situation, they got their heads together to book a unique storyline for the week.

Bret defeated 'Dr D' David Schultz in the traditional qualifying match to become Bockwinkel's babyface challenger in what would be his first ever world heavyweight championship matches – but far from his last. In the week's opener, Thesz would act as special guest referee for the title match.

With two minutes remaining of the 60-minute time-limit match, Bret applied a deep abdominal stretch on the champion; there was no way out of it, no opportunity to reach the ropes. Bockwinkel's only hope to save his title was to make it to the time-limit bell. The crowd were on their feet, willing their local youngster to provide the ultimate upset. The bell rang to signal the end of the match and the fans were heartbroken, but it seemed the bell had rung early. It was then that everyone began to notice who had actually rung it: J.R. Foley.

Foley got in the ring to gloat in Bret's face but was met with the discipline his behaviour deserved in the form of a Lou Thesz elbow smash to the face. The crowd went wild and the culmination of the week back in Calgary would be a dream encounter between two legendary shooters that many fans thought they would never see: Lou Thesz versus John Foley.

Bret and Davey rode together to Edmonton the following day for the second show of the week, where a similar main event took place which continued to stoke the flames. Backstage, whilst congratulating Bret on his stellar performances, Lou asked if he could catch a ride with him and Davey back to Calgary.

Davey sat in respectful silence in the passenger seat as Lou regaled them with anecdotes from his epic career, stories of his fellow fabled heroes, and gave them an education in how professional wrestling came to be. He told them all about how his mentor and trainer Toots Mondt had been the protector and enforcer of kayfabe, a mantle he took on himself as not only one of his generation's greatest workers, but also one of its most feared and respected shooters.

Minute after blissful minute disappeared into the dark sky, as Bret's car hurtled along the illuminated road. Not long after passing the 'Welcome to Calgary' sign on the Edmonton Trail at around 4am, a car screeched out from a side junction at full speed. The wheels of Bret's car squealed like one of Stu's students as he slammed on the brakes and the three of them lunged forward before snapping back harshly when the car came to its abrupt halt.

'You okay, Mr Thesz?' asked Davey.

'Yeah, course. We've all taken worse bumps than that, hey boys?'

Bret got the car moving again and when they reached a red light, the same car was stopped ahead of them. Davey hurriedly wound down the window and yelled, 'Where'd you learn to fuckin' drive?'

Young men of varying shapes, sizes and degrees of drunkenness began to climb out of the car, taunting and jeering Bret and Davey, who took one quick look at each other and nodded – there was no way they were going to lose face in the company of the deity-like Lou Thesz. Babyfaces Davey and Bret ran towards their four real-life antagonists.

'Sorry about that, Lou,' said Bret a few seconds later, as he and Davey climbed back into the car.

'No, I'm sorry boys. These days I fight with my head, not my fists.'

Bret eased the car around the offending vehicle and Davey shook his right hand to relieve its discomfort as he assessed the scene they were driving from: two of the hoodlums were strewn on the highway, one up against the car and one slumped on the bonnet. When Bret put his foot down the rear left tyre seemed to bump. 'Fuck Bret,' said Davey, swinging his head around, 'I think you just ran a leg owa.'

Davey was coming out of his shell and felt liberated to play his own pranks. One night in the small native reservation of Morley, a sparse crowd were deathly silent as Jim Neidhart battled out an impromptu all-babyface match with Hercules Ayala. Suddenly a large 'booooring, booooring' chant began, causing a fiery Jim to yell, 'It is boring isn't it!?' and break his babyface aura. Little did he know that Davey was sniggering in the back, having instigated the chant through the curtain.

Business was up – but so were the overheads. Stampede was still barely breaking even. The youngsters were cutting through the stereotype of the big, lumbering heavyweight wrestlers and they were making their mark. Stampede was becoming cutting edge as their stars entered the fray to rock anthems, blood gushed and steel chairs were wrapped around heads. Rock'n'roll wrestling had arrived in Canada.

One Sunday following the weekly booking meeting that took place after the traditional Hart family Sunday lunch, the newly inseparable quartet of Bret, Tom, Davey and Jim were working out in the dungeon.

Davey spotted for Tom, who was now V-shaped with huge shoulders, as he bench-pressed 450lb with ease, and Davey didn't need to remove much weight from the bar for his own turn. They had both grown to over 14 stone from around 11 when arriving in Calgary. Bret and Jim were busy practising their grappling and bumping in the ring, when the cellar door creaked, and a shard of light illuminated the darkness.

'Boys,' Stu's distinct voice echoed down, 'this is Karl Moffat, we're trying him out. Work him, would ya.'

Down the steps walked a large bald-headed biker with a long grisly goatee. Karl keenly climbed on to the mat, where Jim introduced himself with a tight headlock and takedown, which caused the others to chuckle; they'd all been introduced to the business the hard way, after all. They taught Karl how to take a bump and then gleefully took turns in providing the artillery for him to practise. They joked and laughed as they grunted and perspired – and Karl winced and screamed.

They were all in relationships, Tom and Bret with sisters Michelle and Julie Smadu; Davey and Jim with Hart siblings Diana and Ellie respectively.

They were happy.

10

TIGER MASK

'Realistically, when you watch pro wrestling [today], the thing
you realise is that when it comes to in-ring wrestling, the
modern style that combines some American style with old
British, Lucha Libre and Japanese style had its primitive and
most influential roots in the 1981–83 matches between Tiger
Mask and the Dynamite Kid.'

Dave Meltzer

11 December 1981
Spectrum Leisure Centre
Warrington, England
'Cowboy' Bret Hart v Dynamite Kid
Approximate attendance: 1,500

'DY-NA-MITE, DY-NA-MITE, DY-NA-MITE,' the crowd
chanted constantly for their hometown hero, as he and the villainous
Stetson-wearing foreigner brawled inside the ring. The sub-zero
temperatures and economic struggles of northern England were
temporarily forgotten, as the locals willed on a bruised and bloodied
Tommy Billington.

Every time Tom came home, the fans saw a bigger and better
version of the one they had seen last. For his month-long tour of
England at the end of 1981, he'd secured Bret the relatively lucrative
deal of £50 per night from Max – for whom it was a small additional
price to pay for securing an elongated stint from the now fabled and

lesser-spotted Dynamite Kid, who packed out every venue whenever he was in town. Even Tom's preference for jeers rather than cheers was thawed by his own villagers desperately willing him to finish off the invading Cowboy. To ensure he made Bret look strong and appear to be a genuine threat, he performed his thumb-up-the-nostril blood releasing trick and conceded an early fall. But in the fifth round, with the scores tied at one fall apiece and every member of the audience perched on the edge of their seats, Dynamite scaled the turnbuckle and soared majestically through the air, before his concrete-like body crashed hard on to the mat, and his head gently cushioned into his friend and foe. One. Two. Three.

The crowd went feral; blissfully unaware that the two competitors seemingly from different worlds that they had just seen devour each other had already faced each other countless times, were close friends, and soon to be family.

Before they had packed their bags for the flight to Manchester, as they celebrated one year of courtship, Tom casually told Michelle that they should get married whilst in England. She accepted the less-than-romantic proposal.

Bret and Julie were travelling with them, staying at Davey's family home while Tom and Michelle were just around the corner at his parents'. Bret could see where Davey got his kind nature from in Sid and Joyce, and had become fond of his little sister Tracey, who, even after years of brain surgery to try and relieve her of the cancer she had been born with, always smiled and laughed joyously around the house.

Michelle believed Bret and Julie being there was perfect, as they were going to be best man and maid of honour, but when she suggested to Tom that she would look into booking a church for a traditional English wedding, he snapped at her.

'You know what, we'll just fuckin' get married back in Canada,' Tom snapped, 'I don't want to say "I do" in front of all this lot round 'ere.'

It was a wonderful few weeks for Bret, who was becoming a keen wrestling historian and got to meet and work with some of the British wrestling royalty he'd heard so much about, such as Big Daddy, Mick McManus and Rollerball Rocco, as well as being reunited with former Stampede tourists Marty Jones and Giant Haystacks. Max, using the same stereotype he had for Bruce almost five years earlier, had given

Bret a cowboy gimmick and he was going out to the ring looking like an extra from the line-dancing scene of a budget TV western as black-hatted 'Cowboy Bret Hart', and had predominantly been used to *put over* heavyweight stars such as King Kong Kirk and Pat Roach. He partnered Big Daddy against old foe Haystacks and his partner Kirk in Nottingham, and Halifax saw a now dream contest in Bret Hart and Rollerball Rocco versus the Dynamite Kid and Marty Jones.

Bret wrestled at the historic Royal Albert Hall and he and Julie visited Liverpool and the famous Cavern Club. He met not only Davey's family but Tom's too, as well as Ted Betley, who Tom introduced with the politeness of a choirboy – there was no drinking, smoking or even swearing around his mentor.

Another brilliant series of matches over the month between Rocco and Dynamite climaxed with a high-stakes match at the Victoria Hall in Hanley. Dynamite would challenge for Rocco's world heavy-middleweight championship, but also with the stipulation that the loser would be forced to have his head shaved in the ring after the match. Tom put Rollerball over; in truth, the head-shaving was Tom's idea, as it was his usual *gaijin* look for tours of Japan, which he was resuming immediately after the Christmas break.

Whilst the girls flew back west to Calgary, Tom and Bret headed east for the annual New Japan New Year Golden Series tour. The relatively subdued atmosphere and low fanfare of the small English towns was starkly contrasted immediately, as Bret was mobbed by Japanese fans and reporters, who frantically hoped for a quote from the returning superstar *gaijin* at his side.

The programme set by the New Japan bookers was that they would both be involved in multiple matches of varying types over the month with Tiger Mask. Tatsumi Fujinami had moved up to the heavyweight division and therefore vacated the WWF world junior-heavyweight title. At a New Year's Day special opener, Tiger Mask was to be crowned the new champion, and it would be the Dynamite Kid in the opposite corner. The match was sensational. Satoru Sayama was now so outrageously good he could quite easily have been mistaken for the fictional, animated superhero he was portraying; he would perform impromptu routines involving somersaults, back-flips and spinning heel kicks that would leave the audience audibly gasping, usually followed by appreciative applause more akin to what might be heard after a tenor hits the high note at the opera. Tom Billington was seemingly the only man on the planet that could match him with every flip, roll and handstand.

The championship rematch the whole country was salivating to see would take place on the biggest New Japan show of the tour on 28 January at the Tokyo Metropolitan Gymnasium. Tiger Mask and Dynamite pulled out every move in their repertoire, performing lightning quick acrobatic routines and landing simultaneously on their feet. Submission holds were miraculously countered into snap-suplexes and piledrivers and both men took suicide dives inside and outside the ring.

Tom hobbled his broken body back to the locker room whilst the 10,000 fans still roared at what they had witnessed.

In one of his first matches back in Calgary, Tom blew out knee ligaments again and finally accepted that surgery and some time out of the ring was essential. But New Japan were keen for both him and Bret to go on a lucrative tour of the United Arab Emirates in the spring as they attempted to expand into a new territory and fanbase, so Tom targeted that for his return – just weeks after a major knee operation.

He did decide to do something useful with his time off: get married. He and Michelle quickly and quietly set a date of 25 March and whisked Bret and Julie off with them to Calgary City Hall as their witnesses, and they tied the knot with little fuss.

Despite still walking with a slight limp, Tom joined Bret and they travelled to Dubai together. Tom left his teenage bride a letter: 'Michelle, I can tell you this little secret now, because we're married,' it began. 'I think the next thing on my mind is that we will have some babies, but only when you are ready. I wish that is soon, because when I'm on the road the babies can look after you.

'All for now, I love you more than ever, your ever-loving yard dog, Tom.'

A sandstorm stopped most of the scheduled events from happening in Dubai, luckily for Tom's knee. It was an eclectic bunch that New Japan had put together; as well as the Japanese stars and Bret and Tom, they had asked some veteran European wrestlers and some from the

North American territories. Amongst them was the rotund 6ft 2in heavyweight Texan, Dick Murdoch.

One night, as the wrestlers vociferously bemoaned their situation in the locker room of the near-empty stadium at which they had just performed, Bret noticed a pair of dirty white underpants under the bench he was sat on. He caught Tom's gaze and gestured towards the shit-stained garment. Tom grinned back, knowing there was a prank in the offing. Dick had his immaculately clean clothes, including his pristine white briefs, hung up on the hooks provided. As he dropped his wrestling trunks and stormed toward the shower, Bret picked up the offending item with the lightest pinch-grip he could muster and traded the underpants for Dick's perfectly clean ones that were hanging neatly.

Tom struggled to hold in the laughter as Dick towelled himself down, still remonstrating at the lack of organisation and promotion of the tour.

Bret winced as Dick grabbed the untidy-whities and threaded one leg after the other into them and concluded his tirade with, 'All I know is, there must be a shit freak running around here, because somebody shit in my underwear, and I'm dang sure it wasn't me!' in his deep-south drawl. The veins that so often popped from Tom's head and neck were now doing so as he agonisingly attempted to contain his glee.

'Goddammit,' grumbled Murdoch, as he exited the locker room scratching his behind through his jeans. The moment the door slammed shut, Tom and Bret collapsed into a fit of laughter.

* * *

Back in Calgary, Dynamite and Davey resumed their explosive rivalry. They were on fire. Davey might be the new hero, but he was being made that by the sheer heel perfection of his cousin and J.R. Foley.

'Davey Boy Smith, what I've heard about you,' Foley snarled into Ed Whalen's microphone one night, with Dynamite posing arrogantly beside him, 'always playing with little girls, you should go and join the girls' basketball team. What d'you say, Kid?'

'Let me tell you something Mr Whalen,' Dynamite began, 'd'you remember a few weeks ago, I told you that Boy Smith's mother and father died before he was born?'

'Yes, yes,' Whalen responded, dismissively.

'The answer to that, Mr Whalen,' Dynamite leant forward into the ropes, staring into the camera, 'is Davey Boy Smith was a test-tube baby!' An animated Dynamite began pointing into the camera, 'Boy Smith, you're not human baby! Ya not human … let me tell ya somethin' Boy Smith, you don't deserve a title shot. Why? Because ya not human; ya come from a test-tube baby!'

9 July 1982
Stampede Week
Victoria Pavilion, Calgary
World Mid-heavyweight Championship
Davey Boy Smith v Dynamite Kid
Approximate attendance: 2,500

The packed house for the traditional opening night of Stampede Week grimaced and booed as the Dynamite Kid – the champion – continued to bounce his younger foe hard between turnbuckles, the mat, and the floor outside. Tom bristled arrogantly as he prowled the ring; Davey's fightbacks were spirited but short-lived. He was now almost as muscular as Tom, but as a naturally bigger man, carried the size better.

Dynamite snap-suplexed Davey on the concrete floor by the feet of the wincing front row, then snarled at them before rolling Davey back into the ring. More snap-suplexes followed, which had now become a real Dynamite trademark, as he whipped his opponent quickly over his head and when he slammed him down, the canvas bounced. A bloody Davey Boy sold each one like he'd just fallen from a scaffold.

'Time t' go 'ome, Davey,' Tom whispered as he dragged his stricken challenger up from the floor once more. He raised him up for one more big impact in the middle of the ring, which would surely be followed by the flying headbutt; but Davey skilfully managed to land on his feet behind Tom and in one fluid motion, spin around and perform a perfect belly-to-back suplex and hold the bridge with the champion's shoulders helplessly pinned to the canvas. One. Two. Three.

Pandemonium erupted as an exhausted and pained Davey was declared the winner and joyously held the title belt aloft, while an infuriated Dynamite slammed the mat and kicked the ropes. Little did the ecstatic fans know that, up until a minute or two before the match started, the predictable Dynamite victory was what they were due to be served up.

Tom had placed the booking committee (an ever-moving feast of Hart brothers that, at the time, consisted of Bret, Bruce and Ross) in an awkward position. He was *the man*, the money draw, and the main event. He made up for his ill-discipline and his time out of the territory by being the best and hardest worker around, and yet he appeared to long for Japan and its intensity. He was leaving for Japan the following day, missing the rest of Stampede Week.

'We should put the belt on Davey,' Bret argued in the locker room, while the two competitors laced up their boots opposite each other. Bruce and Ross were aware of Bret and Davey's close friendship and didn't want that swaying business decisions.

'Dynamite's the champ, Bret. We keep him strong tonight and he's money in the bank the moment he comes back with that belt,' Bruce snapped back. 'Shouldn't you be concentrating on your own match?'

'But Davey's ready,' argued Bret, who was once again challenging Nick Bockwinkel for the AWA heavyweight championship in the main event. 'Just think of the pop out there and how strong it would make him; and the belt would be staying here.'

'That's the thing though, Bret,' Ross entered the debate, 'don't you think the fans see it coming? "Oh look, another champion has lost his title just before leaving." We need to treat them with more respect than that.'

'But this will flatten Davey, and with me and Tom in Japan, where does that leave us?'

'He's right,' Tom mumbled. The locker room fell silent and everyone swung around towards Dynamite. 'Davey's ready. He can hold t'fort while we're gone.' He flicked away his cigarette butt and picked up the belt.

Davey looked up towards his cousin – Tom had called him Davey, not Baxter or Bax, and he was insisting on dropping his title to him. Davey knew what this meant. Tom had finally accepted him not just as a friend and a family member, but more importantly, as a worker, and an equal.

'C'mon Dave,' Tom slapped him on the shoulder as he walked past, 'let's make ya.'

11

NEW YORK, NEW YORK

'When I first started wrestling, there was certain people
that we would share tapes of in my wrestling school, and
Dynamite Kid was one of them.'

Rebecca Quin (Becky Lynch)

30 August 1982
Madison Square Garden
New York
Dynamite Kid v Tiger Mask
WWF World Junior-heavyweight Championship
Attendance: 19,908

'INTRODUCING FIRST to my left, the challenger,' began dinner-
suited ring announcer Howard Finkel, in a gentle voice. 'Hailing from
England, weighing in at 200lb, the Dynamite Kid.'

There was a mixture of muted applause and boos – much of the
New York crowd unsure who the muscle-bound, brooding wrestler in
the ring was, and many were unsure yet who they should be cheering
for. Pre-internet and still working within the territory system, almost
all of the fans in MSG were completely unaware of either the Dynamite
Kid or Tiger Mask.

'And ladies and gentlemen, his opponent, from Japan,' Finkel said
with more excitement in his voice, subtly making the audience aware
he was introducing the babyface. 'Weighing 194lb, the world junior-
heavyweight champion, Tiger Mask!' Finkel boomed following a

slow escalation in pace and volume. The crowd cheered, as they had subliminally been instructed to do, but the cheers were still subdued – this was just a warm-up match before the WWF main events they had paid their money to see, after all. Up next after this match was Intercontinental champion Pedro Morales up against Jimmy Snuka; WWF champion Bob Backlund was then in action against 'Playboy' Buddy Rose, and André the Giant and Chief Jay Strongbow were among the participants of a six-man tag team match. The event was being televised on the MSG and the USA networks. In just a few years' time, a card of this quality would be reserved for pay-per-view only.

Sayama removed his championship belt and gestured in appreciation to the crowd.

'We are no doubt looking at a most unusual athlete in Tiger Mask,' began lead announcer Vince McMahon Jr. 'He will not take the mask off, unless Dynamite Kid, err, assists him with that. So, he will wrestle with that most unusual-looking mask on.'

The wrestlers met in the middle of the ring; as far as the crowd were aware, this was the first time they had ever met. The referee checked their attire for illegal objects – Dynamite in red trunks and white boots, Tiger Mask in his usual blue and gold tights.

'Tiger Mask is quite the thing over in Japan, a very popular wrestler,' continued Vince, giving the TV audience the hard sell on Sayama. No words yet to put Tom over. The camera gave a close-up of the glittery and furry mask.

'And there is, err, how would you like to roll over and say, good morning darling, and take a look at that mask?'

No one knew what Vince was saying or why, but his sole focus was on the Japanese champion.

Ding-ding.

There was a sense that the crowd were ready to be thrilled that evening, they just didn't expect it to be yet. Tiger Mask opened by performing a spectacular spinning heel kick into fresh air as a warning shot to his opponent not to come too close, and for the first time the audience let out a mild roar and realised they may be about to witness something truly worth watching.

Tom rushed in and allowed Sayama to reverse leg-sweep him on to his ass. The crowd roared again. 'Oh, look at that!' exclaimed

McMahon. Tom knew this was all about Sayama and making him look perfect. He twisted and wrenched Tiger Mask's arm, and when Sayama performed a forward roll to equalise the twist, it initiated a beautiful and long-lasting sequence of fast-paced and dynamic flips, rolls and handstands, that escalated in drama and ended with Tiger Mask reverse dropkicking Dynamite into a turnbuckle.

'Oh, my!' McMahon screamed. The whole of the Garden rose with a standing ovation and whistled with delight and approval. The match was just one minute old. There would be no let-up in the pace or the drama. They had only been given a short slot on the packed card and Tiger Mask pinned Dynamite to retain his title with what would now be called a moonsault from the top turnbuckle after six-and-a-half minutes of electricity. The match and the display may have been about getting Tiger Mask over with the WWF audience, but the trained eye of Vince McMahon knew what he had seen from the challenger: a job executed with unique perfection.

With the quality television footage, English language commentary and diverse competitors, the match was (and still is, 40 years later) used as the exemplar for smaller wrestlers, young and experienced alike. Previously unattainable perfection had just become attainable to a mainstream audience.

Little did the TV viewer realise that the strait-laced 36-year-old host and commentator McMahon was much more than just that; he was a ruthless businessman with a dream, a dream that was becoming reality as he sat tantalised by the Dynamite Kid and Tiger Mask. He had set the wheels in motion a couple of years earlier, when he established Titan Sports Incorporated and began hosting small events at the Cape Cod Coliseum in Massachusetts. 'Expansion' was a dirty word even in the already murky waters of professional wrestling. The territories and their boundaries were respected by promoters in the same way mafia dons delineate their own turf. In the early 80s, while the AWA, NWA and WWF were in competition, it was indirect and healthy competition, as each one would aim to put on the biggest and best shows, but strictly in their own regions. Talent-sharing was encouraged, as all the promoters knew that a healthy national wrestling scene was good for everyone. The term 'expansion' referred to the desire of one promoter to edge into another territory, be that by hosting a live show there, or by broadcasting on a TV station there. The natural limitations of frequency waves had helped maintain the TV boundaries, but Vince McMahon Jr knew all about the technological advances in cable and closed-circuit TV broadcasting, and knew national syndication was wrestling's future: a monopolising force that would control the industry in the USA.

When his father confided in Vince Jr that his health was failing and he was looking to retire, his son told him without hesitation that Titan Sports was able and willing to buy out his Capitol Sports franchise and take full control of the WWF. Knowing his son's ruthless ambitions, Vince Sr advised him against carrying out the expansion, but knew if he sold to anyone else, his son would probably be cast aside and lose his job.

On 5 June 1982, with an agreed payment of $1 million, the WWF was signed over to Vince McMahon Jr's Titan Sports, and the wheels of invasion were quickly in motion.

12

THE AGE OF DYNAMITE

'The name "Gabe" came originally from Abdullah the
Butcher on tours for New Japan. Abdullah referred to all the
other foreigners as "Gabe" so Tom started calling Bret that
regularly. He also referred to Bret as "the North" for having
won the North American heavyweight title for Stampede.
Bret in turn called Tom "the Wigan Harpoon" for the way he
carved Davey Boy and others on blade-jobs.'

Ross Hart

4 January 1983

Bret and Davey sat relaxing in Bret's house, discussing over a beer what
1983 might bring. Bret's North American heavyweight title belt also
had a seat on the sofa, but it was about to find itself a new home: Bret
was to drop the title to Leo Burke in just ten days' time. Bret and Davey
had grown extremely close, living and travelling together as babyfaces
over the previous 18 months. They would addictively watch and analyse
tapes of their matches, with Bret tutoring Davey on what could've gone
better and why. Always, Davey would improve on that very aspect the
next time out. Whilst, unlike Tom or Bret, he wasn't a natural at calling
matches or ring psychology and needed guidance on these aspects, he
was keen to learn and had an ability to seemingly achieve any physical
feat in the ring after being told or shown just a single time.

Despite working so hard together on their upcoming matches, Bret
and Davey had still not met each other one-on-one in the ring, due to
the fact they were both babyfaces.

'Y' know Davey,' began Bret, 'there's nothing booked for us in Regina next week yet.'

''Aint there?'

'Not that I know of. You know how over we both are there; what if we main evented? Title match. Who knows when we'd ever get the chance to do it, otherwise?'

Davey's eyes lit up and the excitement caused his dimples to appear. With that, they both shuffled forward to the edge of their seats and began enthusiastically planning the story of the match.

When the night came, the Regina crowd looked on in a state of nervous anticipation: they wanted to cheer both men; they didn't want to see Bret lose the belt, but they also wanted to see Davey raise it aloft. Babyface versus babyface matches could be difficult for the viewers, but these students of the game had it all planned out for them.

They began with the ultimate show of respect, a 'may-the-best-man-win' handshake. Davey, in the red singlet with gold stars that had replaced his blue one, locked up with Bret as they began a technical wrestling routine that intrigued the crowd but didn't bring them to their feet. The lockups ended in stalemates but the stare-offs between them got closer and more tense. When they got within slapping distance Bret broke the tension, and Davey's eardrum. They descended into a brawl and the crowd ascended to their feet. Fifteen minutes of hard-hitting action intertwined with flowing wrestling followed. When Davey dove out of the ring at full speed and collided hard with Bret and the barriers, the fans became unglued. They had settled for the predictable ending to a babyface match: the double count-out. But the boys weren't done – they climbed back into the ring in the nick of time and the action continued. Davey was on top and the crowd sensed a title-change as he whipped Bret hard into the corner and sprinted in after him. But Bret popped up from the turnbuckle like a prize gymnast, dropping behind Davey before executing a perfect German suplex and holding on for the pin. One. Two. Three.

The noise level from the claps and whistles of appreciation and respect stayed constant whilst the pair faced off one last time, but the roof was blown from the venue when they shook hands and embraced.

Later that evening, they sat by the bar at the Plains Hotel and smiled with pride at a job well done. Little did they know that just under a decade later, they would get the opportunity to tell that same story once again, but with the stakes, the emotion, and the size of the audience enhanced beyond all recognition.

* * *

Tom returned to the Stampede locker room to find that 'Dr D' David Schultz had installed himself as the locker room leader. In his loud and intimidating way, Schultz was perceived to be bullying everyone from the youngsters to the Hart brothers. He could take liberties with his opponents and ride roughshod over the booking, ensuring he got the results and angles he wished for. Schultz was the only wrestler sanctioned to take his own vehicle on the road trips and would be reimbursed for his transport costs on the proviso that he filled his car with three other wrestlers. But it got to the stage where no other wrestlers would get into his car, as his wide-eyed and highly-strung manner could be unpredictable at best, and violent at worst.

When Tom's friends Bruce and in particular John Foley told Tom of the intimidation they were going through at the hands of Schultz, Tom didn't hesitate but to tell them he would sort the situation out. Despite Schultz's notorious reputation as a tough guy and the fact he was a much bigger man, Tom let it be known he was willing to fight for the locker-room leadership and the position of the ultimate alpha male of the promotion.

The showdown was scheduled for before a show in Red Deer, but Stu got wind of the fight between two of his top stars and rushed there to intervene. Stu fired Schultz for his prior conduct that had led to the escalation and, although Schultz was hired back just a few weeks later, his attitude was far better, because the bully in him had been confronted.

But Tom did walk a fine line between morality defender and being the bully himself. The previous summer American journeyman Ken Wayne came to Calgary and, whilst drinking and getting to know his new locker room, he made the mistake of making a cheap joke about Tom's accent. He soon found himself unconscious and woke up with a deeply blackened eye.

Giant Haystacks returned to Calgary to reprise his 'Loch Ness Monster' gimmick for the summer of 1983, and once again Tom would prove that size offered no intimidation to him as he set about pranking the 500lb behemoth. The giant liked to snooze on the long road trips, but it was a brave man that slept in the presence of the Dynamite Kid.

'Luke! Luke!' Tom would scream into the ears of the slumbering beast, as he also told driver Ross Hart to turn the radio up as loud as it would go.

'I'll fuckin' deck you one Tommy,' the monster would rage when he finally woke up, before snarling towards the driver, who would turn the radio down while Tom sniggered and dramatically feigned being frightened.

* * *

In 1982, having seen the matches between Dynamite and Tiger Mask, a young wrestling-obsessed American journalist called Dave Meltzer began publishing the *Wrestling Observer Newsletter* (WON) as a way to spread news of them and other hidden gems in the grappling world. The newsletter became the original 'dirt sheet', in which Meltzer would analyse wrestling matches and angles as works, rather than would-be shoots. He would get inside scoops on behind-the-scenes gossip, potential upcoming matches and programmes and talent transfers between territories. The publication was initially greeted with anger and suspicion within the industry, which still held kayfabe as its highest order of business, and to wilfully break it was taken with great offence. But it was realised that Meltzer was a great analyst of wrestling and soon, his match reviews were used by wrestlers, bookers and promoters as a reliable source in judging performance. He would give the matches he reviewed a 'star' rating from zero (or potentially minus scores for the truly dreadful) to five.

A singles match that took place between the Dynamite Kid and Tiger Mask on that same tour in Tokyo in April 1983 went down in history as the first ever five-star match; forever the standard-bearer of what a junior- or light-heavyweight professional wrestling match should aim to be. The limitations of what smaller men could achieve in the business were being broken down.

By the end of the decade, the newsletter had expanded and was widely read, becoming much more relevant as the walls of kayfabe continued to erode. In 1987, to celebrate five years in print, Meltzer published a *Best of the Wrestling Observer 1983–1987* magazine, in which his colleague Jeff Bowdren wrote a countdown of the top matches the *Observer* had covered since it began. The number one spot was given to the monumental heavyweight clash between superstars Ric Flair and Kerry Von Erich which packed the Reunion Arena in Dallas.

'Number two took place on April 23, 1983,' wrote Bowdren. 'I think the Dynamite Kid and the original Tiger Mask (Satoru Sayama) had probably the most underrated feud of all-time. Many of the matches these two had may have deserved mention, but this one was the best. I thought long and hard about how to describe it, but it can best be summed up by saying it was a 25-minute-long highspot. They never stopped. They did several things in the ring that would leave you with your mouth hanging open. The highlight of the match had to be the finish. Dynamite had Tiger up for the tombstone piledriver on the arena floor. He does it and Sayama looks dead. The Kid gets up and raises his arms to the crowd. As he turns around, Sayama gets up and gives him a tombstone piledriver on the floor. Both guys then collapse and are counted out of the ring.'

During that April tour, Tom had explained to 'Playboy' Buddy Rose that he would soon have to work outside of Canada for a while, whilst his immigration status was being confirmed. Rose worked for Don Owen's Pacific Northwest territory, based in Portland, Oregon – the closest territory south of the Canadian border. The news that the Dynamite Kid needed some North American refuge was like a lottery win for Owen, who promised Tom more money than Stu was paying him and a spot at the top of the roster alongside the likes of Rose, Rip Oliver and a 25-year-old making a big name for himself, Curt Hennig. Tom, Michelle and their bull-mastiff Duke (named after close friend Duke Myers) would be moving to Portland in the summer. It marked the end of what had become known as the 'Age of Dynamite' in Stampede Wrestling. Tom had been a teenager when he arrived in Calgary to a failing promotion on the verge of closing its doors. In just three years as their main draw, he had transformed it into a thriving territory and the envy of most North American promotions. They were cutting-edge with a revolutionary mid-heavyweight division which contained a fusion of high-flying and strong-style wrestling founded on the perfected styles from three different continents. They had become cult TV programming in the random points around the globe that their signal happened to travel to, including Saudi Arabia, New Zealand, Germany, Singapore, Bangkok, Uganda, Tanzania and Nigeria.

* * *

Alison Hart – the penultimate girl of the clan, with only Diana younger than her – married her fiancé Ben Bassarab at Hart House in May. Ben was a weightlifter and he and Davey had become close friends, working out together daily. Davey was the best man and, now used to stealing Calgary's biggest shows week-in, week-out, invited Diana out on to the balcony and proposed as he slipped a huge diamond ring on to her finger. They cut an adorable picture of perfect young love, but by the end of the year Davey's future in Canada would be in serious doubt.

On a Stampede van journey back to Calgary from a show in Lethbridge at the end of August, a Pontiac Trans Am had shot through a red light, forcing driver Wayne Hart to slam on the brakes and still only narrowly avoid a collision. Emboldened by copious amounts of beer and unaware who the passengers of the van were, the yobs in the Trans Am spun around to pursue and torment the van, which was soon being pelted with empty beer bottles and obscenities. Davey waited for his opportunity to leap from the van and wreak vengeance. That moment arrived at a red light, but the yobs screeched away just in time.

Just a little further up the road though, the Trans Am had been stopped at a police checkpoint. Davey once again jumped out of the van, barged passed the officers and stormed towards the passenger door of the vehicle. In a flash, one cop attempted to wrestle Davey to the ground from behind using his torch across Davey's huge neck. But Davey instinctively performed a hip-toss, and the cop flew almost 20 feet across the road.

As the rest of the babyfaces boarded their van, a handcuffed Davey was being guided into the back of the squad car. If charged and convicted of assaulting a police officer, deportation from Canada could be the minimum punishment Davey would have to worry about.

Meanwhile, Tom was really making his mark in the lucrative American market of Portland. He was instantly aligned with top heels Rip Oliver and 'The Assassin' to form a faction called 'The Clan' that would do constant battle in varied match formats against the babyface trio of Buddy Rose, Billy Jack Haynes and Curt Hennig.

Being the same age and with the same penchant for fierce backstage pranks, Tom and Curt hit it off both personally and professionally. Curt was developing into a truly great worker and the chemistry he and Dynamite found led to some unforgettable moments and matches for the raucous Northwest fans. Curt was the promotion's most popular star and against the perfectly honed heel persona of the Dynamite Kid, they generated amazing heat from the fans. Tom had now added a rather gruesome physical appearance to his arsenal of heel traits: his shoulder muscles appeared to emanate from the back of his cranium; his greasy, unkempt hair was back to shoulder-length; he sported wispy facial hair and his forehead was a mass of scar tissue from all the blading he had done. He also had a black leather waistcoat made with red and white trim on the shoulders and a skull with a lightning strike going through it emblazoned on the back – he truly had mastered the look of the baddest man on the planet.

On 7 September, Tom defeated Curt in Seattle to win the promotion's main title: the Pacific Northwest heavyweight championship – Tom's first heavyweight belt. His thick, muscular physique meant he could not only compete in the top division, but that he could justifiably dominate it too. He dropped the title to Billy Jack after one month so that the promotion could welcome Harley Race as his heel challenger. When Harley landed in Portland, he and Dynamite became reacquainted, and resumed their friendship built on the mutual respect of bad-ass tough guys. Harley still carried a gun; soon, Tom would be doing so too.

Tom's absence from the Stampede roster, and the revolving door of talent as the lure of overseas tours dragged the top stars away, meant that the promotion was once again struggling to maintain its own high standards. There was, however, new hope emerging from the dungeon. Despite not having the natural affection for the industry that his older brothers had, Owen Hart made up for that with the most natural athletic ability of them all. Like Bret, he had excelled in the amateur ranks during his school years, winning all the honours available to him. He had actively sought other career options but helping out at the Pavilion on Friday nights and training in the dungeon with Stu in readiness for his amateur competitions meant he already had one foot in the family business. With the roster threadbare and 18-year-old Owen fit, trained and immersed in wrestling, he volunteered to work some shows around his competitions and his studying.

Also, 16-year-old Chris Benoit was growing into a formidable young talent during his own rigorous training in the dungeon with Bruce and Stu. He hero-worshipped the style cultivated and popularised by the Dynamite Kid and dreamt of following in his footsteps. He had studied Tom so much that he had picked up the style almost instantly and was quickly earmarked as a prodigy.

* * *

Trailblazing superstar Tiger Mask was not only the WWF World junior-heavyweight champion, but also held the NWA's version of the title. But the Japanese wrestling world was left in shock when Satoru Sayama suddenly announced his retirement from the sport. Sayama cited his disillusionment with backstage politics at New Japan for his decision to quit the business. Suddenly, two world championships became vacant.

New Japan and the NWA handpicked 'The Cobra' as the next holder of their belt. Real-name George Takano, the Cobra was a high-flying masked Japanese wrestler billed as being from Uganda. He had honed his skills in Stampede's thriving mid-heavyweight division led by Dynamite and Davey. New Japan decided to introduce 'White Tiger' as a mysterious opponent for the Cobra and selected 20-year-old rising star Davey, who Takano had competed against so often in Calgary, to play the character.

Tired of waiting for his cousin to invite him on to the New Japan gravy train, Davey went into business for himself for the first time by accepting the invitation for the single-match trip against Tom's advice.

On 3 November 1983 at the Kuramae Kokugikan in Tokyo, Davey made his Japan debut wearing a red and white mask. In the locker room before, as Davey pulled on his mask, he felt kayfabe threatened when two men with Canadian accents casually strode in. Davey quickly tied his mask and challenged their presence there.

'Oh, hi there. I'm Bruce Allen, this is Bryan Adams. You might have heard of Bryan, he's about to take the rock music world by storm.

I'm his manager and promoter and we are big wrestling fans and were in Tokyo so, here we are!'

Davey took off his mask and they recognised him as Stampede star Davey Boy Smith. They all shook hands whilst sharing a laugh at the coincidence of their Canadian connection.

Davey and the Cobra tore the roof from the arena. With his physique and brilliant British-style acrobatic highspots, the crowd was going wild and were convinced White Tiger was the Dynamite Kid. 'Keee-do, Keee-do,' they chanted.

The Cobra snatched the victory after 20 minutes of hellraising action. But with his adrenaline pumping, Davey whipped off the mask to reveal himself as a fresh young Englishman for them to love to hate and they roared with delight and turned on the Cobra on behalf of their new sensation.

The fans were missing their 'Kee-do' and Tiger Mask, and with absence forever making the heart grow fonder, Dynamite's sensational talent was inadvertently making him a babyface in Japan.

As Davey settled into his first-class seat home, a newly familiar face appeared next to him: Bruce Allen. They began talking about the current state of the wrestling promotions in Canada, specifically Stampede and its future. Bruce told Davey he'd love to get involved and use his contacts and expertise to help and expand the territory, particularly in his hometown of Vancouver.

When Davey arrived back in Calgary, he excitedly told Stu and Bruce Hart about his acquaintance with Bruce Allen and they saw the potential and made formal contact. Soon, with Bruce Allen running the advertising and publicity, business in Vancouver doubled and even trebled at some shows.

Antonio Inoki and the New Japan bookers saw an instant big-money draw using Dynamite and Davey as a team, making them an offer to return for the new year tour as tag partners – with both also competing in a tournament to take the even more prestigious vacant WWF junior-heavyweight champion's throne.

13

AND THE NEW

'Titles. It would be wrong for anyone to think they didn't
mean anything, that it's all fake. I knew, on that night, the
title meant the world to Tom, but at a price even he couldn't
begin to imagine.'

Bret Hart

7 February 1984
Kuramae Kokugikan, Tokyo
Dynamite Kid v Davey Boy Smith
WWF World Junior-heavyweight Championship Tournament
Semi-final match
Approximate attendance: 12,000

'TOMMY, I'M fucked,' Davey whispered into his opponent's ear
just a few minutes into their match, as the rivetted crowd roared with
excitement at the thought of two of their favourite *gaijin* ripping one
another limb from limb.

They had wrestled as a team for the first time since that impromptu
match in Britain four years earlier against Kuniaki Kobayashi and
Isamu Teranishi on the New Year's Day opener of the 1984 New Year
Golden Series. They gelled instantly; their similar styles and telepathic
knowledge of each other's moves and routines meant they flowed in
and out of double-teams and always tagged at the optimum time to
keep their intensity.

The round-robin tournament featuring Dynamite, Davey, Bret,
Mark Rocco's 'Black Tiger', Nobuhiko Takada, Baby Face, Kobayashi,

Teranishi and the Cobra had seen them all face off against one another. It had provided amazing nightly support to the violent heavyweight contests at the top of the cards, featuring the likes of Inoki and Abdullah the Butcher, and had gained extraordinary momentum as January progressed. As the potential finalists emerged and jockeyed for position, the jeopardy of each match became more palpable.

On the penultimate night of the tournament, with Dynamite's place in the final confirmed, Davey Boy and the Cobra were facing off in a rematch and an effective eliminator, with the winner being installed as Dynamite's final opponent. But when the match ended in a double count-out, a three-way single-night round-robin was declared; with one match immediately following the other. It would be Davey Boy and the Cobra once again, Dynamite versus Davey Boy, and finally, Dynamite versus the Cobra.

The event in Tokyo was sensational, with the explosion of noise loud and constant. To complicate matters further, Davey Boy's intense stalemate with the Cobra continued when, after a brutal ten minutes, both men were once again counted out whilst brawling on the outside of the ring, where bunting and confetti given to the crowd for the coronation of the winner was already mounting. At the final bell, Dynamite had stormed into the ring to battle his new tag partner; he was fresh, Davey was anything but as he continued to perform with hard-hitting intensity. Dynamite had taken control and Davey grasped the first opportunity to tell his cousin he needed a breather. Dynamite changed tactics and did all of the heavy lifting, and slowly got more and more cheers as he turned on the offence.

It's a curious phenomenon in professional wrestling, that the more over you are as a heel, the more the viewing audience despises you; but internally, they know they only hate you so much because of how good you are. Subsequently, the tournament format which saw heels take on heels, babyfaces up against other faces, and all-*gaijin* battles, gave the fans the opportunity to get behind those who they subconsciously respected and admired the most, rather than the bookers dictating who they cheered and booed. And 'Kee-do' was cheered to the rafters.

Once Davey had got his breath back, they launched into the type of hard-hitting but graceful routines that had taken Stampede by storm, and the Japanese fans drank it in and spat it out in the form of roaring appreciation and approval. When Dynamite suplexed Davey high and over the top rope, both men crashed out of the ring. Davey landed hard on the floor, but Tom smashed his already brittle back on the ring apron. Davey heard Tom groan in agony and when he looked up, saw two lumps emerging from his cousin's lower back. Under the guise of scrambling back into the ring to beat the count, Davey helped Tom to crawl under the bottom rope first as the referee completed the ten-count on Davey. Dynamite claimed the victory and the crowd popped – there was no doubt about it anymore, he was the one they wanted to see with that belt around his waist. As Dynamite slumped in the corner of the ring with his back wrecked, Davey got to his feet and wished his partner good luck, before taking his place at ringside in support.

The Cobra, clad in his usual long white blazer, stormed towards the ring, thrusting members of the frenzied crowd out of his way. He climbed atop the turnbuckle like a cat and spun around to face the audience before performing a back-somersault and landing perfectly on his feet in the centre of the ring. Dynamite winced in pain as he dragged himself up to go again. The Cobra tore off his blazer and Dynamite couldn't prevent an early onslaught as the aggressor rained down blows, smelling a quick and easy victory. He whipped Dynamite into the turnbuckle with maximum velocity, and when Tom's thick but shattered back hit the turnbuckle, it made an audibly loud thud. Somehow, Dynamite managed to explode back with a dropkick and the crowd exploded with him. The Cobra bounced back to his feet, but Dynamite performed a nip-up straight into another dropkick, which forced Cobra into the corner; a third dropkick sent him out of the ring and sent the crowd – Davey Boy included – into raptures.

The 'Kee-do' chant was now deafening, with Davey the cheerleader. The match swung back-and-forth with near-falls torturing the crowd, until Dynamite performed a belly-to-back suplex and smoothly rolled over into a brutally leveraged pinning position. One. Two. Three.

The crowd erupted and Davey charged into the ring as the confetti and bunting began to rain down. Grimacing with pain, Tom punched both fists towards the crowd and in a rare moment of weakness, began to show a little emotion. Being the only one to realise just how stricken Tom was, Davey supported him and assisted him through his coronation as world champion. When he was awarded the title belt, Tom raised it skywards in celebration before strapping it around his waist so that he could thrust the huge trophy awarded to him for winning the tournament into the air.

The roars descended into applause of appreciation as little Tommy Billington was helped backstage by the Young Boys. All at the same time he was broken, and he was whole.

Tom laid on his front, still clasping his new title belt and almost using it to press his teeth into in a bid to quell the agonising pain he was in as the Young Boys went to work on his lower back, with packs of ice and deep muscle massaging.

'Great match, brother,' boomed down from above him. When Tom looked up, he saw bright yellow boots stepping over him, followed by the green and gold WWF heavyweight title belt. It was wrestling's gargantuan new megastar, Hulk Hogan.

Real name Terry Bollea, Hogan was 6ft 7in with a mountainous bronzed physique. He had no legitimate wrestling background and little in the way of technical prowess when compared to previous champions, but he did have straight, golden, shoulder-length hair and a thick handlebar moustache to match. He also had enough charisma to electrify arenas all by himself. In the early 1980s, his lack of genuine mat skills was the only thing stopping him from making it to the very top of wrestling. The bosses and bookers of each of the NWA, AWA and WWF had still held the tradition of their champion being a legitimate and believable technician. Hogan's looks and charisma had made him a Hollywood draw in 1981, when he was cast as the arrogant grappler 'Thunderlips' alongside Sylvester Stallone and Mr T in *Rocky III*. But even that stardom didn't convince Vince McMahon Sr that he should make him the champion and the face of his promotion; quite the opposite, he told Hogan he would hold the role against him, as the character was so clearly mocking professional wrestling. So, Hogan went to the AWA and captured the hearts of the fans as the all-American dream and the man to finally dethrone long-term heel champion Nick Bockwinkel. Promoter Verne Gagne attempted to get the best of both worlds, by having Hogan continuously in the main event as the challenger, packing venues with adoring fans desperate to be there when Hogan finally did it – but never actually doing it, as Gagne too didn't see Hulk as champion.

Just as Vince McMahon Jr didn't share the traditional principles when it came to staying out of other territories, he also did not care about the honour and pride of having a supreme worker as his champion. He had seen Hogan fail to become *the man* with the AWA and promised to shower him with all the gold belts he desired. In Hogan he saw money and he saw the vehicle that would drag the WWF through the whole of America and make roadkill out of the competition.

Current WWF champion Bob Backlund had refused to drop the belt to Hogan, resulting in a 'transitional' champion in the Iron Sheik, before the fans finally got their wish to see the hero crowned at Madison Square Garden on 23 January. As part of the ongoing relationship and globalisation of the WWF, Hogan had almost immediately travelled out to Japan to spread what was already running wild: 'Hulkamania', brother.

As Tom lay on the floor looking up, Davey stared across the room at Hogan, dreaming of one day being so huge. As Hogan burst through the locker room door and out to the rapturous applause he himself had just had, Tom knew here was just another example of why he had to kill himself every night, of why he had to take steroids and painkillers and uppers and downers just to stand a chance in this business at 5ft 8in with pale skin and a thick Lancastrian accent. But despite the limitations he felt had always worked against him, he had made his dreams come true, one way or another. Better still, 5,000 miles away back in Calgary, Michelle was pregnant with his first child.

PART 2

THE BRITISH BULLDOGS

'I think the British Bulldogs were more revolutionary in Japan than North America. Their hard wrestling style didn't fit in with a lot of the WWF teams at the time, whereas the Japanese wrestlers and style made them seem more special. I think their impact was strong among hardcore fans and a lot of people who grew up to be top wrestlers. It's funny, because at the time, the Road Warriors were the kings of the tag teams and everyone wanted to be like them … but long term, it was the Bulldogs and Midnight Express who popularised the big move style that the next generation of wrestlers studied.'

Dave Meltzer

14

ALL JAPAN

'Whether it was the constant pounding on my back from
all the suplexes and the piledrivers, or whether it was the
steroids, or a combination of both, at the age of 25, my back
was starting to give me serious pain. Sometimes my ribs, my
kidneys, my whole body, just ached. But I never thought of
cutting the high-risk moves out. Never. They were what the
people had paid to see.'

Tom Billington

August 1984

Mr Hito sat in a Calgary hotel room awaiting his guests for the surreptitious meeting he had put together. Beside him, on the bed, sat a large leather briefcase.

Hito – real name Katsuji Adachi – had long been closely affiliated with New Japan as well as a loyal Stampede Wrestling servant, acting as an agent for younger wrestlers to gain experience travelling between the two promotions. He would put a roof over the heads of the penniless young stars and, even though a stranger to them, would act as a trainer, manager and interpreter.

He had a gentlemen's agreement with New Japan president Hisashi Shinma that he would be financially compensated for this generous work, and a position within the company would be made available to him if and when he decided to return to his homeland. But it had become clear to him that neither of those things was going to happen. New Japan was being slowly run into the ground and many of their top

135

stars – both local and gaijin – were not under contract and had begun jumping to Giant Baba's All Japan, who were happy to pay whatever fee the mutinous wrestlers were demanding. The scales were balancing between the two promotions, and the momentum – and the financial power – was with All Japan.

New Japan had been hit hard by the exit of Satoru Sayama, who had started the exodus. But while he had quit the business, many were joining the arch-rival promotion. Giant Baba had also pulled off an unexpected but ingenious coup: he had bought the image rights to the Tiger Mask gimmick and was carefully choosing Sayama's successor. New Japan did have a couple of things holding the scales firm though: their cross-promotional deal with Vince McMahon's WWF meant that they welcomed the top American stars, including Hulk Hogan; they also had the world's hottest tag team locked down to a lucrative multi-year contract – the Dynamite Kid and Davey Boy Smith.

There was a quiet knock at the door, and Hito rushed to answer it. He opened the door wide to allow the double wide physiques of Tom and Davey through. He quickly shut the door behind them.

'What's this all about, then? What's with all the cloak 'n' dagger stuff?' Tom started.

Hito popped open the briefcase and, gesturing towards the neat stacks of dollar bills that filled it, said, 'Please, Mr Baba would like you to wrestle for him.'

Tom and Davey looked at each other in bewilderment. 'Baba?' Tom asked in astonishment. 'You're a New Japan guy. What's going on here?'

'Not no more. I work on behalf of All Japan now. Here is $20,000 for you to take away today. You get the same again when you arrive in Japan. Then Baba will pay you $1,000 per week more than Inoki pay you.'

'Well fuck me,' said Tom. Davey stayed quiet, allowing the team captain to take the lead. 'You sly old dog, Hito. Well, there's nothing to keep us with Inoki now that Sayama is done and dusted. Tell Baba he has a deal.'

'This must stay completely secret,' insisted Hito, 'no major *gaijin* ever switched in this way. You are supposed to be star attractions for Inoki's tag team tournament at Madison Square Garden in November;

instead you will be in Tokyo for All Japan. They cannot find out just yet.'

'Where do we sign?' asked Tom casually. With that, Hito produced two contracts and a pen. Tom scribbled his name down without hesitation and passed the pen to Davey, who looked nervous.

'C'mon Dave, we're not breaking our backs out there for the fun of it, are we? They pay all the Yanks like Dick fuckin' Murdoch a lot more than us, ya know; and they don't do half of what we do,' Tom said, as he fastened the briefcase back up and put it under his arm. Davey Boy Smith then signed the contract to confirm one of the most controversial talent jumps in wrestling history – and with Dynamite still holding the WWF world junior-heavyweight world title. The deal was for a minimum of three one-month tours each year, but they could do as many as they wished, all on the same lucrative money.

Dynamite and Davey had just returned from their July tour with New Japan as the talk of the tag team world. Their strength, speed and seemingly telepathic communication made them a unique and electrifying spectacle to see in action and they had taken Japan by storm. Their simultaneous high-flying and hard-hitting knew no bounds as Tom would hop from rope to turnbuckle and on to Davey's ample shoulders before crashing to the mat with his diving headbutt. He was guzzling painkilling drugs with complete disregard for their negative impact on his body or their addictiveness, and Davey had started taking them too to keep up the relentless pace, with his lower back and knees already giving him serious problems.

They felt particularly liberated to make such a bold move due to wrestling's political machinations not just in Japan, but in North America, too. Stampede Wrestling was in the process of winding up its business and closing its doors, having become the latest NWA territory to be muscled out by Vince McMahon's WWF. Vince had offered Stu a 'take-it-or-leave-it' offer of $1million plus ten per cent of the gate whenever the WWF ran a show in the territory. Vince would get Stampede's western Canadian television slots to air his new glitzy wrestling programming, which was on its way to becoming nationally syndicated. Stu had little choice but to accept; Vince hadn't been so polite and respectful in other territories, instead simply running shows there and leaving their top talent no option but to jump aboard his expanding empire. The promising connection with the promotional office of Bruce Allen in Vancouver, which had seen one show sell out a 10,000-capacity arena that summer, was also ended with the sale of Stampede. Davey and Diana would remain friends with Bruce and would always get tickets to see Bryan Adams when he came through Calgary.

Vince promised jobs to Stampede's three top stars: Bret, Dynamite and Davey. Stu also negotiated the promise of a job for another son-in-law, Jim Neidhart, who was wrestling for Eddie Graham's Florida territory (but Stu knew it was only a matter of time before Vince's crosshairs pointed in that direction), and a potential office job for his son Bruce, whose recent successful booking of Stampede had garnered him respect in the business. But Wayne, who was a great referee, and Ross, who produced the TV show, would be out of jobs. Tom and Davey's friend Ben Bassarab, who had been rising through the Stampede ranks, would see his dream career suddenly in tatters, and popular veteran residents such as Leo Burke, Mr Hito, the Cuban Assassin and Gerry Merrow would struggle to find work outside of Stampede.

* * *

With baby girl Bronwyne born in May that year, Tom and Michelle had already moved back to Calgary from Portland at the turn of the year, with perennial heel the Dynamite Kid making a dramatic return to Stampede as a babyface to join forces with Bret and Davey. They would stand together to challenge the formidable heels of Killer Khan, Cuban Assassin and the brutal and demonic new acquisition 'Bad News' Allen. Real name Allen Coage, Bad News had been spotted in Japan by Bret as a monster heel of African-American descent with a legitimate and marketable background as a bronze medallist in judo at the 1976 Olympics.

Dynamite's subsequent street fights and cage matches with Bad News became so frenzied and notorious that venues could have sold out twice over from the moment the main event was announced. On one occasion, after Bad News used a broken bottle as a weapon at the Pavilion, the Alberta Athletic Commission suspended Stampede from the venue, forcing them to find a temporary home at a nearby First Nations.

Now both babyfaces, Dynamite and Davey were free to wow their hometown crowds with the revolutionary tag team action that had previously being reserved for the Japanese audience, and they had won the International tag team title at a tournament in March.

Tom also won the North American heavyweight title for the first time from Killer Khan on his return, before dropping it to Bad News. Davey Boy established himself as the promotion's top star when he made the title his own maiden heavyweight crown by overcoming the evil Bad News in front of 7,000 fans in Vancouver. He remained the holder of the belt until Stampede closed its doors at the Edmonton Fieldhouse on 15 September.

The promotion went out with a typically bloody cage match which fittingly saw Dynamite and Bret team up to defeat Bad News and 'Rotten' Ron Starr.

The bloody in-ring battles between Tom and Ron Starr had merely been art imitating a recent real event. Starr was an American Vietnam war veteran and a two-time NWA junior-heavyweight champion, but was an outspoken locker-room agitator. Word got to Tom that while they were in Japan, Rotten Ron had been accusing them of being selfish by leaving the territory struggling while they so regularly jetted off for their lucrative tours on the other side of the world.

'It's good to see you, Tom,' Ron said the first time he saw Dynamite in the Pavilion locker room following their return. 'I wasn't expecting to see you tonight.'

Tom looked at Ron coldly. 'Well, I came to fight.'

'Damn! Well I sure hope it ain't with me!' Ron joked.

'Well, don't be too damn sure of that,' Tom said before instantly unleashing a rapid and ferocious barrage of punches to Starr's head and face. A lacerated Ron protested his innocence. Some onlookers believed Tom had used the situation to take a cheap shot at a defenceless Ron and therefore reinforce his status as locker-room leader and enforcer, although few had much sympathy with Ron.

Not only was Vince McMahon bolstered with another territory, but two years after salivating over the Dynamite Kid in Madison Square Garden, it appeared he finally had his man. Tom and Bret were summoned for two days of TV tapings in New York, where Vince would watch them intently to see where they would fit into his ever-expanding roster.

Dynamite and Bret won a short tag match followed by singles matches the next day. As well as Vince, road agent Chief Jay Strongbow gushed over Tom's physique and talent. They only got paid $100 each in total – not even enough to cover expenses. Bret had been made aware previously that WWF TV tapings were notoriously low-paid, with the office deeming that the wrestlers should be grateful for the exposure. But Tom, in typical fashion, didn't hide his disappointment. He brooded over what he saw as disrespect, so much so that when they arrived back at Hart House with their bags, he told Stu to pass on the message to Vince that he could go fuck himself; that his and Davey's lucrative new All Japan contracts were enough, even if they only worked six months of the year.

They did honour a few WWF Canadian bookings before they were due to cause their Japanese shock, but once again, Davey trusted Tom's judgement and rejected the WWF offer without question. They were becoming an elusive thorn in Vince's side, but while he believed they were still under the New Japan contract, he knew it was unlikely they would sign for the AWA or NWA, as the stakes continued to rise in the American wrestling war.

* * *

All Japan flew Hito out to Tokyo to continue his own personal espionage. He was at the airport to meet Dynamite and Davey for their first tour in late November, escorting them to a hotel and staying there himself, drip-feeding them just enough yen to get by but not enough that they might get tempted to go out and make themselves known around town.

At a press conference on 14 November at the Tokyo Capital Hotel, two days before the tour was scheduled to start, Giant Baba shocked the wrestling world by announcing the team of the Dynamite Kid and Davey Boy Smith for the upcoming tournament. Industry crisis meetings began in earnest. Suited representatives thrashed it out with talk of lawsuits, countersuits and vast amounts of compensation. Vince McMahon even scrambled himself a flight out to Tokyo to add to the

New Japan bargaining power in an attempt to reverse the move and avoid Dynamite and Davey moving further away from the WWF and a step closer to his domestic rivals, with All Japan being affiliated with the NWA.

But when Tom did the honourable thing regarding the treasure he had stashed amongst his luggage, and posted the championship belt to the New Japan office with a note saying 'thank you', everyone accepted the inevitable.

The Dynamite Kid had been the WWF junior-heavyweight champion for nine months and retired the belt undefeated.

Compensation and a media blackout of that initial tour was agreed on to give New Japan time to regroup and soften the blow to their loyal but expectant fans during their own simultaneous tag team tour. But the media blackout didn't stop the fan frenzy. Dynamite and Davey debuted a week later against *gaijin* icons Terry and Dory Funk Jr at the Korakuen Hall. The Funks were the most successful *gaijin* tag team in history.

Every night but one of that tour sold out, with Dynamite and Davey competing in dream matches against such teams as Bruiser Brody and Stan Hansen, and Harley Race and Nick Bockwinkel, as well as fans flocking to see if the Dynamite Kid and the second iteration of Tiger Mask – Mitsuharu Misawa – could improve on perfection.

* * *

Davey had finally been formally charged for assaulting the cop a year earlier. The delay meant nothing would prevent him marrying Diana. On 7 October Hart House was presented as a candlelit palace and a glittery ballroom, as a harpist serenaded the 800 guests. Tom stood beside Davey as his best man and was just one of dozens of high-profile wrestlers who stole the attention of the photographers from the beautiful bride; but the only one that told one of them to 'Fuck off' as he guzzled down his beer.

Christmas brought about a very different mood at the mansion. Davey had been found guilty but, much to everyone's surprise and relief, had only been fined and placed on probation. Behind the scenes, Stu had used his connections and the respect he held locally with long-time contact Bill Phillips, who worked at the Immigration

Department, to secure and retain foreign wrestlers' visas, ensuring Davey's residency, career and marriage in Canada weren't brought to an abrupt end.

Tom and Davey remained coy about where their futures lay – the media blackout in Japan meant they hadn't had to break the news of their treachery at home either. Bret bemoaned his position on the bottom rung of the WWF, but he sounded out Tom and Davey to join him on behalf of the office. He tried to sell it by informing them of the rumours that were spreading wildly about the spring extravaganza that the WWF were putting together – *WrestleMania*, which was to be a celebrity-laden prime-time show full of glitz and glamour that would be broadcast nationwide via closed-circuit television. Vince had seen the MTV demographic emerge and felt he could capitalise on it.

Beginning with the Korakuen Hall in Tokyo, Dynamite and Davey blew away any New Year blues as they put on astonishing performances country-wide to electrified crowds of several thousand every night. They were a sensation, becoming viewed as a modern but mythical second coming of previous deity-like Wigan natives Robinson and Gotch. Tom, especially, continued to crash around the arenas with reckless abandon and complete disregard for his own health to entertain the fans. The fast-flowing and high-flying innovative moves made them the star attraction and cemented their position as one of the most valuable assets in the business.

15

WRESTLEMANIA

'Sadly, under Tom's influence, Davey was developing a bit
of a mean streak. The two of them reminded me of a set of
genetically altered, raging pit bulls.'

Bret Hart

March 1985

Dynamite and Davey were whisked the short distance from Toronto
Airport to the Howard Johnson Hotel in a shiny black stretch limousine.
Their airfare and the limo had been paid for by Vince McMahon, who
sat waiting for their arrival in the conference room he had booked.
The WWF and the world's hottest tag team were in the same country
at the same time, and McMahon wasn't going to let the 2,000 miles
between Calgary and Toronto stop him from arranging to meet them
at the hotel his wrestling delegation were using.

'Hey, guys!' a sharp-suited Vince, escorted by his right-hand man
George Scott, greeted Tom and Davey as they entered the room. He
stood and shook their hands and told them to take a seat.

'I'd like you to come and represent the World Wrestling Federation,'
said Vince, cutting to the chase.

'Yeah, thought that's why you flew us 'ere,' Tom replied, nonchalantly.
Davey stayed quiet, trusting Tom to do any negotiating. The WWF
had all the momentum and the NWA and AWA were ailing in Vince's
wake. All three promotions were interested in the Bulldogs, whose
affiliation with All Japan and their scorning of New Japan made any

WWF deal tricky. But Stu had convinced them, stubborn Tom in particular, to meet with Vince for the sake of their own futures. The Bulldogs had been ahead of the curve in Japan, as the struggles of New Japan continued and more of their top stars jumped ship. The New Japan–WWF alliance was inevitably going to end as the WWF's stars were being priced out of the market. Stu recognised this and advised Tom and Davey to go and get the best of both worlds.

'You heard what we're doing at the end of the month, right?' Vince grinned and leant forward with his eyebrows raised in excitement.

'Putting a big show on at Madison Square Garden, so I hear.'

'Big? This is *WrestleMania* pal!' Vince's eyes widened a little further as he leant back, as if bowled over by his own announcement. 'And you guys would've been on the show, earning big bucks, if we'd got something agreed. Which is why I've brought you here today. Tell me, is it true that you guys are first cousins?'

Tom and Davey both nodded.

'Jeez. Those guys in Calgary sure know how to kayfabe, eh? Who knew?!' Vince's excitement grew. 'I can see it now; you guys will be the British Bulldogs!' his eyes were now stretched open as he stared up at the ceiling, visualising roaring arenas and bulging ticket sales.

Tom and Davey afforded themselves a grin in each other's direction.

'We'll have those tag belts on you within a year and you'll be wealthy young men. What d'ya say?'

'What ya think, Dave?' Tom asked.

'The British Bulldogs?' Davey asked rhetorically.

'Well, you look like a pair of Bulldogs!' Vince yelled, followed by his yuk-yuk chuckle.

'Okay, we'll give it a try,' confirmed Tom.

'Alright!' Vince stood and offered his hand for them to shake. After they did, he climbed atop the conference table and began to dance like the bride's uncle at a wedding. He finally had his man (and his even bigger partner).

The newly-titled 'Bulldogs' left the room and headed down in the elevator. They decided to toast their new lucrative employment with a beer, so stepped into the hotel bar. The security of employment was a relief – not only was Tom now a father, but Diana was expecting Davey's first child too.

'Well look who's here!' came the brazen voice of Jim Neidhart, who was sat beside Bret.

The four friends and brothers-in-law got reacquainted over a beer. Only weeks earlier, Bret had been alone and jobbing in the WWF, while Jim was working hard for little pay in Florida and Tom and Davey looked on the verge on isolating themselves in Japan. Suddenly, they were all back under the same roof – literally and symbolically.

'We're gonna be the fucking British Bulldogs, Gabe,' laughed Tom. 'We start next month.'

'We're a tag team too,' said Bret. 'I was scratching around for loose change here until they brought Jim in. They found out about our connection and now they've given us Jimmy Hart as a manager, turned us heel and called us the Hart Foundation.'

'Well, the Bulldogs are babyfaces, apparently,' Tom replied. 'You know what that means? We'll be back in the ring together soon, Gabe.'

Throughout March, 'Rule Britannia, Britannia rule the waves' boomed out to finally welcome Dynamite and Davey to a WWF audience. The British Bulldogs were clad in dark red tights with Union Jacks embroidered on the rear and the word 'BULLDOGS' up the legs. The crowds were going crazy, as were Vince and main booker George Scott watching on the monitors in the back.

After TV tapings in Poughkeepsie, George approached Tom with contracts. They were five-year deals worth up to $10,000 per week (depending on which cards they were on and their position on them) plus pay-per-view bonuses and merchandise royalties. But after scanning over the text, Tom handed the contract back and shook his head. It claimed exclusivity. No Japan. Tom told George to pass on to Vince that he and Davey would still be honouring their minimum three tours per year for the unaffiliated All Japan. Vince McMahon begrudgingly allowed them to have the unique position of being WWF tag team headliners and yet still leave multiple times each year to represent a rival company – anything to get them signed up and avoid them joining the NWA.

Tom had developed into a savvy businessman who knew the industry and his own worth. Honouring their All Japan deal enabled them to keep their roles as fearsome *gaijin*, to maintain and enhance their now legendary status there and guarantee themselves the thick end of $100,000 for three months' work. They could then have their cake and eat it, touring the USA with the WWF as the smiling, honourable and all-conquering heroes the British Bulldogs – and rake in another six-figure sum for that nine months' work.

Just six days later, on 31 March, to the relief of everyone associated with the WWF, *WrestleMania* was an unprecedented success. As well as a capacity audience at MSG and with tickets at a record price for a wrestling show, over one million viewers tuned in via closed-circuit television to see the *Rocky III* co-stars Hulk Hogan and Mr T team up to defeat Rowdy Roddy Piper and 'Mr Wonderful' Paul Orndorff with Muhammad Ali as a special guest referee.

The Bulldogs, as well as Bret and Jim, who hadn't climbed the ranks high enough yet, had missed out on the extravaganza and the huge payday it provided, but set about ensuring they weren't to miss out on the next pay-per-view event Vince added to the calendar. Dynamite and Davey began by wrestling the heel tag teams, including the Moondogs, the Dream Team (Beefcake and Valentine), and the Iron Sheik and Nikolai Volkoff. Even in *house shows* with small audiences against jobbing tag teams, the Bulldogs would flail around in dramatic fashion for the crowd's amusement. At TV tapings they would pull off their ultimate dangerous manoeuvre, as Dynamite would climb from the top rope on to the back of the opponent Davey had straddled across his shoulders, balance there and then perform his dynamic diving headbutt on to the opponent fallen on the mat. 'We've never seen anything like this ever before!' Vince would shriek on commentary.

Initially, they would rarely face Bret and Jim, being distinctly above them in the pecking order and often touring the big cities and venues on the same card as Hogan, with the Hart Foundation on the 'B' tour.

But on 27 April in Philadelphia – the city of brotherly love – the four brothers in-law met on the British Bulldogs and the Hart Foundation for the very first time. Earlier that same day, after much agonising over a nickname to go well with Jim 'The Anvil' Neidhart, Bret imaged himself as a cold-blooded technical wrestling executioner, and Bret 'The Hitman' Hart was born and would be making his first appearance in the match.

The four agreed to really go the extra mile and make each other look as great as possible and show those backstage what the Stampede boys were all about.

Bret and Jim looked cocky and arrogant in their reflective shades as they waited in the ring, as the 'Mouth of the South' Jimmy Hart, a diminutive but obnoxious heel manager who shouted through a megaphone and still managed to wear suits louder than his voice, jumped around the ring like a frog on a volcano. When 'Rule Britannia' hit, the crowd popped and the mayhem began, as 30 minutes of intense brawling, hard bumps and perfectly coordinated and flowing highspots had the audience enthralled. The match needed a spectacular ending, and it got one when Dynamite launched his flying headbutt from a dazed and stumbling Jim's back on to a stricken Bret. With both Jim and Jimmy scrambling to break up the pin, Davey launched the Anvil over the top rope, squashing his loudmouth manager on landing.

'Thanks, Gabe,' Tom whispered into his friend's ear as the referee's hand pounded the mat for the third time.

George Scott was at the venue and was blown away; he already knew the Bulldogs were that good, but now he knew the Hart Foundation were too, and that the chemistry between the two teams would make for an exceptional feud at the top of the division.

The British Bulldogs and the Hart Foundation opposed each other relentlessly, and redefined tag team wrestling in the USA. Gone would be the older, rotund stars who were in the tag team division for the natural breaks which that type of match gave them to recover, and in came the young studs using each other's skillset to create unique highspots and relentless pace.

In October, Bret and Tom performed a singles match on the mid-card of a TV show in Denver that is still remembered and re-watched today.

But George and Vince saw the Bulldogs' Achilles heel emerge when they put a camera to their faces at TV tapings and asked them to shoot promos. They had never been naturals on the microphone, but Tom had been so in tune with his cocky heel persona in Stampede that he gained a natural confidence that transcended into good mic skills; as a smiling and polite babyface, he was lost. They appeared awkward and clumsy and their thick Lancastrian accents almost made them sound dim. Vince decided to put 'Captain' Lou Albano with them as their manager. Captain Lou was a veteran personality of the wrestling scene, a hairy, roly-poly figure with needles and pins emerging from various parts of his face.

Captain Lou instantly had the desired effect on the Bulldogs and saved them from having to do too much talking. The problem was, they were already beer-drinking, drug-using pranksters, and Albano was certainly not the man to set them on any kind of righteous path.

Diana gave birth to Davey's son Harry on 2 August 1985.

* * *

Despite booming business throughout the USA, the WWF's forays into western Canada had initially proven unprofitable. In typical ruthless fashion, Vince decided to pull the plug on his deal with Stu, having paid him only a tiny fraction of the fee they had agreed and having taken all of his top talent. Stu decided to bring the band back together – even if it was without the frontmen that had made them chart-toppers. In the summer of '85, Stampede Wrestling was on its way back. In truth, Stu had been given little option, with legal action against Vince not plausible. Vince employed multiple family members and also knew that the first violation of the deal had actually come from Bruce Hart the previous year, who had supported a local opposition group in briefly and unsuccessfully reforming Stampede Wrestling, breaking the no-competition clauses built into the deal. Free agents at the time, Dynamite and Davey had signed up to be the flagship stars of the renegade promotion, but when Bruce wasn't given the role of booker that he had assumed he would when helping the upstarts and securing them a TV slot – which would also run against the WWF – all three pulled out, leaving the new-look Stampede with no Hart lineage to promote and no true headline act. It was destined to fail, and it did.

But the newest incarnation of Stampede Wrestling was built around the latest group of dungeon-trained talented young rookies: Owen was now 20 and already looking like a real superstar; another Hart brother-in-law and Davey's best friend Ben Bassarab resumed his training; John Hindley, Ted Betley's typically well-trained nephew, had moved to Calgary under the name 'Johnny Smith' – Davey's 'brother'; Brian Pillman was a budding NFL star who had narrowly missed out on a 1984 draft selection so had decided to turn to pro wrestling; and then there was the apparent second-coming of the Dynamite Kid in the almost identical form of the now 18-year-old Chris Benoit. Complete with shoulder-length fair hair and a move repertoire that included the snap-suplex and the flying headbutt, his inspiration left little to the imagination for the returning regulars to the Pavilion. They also attracted a new set of Japanese youngsters to continue their training and development in Calgary, one of whom was Keiichi Yamada, who soon thereafter would burst on to the New Japan scene as Jushin 'Thunder' Liger.

16

THE WRESTLING CLASSIC

'If ever there was a time when I should have stopped to think
about what I was doing it was the time I ran out of my usual
steroids and took some horse steroid instead. I got it from a
vet who lived close to my home in Calgary. He told me it was
for horses. The label even read, "For intra-muscular use with
horses only" and there was a picture of a horse on the front.
But I didn't care, I was desperate.'

Tom Billington

The Wrestling Classic
7 November 1985
Rosemont Horizon
Chicago, Illinois
Attendance: 14,000

'HELLO EVERYONE and welcome to the beautiful Rosemont
Horizon in the suburbs of the windy city Chicago,' began a raucous and loud
Vince McMahon. 'We are looking forward indeed, as it was outlined
earlier, to the 16-man elimination tournament – a most spectacular,
one-of-a-kind happening in the World Wrestling Federation.
Notwithstanding that, also we'll announce the winner of the Rolls-
Royce Silver Cloud III, and then from there, Hulk Hogan in his title
defence against Rowdy Roddy Piper.

'With me at this moment, my colleague Lord Alfred Hayes along
with Susan Witkes, and here we have this extraordinary tournament

line-up; the drawing was held this afternoon and a most interesting one indeed it was.'

McMahon and Hayes continued to analyse the tournament format at this latest pay-per-view event that Vince had masterminded. Unable to wait the whole 12 months for *WrestleMania II* to further put his rivals to the sword, he had devised another extravaganza to split the year-long gap.

Mug-shots down the left-hand side of the giant blue board showed who would face off in the opening round. The Dynamite Kid would meet Nikolai Volkoff and, further down, Vince displayed a jolt of excitement when he announced the 'scientific match-up' between Davey Boy Smith and Ricky 'The Dragon' Steamboat.

In the second match of the tournament, 'Mean' Gene Okerlund introduced the Dynamite Kid to a small but rousing reception, before asking the audience to stand for Nikolai Volkoff's rendition of the Soviet national anthem – which was predictably met by boos and derision. Volkoff took off his native karakul hat, proudly saluted and began to sing. Having seen enough, Dynamite climbed on to the turnbuckle and perched there like Batman atop a gargoyle, stalking a Gotham crook. As Volkoff, unhappy with the disrespect of the American public, angrily handed the microphone back to Okerlund, Dynamite soared through the air and hit the perfect dropkick, once more landing hard on the small of his back, before pouncing on his shocked foe for the one, two, three and one of wrestling's quickest ever wins. The crowd – who had been booing just seconds earlier – were in raptures.

Davey Boy and the highly-decorated Ricky Steamboat put on a respectful all-babyface wrestling clinic, making each other look phenomenal. Steamboat was literally and figuratively on the ropes when Davey attempted a dropkick, which Steamboat evaded. Davey crotched himself on the ropes, causing an early end to the match as Davey clasped his supposedly torn groin muscle.

Dynamite defeated the 300lb Adrian Adonis in the second round. As Tom and Adrian had paced the corridor and awaited the cue for their ring walks, Adrian – a rotund veteran and reputable bully himself – said, 'Tommy, you just follow my lead in the ring, and we'll be okay.'

'Look,' Tom began his reply, 'if you want to piledrive me, backdrop me, suplex me – whatever – that's okay, but do not tell me what to do and how to do it in that ring. Nobody does. You do what you want, and I'll do what I want.'

The Dynamite victory qualified him for a semi-final match against 'Macho Man' Randy Savage.

Despite being with the WWF less than six months, Savage had already become one of the top heels in the company. He was arrogant and flamboyant, wearing garish leopard-print outfits and oversized sunglasses to the ring. The main cause of the fans' ire towards him though, as well as his flagrant rule-breaking, was his misogynistic treatment of his loyal and beautiful 'valet' (and real-life wife) Miss Elizabeth. A second-generation star, Savage had stayed loyal to the territories his father, Angelo Poffo, was so ingrained in, and his 12-month feud with Jerry Lawler in Memphis is remembered as one of the final great rivalries of the regionalised system. But when Lawler won their 'Loser Leaves Town' match in Tennessee on 7 June 1985, there was only one place Savage could be heading; once again, Vince had his man.

With Dynamite waiting in the ring, the Macho Man made his elaborate ring walk to his 'Pomp and Circumstance' entrance theme – the same one the heel Dynamite Kid had been using in Stampede several years earlier. Whilst the match only lasted five minutes, the pair really did put on a mini-wrestling classic, as they realistically brawled and jostled for leverage, and every time it appeared the bigger man had gained it, Dynamite would counter to the delight of the fans, and to the frustration of Savage.

Savage went to the top rope and was poised to deliver a high-flying move, but Dynamite leapt to his feet and joined Savage on the turnbuckle. He clutched his opponent tight before delivering a huge superplex and rolling over into a pinning position. As the referee began the count, Savage cleverly hooked his own leg around Dynamite's, which naturally raised one of his shoulders off the mat and pressed both of Tom's against it. The referee continued his three-count and Dynamite jumped to his feet believing he had won the match but was left bemused when Okerlund announced Macho Man as the winner. The unique and brilliantly executed ending would become forever known as the 'Dynamite-Savage-finish'.

Randy Savage was left rolling around in agony on the outside of the ring with Elizabeth tending to her broken and battered man, whilst the Dynamite Kid was on his feet in the ring, looking fit and strong and still claiming to be the victor. Tragically, the short match would be the only time the two men – for so many years earlier regarded as the hidden gems of professional wrestling – would meet in the ring.

The toll taken on Savage was the storyline of the grand final, as he struggled to compete with the comparatively fresh Junkyard Dog and was eventually counted out, giving the fans their babyface winner.

In a tournament that also featured Paul Orndorff, Bob Orton Jr, Terry Funk, Don Muraco and then-Intercontinental champion Tito Santana, both Davey and Dynamite had been firmly put over as top-level contenders – the latter in particular. Their stocks were rising, both individually and collectively.

Their strong booking and momentum were in spite of their unique situation. Almost immediately after the event the Bulldogs were off for another adrenaline-filled tour for All Japan, on the completion of which, Tom asked the office staff to tell Giant Baba that they wanted the $20,000 advance that had been agreed to confirm their deal continued into 1986. The message was passed back that Baba would pay them on their January return. Tom knew something was amiss – Baba was always good for the money up front. Vince and the WWF had grown further in stature and monetary power and had done a deal with Baba for the Bulldogs' exclusivity. Word was out within the industry that the Bulldogs were going to be the WWF's next tag team champions and would be holding the belts for the foreseeable future.

The WWF's 'A' team wasn't the only one on which the Bulldogs were to feature, as alongside Hulk Hogan and others, they made a guest appearance in an episode of hit TV show *The A-Team*, with Tom volunteering to deliver the headbutt required to vanquish one of the villains. Suddenly, the Dynamite Kid and Davey Boy Smith were becoming household names.

The WWF was an institution. They even had their own resident doctor in George Zahorian. He was based at a regular venue at Hershey, Pennsylvania, and would be there to perform heart rate and blood pressure testing for all the wrestlers before the show, and was on hand for any emergency that may occur. There was a curious phenomenon though: all the wrestlers seemed especially keen to have these seemingly tedious tests carried out and would form a long queue outside Dr Zahorian's office in anticipation. Once seen, they would emerge with a brown paper bag, which would contain the ingredients to that particular wrestler's daily drug cocktail. As well as the full range of steroids, Dr Zahorian was armed with the complete arsenal of uppers and downers and prescription painkillers such as Percocet and sleeping pills including Valium, Halcion and Placidyl. The premature deaths of young wrestling stars David von Erich and Jay Youngblood in 1984 and '85 respectively, had done nothing to curtail the institutionalisation of daily substance abuse. For Tom and Davey, access to the drugs they had become dependent on had just become easier.

THE NIGHT PATROL

'I saw Dynamite Kid give himself injections of steroids in the
locker room and when he'd given himself a shot in the hip,
he'd just throw the syringe against the wall ... he left a trail
of syringes across the whole entire territory and just went
about his business. He was really vicious.'

Superstar Billy Graham

7 April 1986. Chicago

Whilst Hulk Hogan was posing to his delirious *WrestleMania II* crowd
following his cage match victory over King Kong Bundy, the Bulldogs
and the Harts were in the Chicago Hyatt bar. They were amongst the
final few wrestlers that still kayfabed, and so sat at opposite sides of the
crowded bar. But when Bret and Tom's glances met, they smirked and
held up their beer bottles. They had been there together from the very
start eight years earlier; now, after all the literal blood and sweat, their
careers were finally taking off. Tom and Davey had been paid $20,000
each for their 15-minute tag title match and were now firmly installed
as champions and headliners. Bret and Jim had been the final two men
eliminated by the eventual (and predictable) winner of the 20-man
Battle Royal – André the Giant. When Bret excitedly told Tom that
he believed this was the first sign of them getting a push up the roster,
the ever-mocking Dynamite Kid nicknamed them the 'Push Brothers'.

But Tom needed more painkilling substances than ever in the
aftermath of *WrestleMania*. Going typically over and above the call
of duty for the pay-per-view audience, after the 'sacrifice bump' spot

(as that particular finish is known), which had seen Dynamite thrust his head into the incoming Greg Valentine whilst perched on the second rope, Tom had launched himself far and wide and intentionally smashed himself into the steel barriers. His fragile spine had absorbed another devastating blow.

Both Tom and Davey bought big mansions on the outskirts of Calgary to raise their families – even though they knew they weren't going to be there much to see their kids grow up. The WWF schedule was relentless, which only served to encourage their rampant lifestyles. It was a daily routine of travel (usually whilst having a few beers), workout (with speed and steroids), perform, go to the bar and party all night (more uppers, beers and possibly even cocaine), then some Valium or Halcion to ensure a few hours' sleep before doing it all over again. Tom was even injecting cortisone into his injury-ravaged joints to mask the pain for long enough to be able to perform. Cortisone, if used too often, causes deterioration of the tendons, ligaments and bones.

Although they were rarely there to enjoy them, they had provided great atmospheres in their homes for their young families. Bull-mastiff Duke was joined by Duchess and eventually Tigger in the Billington household as Tom and Michelle intended to breed them on their expansive land, where they also kept cats.

Davey and Diana would have a house full of pets, including rottweilers Brutus (named after friend Beefcake) and Holly, a shih-tzu called Dante and several cats.

* * *

'What the fuck are you doing 'ere?' Tom said as he checked in at the Howard Johnson Hotel in Toronto once again. He had spun his head around when an unmistakable gentleman walked up beside him to check in.

'Tommy!' replied Harley Race, joyously. 'Well, Kid, if you can't beat 'em, join 'em, eh?'

Harley had been amongst the rebels against Vince's national takeover, standing firm alongside the likes of fellow NWA stalwarts Ric Flair and Dusty Rhodes. The remaining territories, promoters and wrestlers had pulled together to form their own nationally syndicated company under the umbrella of Jim Crockett Promotions.

Harley's defection to the WWF was somewhat symbolic. He was an eight-time NWA heavyweight champion and a universally respected figure. But despite his standing within the wider business, Harley would, for the most part, be a mid-carder in the WWF. He was a relative unknown to the legions of youngsters Vince had recruited as his fanbase, and the sheer size of the roster meant that Race went from being a big fish in a shrunken pond, to average-sized in a continually expanding one. The amount of talent at the WWF's disposal meant that they could put on simultaneous tours in different parts of the country and multiple shows each and every night. They were a relentless juggernaut.

The tours were equally relentless: three weeks long, with the stars wrestling every night and often multiple times per day at weekends and at TV tapings. The three days off at the end of each tour included the several hours it would take to travel home, and up to a day they would have to allow to pack and travel in preparation to start the next tour. They would zig-zag across the vast country and its different time zones for 300 days per year.

Harley was a welcome locker-room and bar-stool ally for Tom, who loved the lifestyle. The drugs were dragging him towards breaking point, both physically and mentally, but the vicious cycle was formed by the fact that those same drugs were masking the symptoms. He was becoming nasty and more temperamental. His pranks and ribs were becoming more malicious and were often targeted towards those less likely to give him a comeback, or a 'receipt', which was getting him the reputation of a bully. He thought nothing of spiking drinks with sleeping pills or laxatives, cutting up wrestlers' apparel or clothing in the locker room, using the head of an unsuspecting colleague as an ashtray or even defecating in a colleague's travel bag. Davey Boy, like he had for a decade, simply followed the lead of his team captain.

Tom had always just wanted to wrestle and put on electric performances for the fans; he didn't like the commercial side of the WWF, and being top babyfaces, the Bulldogs were expected to regularly appear in family-friendly TV commercials. Despite being lucrative to be a part of, Tom found himself getting fined as a result of turning up late or not at all, and soon the Bulldogs were in Vince's doghouse and they stopped getting invited along to them at all.

Outside the ring, Tom and Davey formed a four-man stable with two other wrestlers – 6ft 7in blond giant Dan Spivey and Gary Portz, who wrestled as Scott McGhee and had originated from Shipley, West Yorkshire, before he moved to the States in his late teens to pursue a wrestling career (his father, Geoff Portz, had been one of the original Brits on the Stampede roster). Both Dan and Gary were mid-carders at best but were top tier talent in the extracurricular exploits that the Bulldogs also enjoyed. They adopted the name the 'Night Patrol', and they were proud to be the last ones to retire from the bars each and every night. Only André the Giant's legendary drinking feats could eclipse those of the Night Patrol members and, in particular, their 'Squadron Leader' Tom and second-in-command, 'Little Dog' Gary.

Dan Spivey and Gary Portz became the latest inductees into Tom's sacred inner circle, a club that earned you an unconditional friendship and unending loyalty.

* * *

Stampede and the WWF worked together to put on a jointly promoted show at Calgary's Saddledome for the 1986 Stampede rodeo week. The card was reminiscent of the *WrestleMania II* show that had preceded it just a few months earlier, as Hulk Hogan battled King Kong Bundy for the WWF title and the Bulldogs defended their belts against the Dream Team. Bret was in singles action as the hometown hero, despite his heel status, against Siva Afi. The undercard was made up of Stampede stalwarts, as Owen and Ben Bassarab were in tag team action against Duke Myers and Kerry Brown, and Wayne Ferris showed off his charismatic showmanship in his heel persona 'Honky Tonk Wayne' as he defended his North American heavyweight championship against veteran local favourite Dan Kroffat.

Ferris would vacate the title in the following month of August as the WWF signed him up and made him the 'Honky Tonk Man'.

HAVE A NICE DAY

'"Hey Dynamite, it's nice to meet you," I said to the man who
pound for pound may have been the top wrestler in the world
... "You can give me that snap suplex if you want," I offered
the man who had been responsible for bringing high risk into
WWF, and who would also be responsible for my inability to
eat solid food for the next month.'

Mick Foley

26 August 1986. The Providence Civic Center, Rhode Island

'What's your name?' Pat Patterson asked the hairy 21-year-old local
they'd booked to partner Les Thornton against the British Bulldogs.

'Cactus Jack,' replied Mick Foley, enthusiastically.

'Well, we can't use your gimmick name. We'll use your real name,'
Pat said, scribbling down on a clipboard. 'Also, kid, you'll have to get
rid of the bandana.' Mick's mannerisms and nervous energy gave Pat
concerns over just how green this kid he had been sent was.

'How many matches have you had?' he asked.

'Just one,' Mick replied, causing Pat to shake his head in disbelief.

Enhancement talents were supposed to appear like average joes
dragged in from the street, so as not to take any attention at all away
from the stars they were being paid to make look good in the fans'
eyes. This was a TV taping of *WWF Superstars* and Mick was a huge
boyhood wrestling fan with a dim and distant dream of becoming a
wrestler himself. Following a year of hard training, Mick had learnt
very little offence, just a spinning elbow into the face of an onrushing

opponent. He had, however, mastered the art of taking bumps with his wide, unathletic body. This skillset made him perfect cannon-fodder for the WWF stars.

Mick's gaze suddenly turned starstruck as the world tag team champions strolled into the corridor to meet their prey. He introduced himself to Tom and told him that he was able and willing to take his best moves.

'Thanks mate.' Dynamite turned and winked at Davey.

'Hey Davey,' Mick continued to dig his own grave, 'I throw this really great elbow, and I was going to try and work that in. Is that okay?'

'Yes mate,' replied Davey as both he and Tom struggled to contain their laughter, 'I think we'll do a lot of great stuff out there.'

Les Thornton and 'Jack Foley' were introduced to the 18,000-strong but silent audience before 'Rule Britannia' hit and got them off their seats.

Thornton started the match and after a minute or two of exchanging respectful British-style wrestling with Davey he tagged his rookie partner into the lion's den, as Davey tagged in Dynamite. A stiff snap-suplex, backbreaker and falling headbutt routine saw Mick down, so Tom decided to let his cousin also have some fun. Davey raised the 235lb Foley up on to his shoulder with ease and powerslammed him back down, before raising him up for a long vertical suplex and another huge crash to the mat. Kicking out of the pin would be something Mick would regret, as he began hitting Davey with punches to the stomach as he was being raised from the canvas. He then shot Davey into the ropes and launched his patented flying elbow, only for Davey to stand there disgusted as though a moth had flown into him. Tom immediately asked to be tagged back in. When he was, he venomously shot Mick across the ring and spinned just a step behind him. When Mick came off the ropes, his jaw was crushed by Dynamite's rock-solid bicep. A thunderous belly-to-back superplex then made the ring bounce and, mercifully, Dynamite pinned the rookie Mick Foley for the one, two, three.

* * *

1 November 1986. The Boston Garden

The Bulldogs and the Hart Foundation got together in the locker room before they went out for yet another tag match which would spark a new series between the two and result in Bret and Jim finally ending the record-breaking reign of Dynamite and Davey as WWF tag team champions in the new year. Vince had told Tom that he wanted them to drop the belts to Sheik and Volkoff, but Dynamite refused. He told Vince they would only drop the belts to the Foundation, saying they were the hardest-working and best heel team in the company. In a rare show of humbleness, Vince had agreed.

Their matches were always spectacular, and the office now trusted them to main event any show in any town. Bret and Tom, as usual, discussed the highspots and the finish as Jim listened intently and Davey did his best to do the same whilst entertaining their new mascot, Matilda the real-life English bulldog, who had made her debut three weeks earlier. Before they left for the ring, Tom threw two Percocets in his mouth and gulped them down with his coffee.

For the first time in wrestling history, the WWF was openly marketing towards children. As well as a Saturday morning cartoon featuring all the top stars – whose gimmicks were becoming more cartoonish by the week – they also featured many animals on the live action product. Koko B. Ware brought his pet macaw Frankie to the ring, Jake 'The Snake' Roberts carried a large sack containing his giant python Damien, Ricky 'The Dragon' Steamboat had a baby Komodo dragon, and now, the British Bulldogs had Matilda.

Matilda had effectively replaced Captain Lou. Lou was a notorious drinker and would knock back full bottles of vodka and whiskey backstage. During a conversation about Vince's new hard disciplinary line towards recreational drugs and any reports of hotel room damage, Lou bragged obnoxiously that he was unsackable, as he had been part of the family since the late Vince Sr had been in charge. Tom dared him to tell Vince Jr to go fuck himself the next time he brought it up. He did. Vince fired him.

The Hart Foundation swaggered to the ring sporting their new black attire with thick pink trimming. 'Rule Britannia' hit and the three bulldogs marched out to the delight of the crowd. After another 20-minute barnstormer, the match neared its end and manoeuvred towards its pre-planned finish, but the Anvil slammed Dynamite hard into the canvas only for Tom to grimace and moan, 'Ooh me fuckin' back!'

After the match that night, Tom guzzled Percocets hourly to make the pain go away.

The British Bulldogs defended the tag titles multiple times each week, against representatives of the 'Heenan Family', Sheik and Volkoff, the Dream Team and, of course, the Hart Foundation. Transporting, walking and feeding Matilda only added to the burden of life on the road, and Davey took her in as the Smith family pet to provide her with some stability. But a wrestler's life was no life for a dog, and she was soon living on a diet of arena hot dogs and was unable to drink for hours before show time so that she didn't urinate in the ring.

19

INEVITABLE

'Some of the boys had to blink back tears as Davey helped
the frail shell of the Dynamite Kid through the backstage
area. When Tom painfully pulled on his gear it hung on him,
and even I felt tears come into my eyes at seeing this broken
machine that once ran like no other.'

Bret Hart

13 December 1986. Hamilton, Ontario

'Tommy, will you crack my back?' asked 6ft 4in, 300lb Nikolai Volkoff
as the Bulldogs stood behind the curtain waiting for 'Rule Britannia' to
cue them in. Davey was holding Matilda's lead, leaving Tom the only
man available for the job. The music started as Tom wrapped his arms
around the topless Yugoslavian.

'C'mon, Tommy,' said Davey, opening the curtain. Tom quickly
yanked Volkoff up from the floor but felt a twinge in his own back.
He wasn't really concentrating on the task or even the match in hand;
he was preoccupied with the following night's cage match against the
Dream Team, where he was intending to put a stiff beating on Brutus
Beefcake.

A few weeks earlier, Ted Betley had arrived from Warrington
for an extended holiday, much of which he was to spend touring
with Tom and Davey. They had introduced him to all of the stars,
almost all of whom had posed for photographs and signed tickets and
programmes for an often starstruck Ted. But when Ted innocently
mentioned that Beefcake had shunned him, Tom was furious and

planned to sort Brutus out in the locker room the next time he saw him. But out of respect for Beefcake's tag partner Greg Valentine, Tom instead decided to take his revenge under the guise of the worked match they had coming up inside the confines of a steel cage. He was looking forward to it, and just had to get through the Bulldogs' match at the Copps Coliseum against 'Magnificent' Muraco and Bob Orton Jr.

Dynamite and Davey, wearing their sky-blue tights, looked typically dynamic in the opening minutes of the match, but then the time arrived for the heels to take charge.

Immediately after an insignificant leap over the flattened Orton, Tom's spine finally crumbled. His momentum and instinct took him into the opposite ropes, where 'Magnificent' Muraco put a sly knee into Tom's back – the move that was supposed to trigger the villain's big comeback. When Dynamite crumpled down in a heap, even his fellow wrestlers thought it was part of the act. Muraco began to rain down blows, forcing Tom to drag himself out of the ring using his upper body; he slumped to the floor outside, a complete dead-weight and in very real agony. The referee was left with no choice but to count him out, as even Davey Boy watched on from the corner in bemusement and the disgruntled crowd began to boo and jeer, feeling they had been cheated.

Tom was known as one of the best and most realistic sellers in the business, therefore no one believed he was actually hurt, so innocuous had been the incident. Mr Fuji – Muraco's manager – began to attack him on the floor with a steel chair in an attempt to rescue the audience reaction. When Fuji realised that Tom's agonised groans were actually him attempting to speak but failing because of the pain, he finally stopped the assault and began to signal to the back.

The paramedics had to cut through Tom's wrestling tights as his leg began to shake violently. When they reached the hospital in Hamilton there were no spare beds, so the doctors pumped him full of painkillers and morphine and left the Dynamite Kid strewn across a stretcher, parked in a corridor, his wrestling gear hanging off him in tatters, his left leg still twitching involuntarily every once in a while.

An ambulance eventually collected him and transported him to Toronto Airport, where he was to board the next flight home to

Calgary. Vince had paid for three seats on the plane, so that Tom could be strapped across them on his stretcher. With the painkillers wearing off, the bumpy four-hour flight became torturous.

Another ambulance was waiting in Calgary and whisked Tom to the Holy Cross hospital, where he would spend the next ten days. After having scans, X-rays, injections and tests, the results predictably showed the true extent of the damage, and emergency surgery was needed. By this point, Tom's left leg was no longer twitching, but worse, he had lost all feeling and movement in it. As well as the two ruptured discs (his fourth and fifth lumbar, which were to be completely removed), he had severe nerve damage. The doctors assured him that the feeling would return slowly, but sternly told him he should find a new line of work. He had only turned 28 the week previous.

'I'm sorry, but no, I will be getting back in that ring,' Tom told them, with equal resolve. They told him that his steroid use had caused drying and shrinking of his tendons and soft tissue, and he would be prone to further bad injuries whenever he wrestled.

When Bret visited the hospital a few days before Christmas, he commented that Tom, who was visibly shrinking by the day, looked surprisingly well.

'Yeah, on t'outside maybe, but not inside. I'm not being funny Gabe, but I'm fucked.'

'Well yeah, you're gonna be out of it for a while, that's for sure. Actually, Vince asked me to get the tag belt off you to take back for him to use.'

'Oh, right. Well, ya can tell Vince 'e can fuck right off,' Tom responded.

'Look Tom, Vince needs those belts, we're gonna start running up to 'Mania as soon as we go back.'

'Sorry Bret, but no means no. Not like this.'

Despite barely being able to put one foot in front of the other and still in immense pain, Tom checked himself out of hospital on Christmas Eve. Michelle, along with Stampede wrestler and Tom's close friend Duke Myers, collected him and they had to drive at walking-pace, as Tom grimaced in pain with every bump and turn. He crawled out of the Bronco and up the two steps into the house. He slept on the sofa and would use little Bronwyne's potty rather than have to be carried upstairs.

Michelle had been unaware that Tom's back problems had escalated so badly, particularly in the previous few months. She knew he had a mobile drugstore and a cabinet full of prescription pills at home, but he hadn't told her the extent to which he was taking the painkillers and exactly what for. She had been more concerned about his drinking, as he had been downing a litre of vodka every night he was at home to knock himself out at bedtime.

Tom drowned his pain and his sorrows in alcohol that whole festive season and opted not to tell Michelle of the doctors' advice to quit wrestling immediately. He had gone under the knife for extensive back surgery on Christmas Eve. The doctors advised him to stay in the hospital for six weeks and follow a pre-prepared physical therapy recuperation plan. Instead, he went home and attempted his own rehabilitation: a daily regimen of steroids, relentless gym work, painkillers and alcohol.

Vince called periodically to check on Tom's health and to hint about the title situation, 'I don't blame you for keeping it, Tom. You did the right thing, really. But I am going to need you and Davey to defend those belts on TV.'

Davey had been tasked with keeping the Bulldogs' feud with the Hart Foundation going for four weeks' worth of house shows, valiantly taking on Bret, Jim, Jimmy and heel referee Danny Davis – who Jimmy Hart supposedly had on the payroll in the same way J.R. Foley used to have Alexander Scott in Stampede. The WWF continued to bill championship tag matches featuring the British Bulldogs at house shows far and wide, with the audience bewildered when Davey would have a guest partner, some of whom included Tito Santana, Junkyard Dog and Roddy Piper.

TV audiences were still blissfully unaware that one Bulldog was firmly licking his wounds, as Vince spread out pre-taped Bulldog matches across the broadcasts, but they were now down to the final one. The next TV tapings were at the Sun Dome in Tampa, Florida, on 26 January.

'I'm sorry Vince, but I'm not ready. I mean, really, I can't walk,' Tom told Vince.

'Tom, I know you're not well, but one way or the other, I need those belts back.'

Tom strongly suspected that if he and Davey vacated the titles, Vince would revert back to his original plan of giving them to the Sheik and Volkoff.

'Okay,' said Tom, 'we'll be there for TV in Tampa to drop the belts – to t'Hart Foundation.'

26 January 1987
Sun Dome
Tampa, Florida
WWF Tag Team Championship
The Hart Foundation v The British Bulldogs
Approximate attendance: 10,800

The locker room fell silent as the Dynamite Kid entered. He was a frail shell of the superhuman wrestling machine they had last seen six weeks earlier. He wasn't even walking under his own strength; Vince had paid for the expenses of road agent Arnold Skaaland's son George to travel with Tom the whole trip, to carry his bags – and his body – from Calgary to Florida in a wheelchair. Gary Portz had moved back to Florida, so Tom and George had arranged to stay with him for a couple of nights either side of the show. Gary, who was on crutches himself, was needed as a second pair of hands to help Tom get around the house and even to the bathroom.

The wrestlers in the locker room tried not to watch as this once great stallion was helped into his wrestling gear, which duly sagged on him. Even the extraordinary amount of prescription drugs he was taking could not mask his agony. Tom's name was etched into Canadian medical journals – no one on record had ever returned to work inside six weeks after that level of spinal surgery, let alone if their job was a professional wrestler.

As 'Rule Britannia' began to play, Davey took his cousin by the arm and supported him out towards the ring, holding Matilda's lead in his other hand.

The Hart Foundation circled the ring like vultures as a solemn crowd cheered support in Tom's direction – there was no fooling the fans on this occasion. They knew something was obviously wrong with the Dynamite Kid.

Davey allowed Tom to support himself on the ring apron before chasing Bret, Jim and Jimmy out of the ring with the suddenly blood-lusting Matilda. The crowd began to go wild as the Harts scrambled in different directions, Jimmy ran towards the corner where Dynamite was propped and clubbed him around the back of the head with his megaphone – something the Hart-supporting referee Danny Davis conveniently missed happening. When the camera finally cut to him, Tom was face down on the blue mats holding his head; he just had to stay there for a few minutes while Davey put up a valiant and heroic effort, before the inevitable happened. Bret and Jim took control and when they hit their Hart Attack finisher for the one, two, three, it was mercifully over.

The Hart Foundation celebrated joyously before making a quick exit. Tom Billington may have been unable to walk, but he had just given the 'Push Brothers' the biggest push of their careers. Davey carefully picked up his broken cousin and walked him to the back. As they emerged through the curtain, the superstars and the staff had formed an impromptu guard of honour, giving Tom an emotional standing ovation. Even Vince looked on in disbelief.

He had always wanted to be the toughest and most respected guy in the locker room, and now Tom Billington certainly was – ironically, it had come at the point he was at his weakest and most vulnerable. Most of those applauding and wishing him well believed they were witnessing the end of the road for the Dynamite Kid. Really, they should've been right.

20

BIGGER! BETTER! BADDER!

'I was still having a lot of problems with my back, and there
was no doubt that wrestling was aggravating it. But I hadn't
changed anything in my style. I still dove off the top rope,
still did the snap suplexes, and still took the brunt of the
landing from a superplex. And all of it was only possible
because of the painkillers; I was addicted to them.'

Tom Billington

WrestleMania III
29 March 1987
Pontiac Silverdome
Pontiac, Michigan
The Hart Foundation and Danny Davis v The British Bulldogs and
Tito Santana
Official attendance: 93,173

THE ROAR of the crowd echoed and sounded like the ungodly
rumble following an explosion. As the superstars, road agents and
production staff excitedly bustled around the backstage area, Davey
Boy Smith stood solidly behind the curtain, holding Matilda by the
lead. Next to him stood Tito Santana, one of his tag team partners
for their revenge-fuelled six-man tag team match against the Hart
Foundation and former referee, Danny Davis – who had been banned
from officiating for 'life plus ten years' after his clear bias cost the

Bulldogs their belts and also Santana his Intercontinental title to the Macho Man Randy Savage.

The third member of their team stood casually leaning against the wall and when 'Rule Britannia' hit, he swilled down the last of his coffee, took a huge final drag on a cigarette and discarded the remains, before joining the team and climbing aboard the motorised cart that had been installed to transport the wrestlers on the mammoth journey through the crowd to the ring. The main reason the cart was needed was that one of the men in the main event later had a back in even worse condition than that of the Dynamite Kid.

The match ended when Danny Davis clobbered Davey over the head with Jimmy Hart's megaphone and the contest descended into chaos. But the only result that mattered was that the boys picked up their biggest pay-cheque of their careers to date.

Just two months earlier Tom had needed to be carried around the country. He had been advised repeatedly that his wrestling days were behind him. But with *WrestleMania* and another huge payday around the corner, Tom had doubters to prove wrong once again. The six-man tag match, scheduled for less than ten minutes, had been booked largely to limit Tom's workload, yet his body looked almost back to its biggest and most sculptured, and during his cameo appearances in the ring he looked as hard-hitting as ever. To the naked eye, it appeared that the Dynamite Kid was back. But the truth was, he was more fragile than ever. He had dragged himself heroically but recklessly to a position in which he was able to appear at *WrestleMania* and collect the pay-cheque his expensive lifestyle and young family needed him to provide. The somewhat heroic recovery had come at a cost physically and mentally.

Tom's mother, father and 12-year-old brother Mark had stayed with Tom and Michelle for a rare two-week visit from England in the lead-up to *WrestleMania*. Mark understandably hero-worshipped his older brother and loved spending time with him. One night, they sat side-by-side on the sofa and watched *Rambo: First Blood*. Half-way through the movie, Mark felt Tom slump against him and assumed he had fallen asleep – little surprise given Tom's daily routine at the time – but when young Mark glanced to his side, he realised Tom was shaking frantically. Already accustomed to Tom's pranks, he told him to stop messing around, but then noticed his eyes had rolled backwards and that he was beginning to foam at the mouth. Mark frantically called for help and the panicked family attempted to stop Tom convulsing and called 911.

Tom came around after about ten minutes, just as the ambulance arrived, and had zero knowledge or memory of what had happened. The emergency medical staff insisted on taking him to the hospital, but Tom played down the incident and was soon back home. He made the decision that the seizure should be kept quiet, so as not to jeopardise his lucrative position at *WrestleMania* and risk undoing all his hard work so far to be there.

WrestleMania III had been the culmination of the momentum created by the WWF's expansion, which was now transcending its own national agenda, and going international. Vince knew that the timing was perfect to create the biggest wrestling show of all time, which would further confirm their supremacy and domination.

Needing the ultimate monster heel to challenge Hogan, and one that would legitimately make the adored champion the underdog and create real fear that he could lose the title he had held for three glory-filled years, Vince had turned the beloved André the Giant into a green-eyed villain. Hulk Hogan versus André the Giant was a match the fans never dreamed they would see; it simply didn't seem possible. The tagline of the event was soon created: *'BIGGER! BETTER! BADDER!'*

The stadium erupted and Hulkamania ran wild like never before when Hogan picked up and slammed André and then hit his big leg-drop to achieve the so-called impossible one, two, three. André had been on the cusp of retirement; his back was so twisted and broken from 20 years spent relentlessly pounding the ring and his acromegaly was beginning to really take hold. After his successful movie appearance alongside Billy Crystal and Robin Wright in *The Princess Bride*, he was considering the comparative retirement of life on his farm and the odd acting role. But Vince offered him one last mega-lucrative run.

Yet again, McMahon and WWF had outdone themselves. Filling stadia like the Pontiac Silverdome couldn't even have been dreamt of in the wrestling business just a few years earlier. The event had also raised over $10 million in pay-per-view sales.

But the money being generated by the industry was making its sought-after stars greedy and encouraging them to make decisions about their lifestyles many of them would live to regret. Worse still, many would not live long enough to regret them.

'Corporal Kirchner' (Michael Penzel) was suspended by the WWF in the summer of 1987 following a failed drugs test. When his suspension ended, he rejected the option to return and signed for Stampede Wrestling, making his debut there in September. Tom liked Kirchner and had made the recommendation to the Harts, believing it would be good for both parties. Tom had subsequently sold one of Duchess's puppies to Kirchner.

But Tom was back home in Calgary in November and heard that Kirchner had put a pistol in the mouth of his friend, Johnny Smith, in a hotel room whilst the Stampede crew had been on the road. Always loyal and eager to stand up for his close friends, the following Friday evening Tom quietly and deliberately strode into the Pavilion locker room, with a revolver concealed under his leather jacket.

Fortunately, Kirchner was already prepared to move on from Calgary and no-showed the event and was never seen or heard from there again.

Of Tom and Davey's 'Night Patrol' buddies, Dan Spivey had spiralled further down the roster, meaning he wasn't on the same shows as the Bulldogs very often; meanwhile Scott McGhee (Gary Portz) had been let go but Tom had insisted he move to Calgary and live with him, Michelle and Bronwyne on their huge acreage and work for Stampede.

Davey became a father for the second time in September as Diana gave birth to a baby girl, Georgia. Fatherhood suited Davey, as it gave him the perfect opportunity to show his playful side; even more so, over the coming years it would allow him to indulge in another passion of his: video games. Davey's extraordinary hand-eye coordination and ability to learn anything quickly meant that from Nintendo to Sega and from *Pacman* to *Mortal Kombat*, no one could get the better of a chuckling Davey when he had a game controller in his hand. On family holidays in British Columbia, Davey would become reacquainted with the hobbies of diving and swimming he had excelled in as a youngster, and easily picked up the skill of water skiing.

NOTHING IN MODERATION

'I couldn't wrestle without taking … Percocets, which are
very strong, narcotic painkillers. I took them more or less
every night before a match. And when they wore off later in
the evening, my back would be screaming out in pain … A
normal working day for me was: speed to wake me up in the
morning to catch an early flight, Valium to make me sleep on
the plane, Percocet just before the match, then we'd wrestle,
hit the beer and the cocaine until the early hours, before
taking another Valium to put me to sleep at night.'

Tom Billington

February 1988. San Francisco Airport

A fleet of musclebound wrestlers dispersing through an airport after
their plane had touched down had become a daily sight across America.
They carried huge bags that would accompany them everywhere
throughout their multi-week, non-stop tour. Many of them would
go immediately to the car-hire desk. Tom was sweating heavily as he
collected the keys and charged off towards the escalator. His travel
partner for the tour, new WWF recruit Jim Hellwig – the Ultimate
Warrior – followed behind.

Tom suddenly stopped in his stride and began to rub his temples.
'I don't feel so good,' he said.

'You don't look great,' Warrior replied, 'go outside and get some air.
You'll be alright. I'll wait for you up there.'

'Nah, I'll be fine,' Tom stiffened and with a shake of the head followed on. As he climbed on the escalator, red dots began to appear in his blurred vision. He lost consciousness and fell backward all the way down to the floor.

He awoke in the local hospital, an intravenous drip attached to his arm, almost unable to move any part of his aching body. A doctor told him he'd had a seizure, and that they had no way of knowing at this stage if it would be a completely random, singular occurrence, or something that may reoccur, urging Tom to rest and recuperate. Tom went straight back and re-joined the tour and every bit of the lifestyle that came with it, never mentioning the fact that something similar had happened less than a year earlier.

For almost all of that year, since returning to wrestling too soon following his crippling back injury, Tom and the Bulldogs had been wrestling a full schedule for the WWF. With Stampede ailing, when they did go back to Calgary for a rare few days at home, a combination of either of them and Jim or Bret would also wrestle a match at the top of the card for Stu to cash in on their popularity and the nationally notorious rivalry. In April, shortly after *WrestleMania III*, Bret and Davey had headlined at the Corral in a 'four-corner chain' match, in which the two competitors are chained to each other and the winner is the first person to touch all four corner pads. With no intention of taking it easy whilst working back for Stu, Bret and Davey beat one another senseless, both spilling their own blood all over the mat and near throttling each other with the chain. They turned the Corral into a raging inferno of cheers and jeers as the bloodthirsty Stampede crowd welcomed back their homegrown stars.

Their cameo appearances alone were not proving to be enough to turn around the ever-struggling Stampede, and Vince then suddenly embargoed his stars from performing at these shows during their time off, citing that they were enhancing competition. Vince was proven right, as the next time the WWF returned to Calgary they sold out the Corral with a cage match between the Bulldogs and the Foundation.

Owen was Stampede's undoubted star. Despite his reservations about the wrestling business, he had little choice but to take the ball and run with it. He too knew the art of wrestling via osmosis, having been brought up as the youngest Hart brother, spending so much time in the dungeon. He had studied Tom and Sayama's masterpieces until the priceless tapes he owned broke. He had managed to replicate both Dynamite's acrobatics and Bret's grappling, all the while being free of any drug or alcohol consumption – his naturally thick frame meaning steroids had little incentive for him, either. He was a sensation, receiving *Pro Wrestling Illustrated*'s Rookie of the Year award for 1987, but there was a sense of *déjà vu*, similar to Dynamite a decade earlier, as Owen was garnering attention from North America, Europe and Japan. He had already used the connections ingrained into Stampede with the UK wrestling scene and toured for Max Crabtree, appearing on *World of Sport* and also at the iconic Royal Albert Hall, with Max once again sticking to the Calgary-cowboy stereotype and billing him as 'Bronco' Owen Hart.

He wasn't the only young Stampede star to be bringing about nostalgic reminiscence of the teenage Dynamite Kid, as Chris Benoit now cut an almost physically identical figure who had so clearly modelled himself on his hero.

Brothers Bruce, Ross and Wayne Hart continued to live and breathe the Stampede cause, valiantly fighting a losing battle. Brian Pillman was another potential star, and biker Karl Moffat was playing a maniacal heel in 'Jason the Terrible', his bloodletting a little too extreme even by Stampede's standards. Bad News Allen (soon to be Bad News Brown) was the latest headliner to be lost to the WWF, as Vince signed him on the promise of building him up as the next monster heel from the conveyor belt, to challenge Hogan.

The Bulldogs and the Harts were still pitted against each other regularly on the WWF roadshow. Throughout 1987 they had a series of similarly violent and all-action cage matches which served to further redefine the tag team division. They also provided a little mercy on Tom's back, as they conjured up original and innovative highspots and finishes without the need for Tom to crash around the ring with his usual reckless abandon.

Tom did perform in that usual manner, though, when the Bulldogs regularly faced off against the new monster heel tag team 'Demolition' – Tom once again putting his failed back through torturous high-impact bumps to make others look as strong as possible.

On Boxing Day 1987, WWF *Superstars* aired a match between the Bulldogs and the 'Islanders' – Haku and Tama – who were managed by

Bobby 'The Brain' Heenan. During the match, the dastardly trio took Matilda from the little podium from where she quietly watched her fellow Bulldogs perform, running up the aisle and into the back. Davey gave chase, with Dynamite following behind. As he ran through the doors into the corridor backstage, in an unplanned comedic moment, Davey slipped and tumbled to the floor, and a sprinting Dynamite then fell over Davey. Needless to say, by the time they had scrambled back to their feet, Matilda was long gone. This set up a feud leading to *WrestleMania IV*, as they spent months attempting to track down the whereabouts of their 'beloved' pet.

In Atlantic City, they were joined by fellow animal-lover Koko B. Ware to take on the Islanders and Heenan in front of a crowd of 20,000. In a match that was distinctly more entertainment than it was sports, Heenan donned a dog-handling suit as Matilda was supposed to be hell-bent on her own retribution. In truth, the storyline had been largely designed to give her some time off – the schedule having been deemed too punishing for a canine, if not for the drug-fuelled human beings. But Matilda's return to action didn't go according to plan, as she didn't seem interested in chasing down her dog-napper and had to be dragged around the ring by Davey.

The fact that the Bulldogs were in a match that provided some light entertainment in the middle of an intense four-hour show that included a 14-man knockout tournament for the vacant WWF heavyweight championship, matches for the tag team and Intercontinental titles and a 20-man Battle Royal, displayed the first signs that maybe the British Bulldogs had become a tired act. If there was one thing that Tom felt he needed to be, it was a serious wrestler in the upper echelons on the big shows. However, on this occasion the huge $24,000 payoff each for this show would soften the blow taken to their art.

The Macho Man won the tournament as Vince made his first attempt to pass the torch from the Hollywood-bound Hogan. Bad News Brown won the Battle Royal, eliminating fellow heel Bret after double-crossing him after their supposed pact to share the prize. Bret then dropkicked Bad News out of the ring just as he was being awarded the 7ft tall trophy, which Bret subsequently destroyed. This incident was designed to turn Bret Hart from tag team heel to singles babyface as his unrelenting perfect match execution, ability to wrestle either technically or in a brawling manner, willingness to shed his own blood, and his natural charisma and good looks meant he had become popular with every demographic of fan and it was time for him to have a push up the roster as a heroic underdog against the monstrous bad guys.

With the tag team division red hot off the back of the Bulldogs and the Harts, more young and explosive teams were signed to bolster the ranks: Jacques and Raymond were the 'Rougeau Brothers', a clean-cut second-generation babyface pairing from Montreal; and the 'Midnight Rockers' (soon shortened to simply the 'Rockers'), who were the dynamic but volatile young pairing of Marty Jannetty and Shawn Michaels, recruited from the ailing AWA.

The Rockers came with a reputation as arrogant party-animals, who relied on their youth and natural athletic ability to enable them to perform even when hung-over; they also had form for trashing hotels rooms and bars – the kind of behaviour reserved for seasoned veterans who had paid their dues. They had in fact already signed for the WWF the previous year but were fired after immediately living up to the troublesome reputation that preceded them. But their talent could not be ignored, so Vince had given them a second chance. They appeared standoffish with all of the other wrestlers on their return, fearing that the established wrestlers had already made up their minds about them. Ever the locker-room leader, it was Tom who approached them in a bar after a show to break the tension. He told them they had to make an effort to win the guys' trust and respect, or they wouldn't last long this time either. Tom had seen the talent they had, especially Shawn Michaels, who was only 22. The Rockers took Tom's advice and were soon well-respected members of the roster – with Michaels' extraordinary selling ability making them a joy for established stars to work with.

Tom's close friend Harley Race was suddenly missing from the tour after *WrestleMania IV*. Harley had been rushed to the hospital for emergency surgery on a failing intestine. In the locker-room one night, Intercontinental champion the Honky Tonk Man, who didn't hold much respect with the boys (it was believed he had made it so high up the pecking order due to who he knew rather than his talent and he was also considered one of the very least legitimate tough guys), made a crass gag about Harley no longer having the guts he used to.

Tom stood up, walked over and backhanded him off his seat. 'Don't you ever say anything about the King ever again!' Dynamite yelled as Honky pleaded for forgiveness.

'Tommy, I thought you and me were friends.'

'The King's my friend, you're nothing but a piece of shit!' Tom replied. No one rushed to Honky's aid.

Despite his brave efforts to show no signs of slowing down, the truth was, the Dynamite Kid had lost the slight edge that made him so special. Davey Boy, meanwhile, was approaching the peak of his abilities. Still only 25 but with ten years' experience already, he seemed to be the perfect blend of power and speed; of strength and agility; of youth and experience. It was Davey that now performed the majority of the highspots in the Bulldogs' matches – he was the star now.

* * *

Tom became a father for the second time on 5 May, 1988, when Michelle gave birth to his first son, Marek Thomas. It was Bronwyne's fourth birthday three weeks later. She had become daddy's little girl. When she had been a tiny baby, Tom hadn't dared to even hold her, so fragile she looked to a man whose bulging, rock-solid body was more used to causing physical damage than doling out cuddles. Instead, he would lovingly hold her hand and allow her to grip on tight to one of his fingers. But now she was sturdy and fun-loving, he wanted to give her anything she desired. When most four-year-olds ask for a pony for their birthday, they have to make do with a toy version, but when Bronwyne was ushered into the field of their acreage, strolling around the land near the full-size wrestling ring was a real-life pony. Smitten, Bronwyne named her new pet Starlite after the talking horse in her favourite cartoon *Rainbow Brite*. But the pony had been an impulsive one by Tom, and Starlite was able to escape from their land into the neighbours' yard. Luckily, the neighbour was an equestrian vet so knew how to handle the situation, and eventually homed Starlite in his stable for Bronwyne to visit.

Tom would cut the grass on his ride-on mower, taking Bronwyne and Marek on exciting tours of the land or dragging them behind on a sledge, then they would play wrestling in the ring Tom had placed outdoors for training and for fun. But the 20-acre expanse was rarely the scene of such perfect family serenity; more often, a staggering Tom could be seen and heard blasting gophers dead with the choice of weapon from his arsenal, which by now included a sawn-off shotgun, a 30-30 Winchester rifle and a 9mm semi-automatic pistol.

He would often be joined in his own brand of conservation by pals including Davey or Duke Myers. But his most loyal shooting companion emerged when Gary Portz tragically suffered a huge stroke at the age of just 28. With Gary unable to walk, Tom picked him up from the hospital and took him directly to a Calgary bar to prove to him that life goes on. Gary's wrestling career appeared over and he found it difficult to motivate himself for the tough road to recovery from his stroke. But Tom taught him how to hold and shoot guns and the pair bonded further over hunting trips. The concentration and coordination required for his daily target practice helped Gary rehabilitate successfully, and he went on to retrain as a nurse and get his life back together.

BAD COMPANY

'Unfortunately, [Outback] Jack rubbed a lot of the boys
here the wrong way when he indicated openly that he was
only capitalising on Stampede to get into WWF, where
he expected to get a big push and make big money. It was
sort of the idea that working in Calgary was just a minor
league stint. His image certainly preceded him to WWF
as Dynamite, Davey and other Stampede alumni stars kept
regular tabs on the Stampede territory and targeted him.'

Ross Hart

PETER STILSBURY was a 28-year-old Australian rookie who,
almost, found himself in the perfect place at the perfect time towards
the end of 1986. Standing 6ft 5in with a loud, brash personality, the
WWF brought him to America in a typical attempt to cash in on the
huge success and popularity of the recent movie release, *Crocodile Dundee*.

A respectful and healthy working relationship between Vince and
Stu had survived the attempted Stampede takeover, so Vince sent
Stilsbury to Calgary for a crash course in the North American style
and to practise his mic skills before donning the stereotypical Aussie
garb the WWF had in store for 'Outback Jack'.

His perceived obnoxious and arrogant nature had riled some of the
hard-working Stampede veterans, so his reputation preceded him when
he swaggered into the WWF locker room. There were particular traits
that especially pushed Tom's buttons and being a poor worker with
no legitimate background who bragged constantly, just about pressed

them all simultaneously. Tom had been brought up as a shooter and he had been stretched and bullied as a trainee; he held resentment for those who he felt hadn't paid those dues and were just riding on the coat-tails of those that had.

The Bulldogs had become the most notorious 'ribbers' in the locker room and were beginning to get a reputation as bullies as their pranks became more extreme and damaging to their victims. The mobile pharmacies they carried around with them everywhere meant that they always had a prank to hand when called upon. Slipping pills into unsuspecting wrestlers' drinks had become Dynamite's calling card almost as much as his flying headbutt. Once targeted, a colleague would rarely leave a bar conscious as Tom would stealthily, and often recklessly, drop as many Halcion sleeping pills as required to witness a crash to the floor. Outback Jack spent much of 1987 as the target.

Jack would often challenge members of the clan to drinking contests, which led to him being as exposed as Hulk Hogan's scalp to Dynamite's favourite trick. He was often found slumped in corridors and bars in various stages of undress, urinated on, eyebrows shaved, clothes shredded. When Jim Neidhart nonchalantly strolled past an infuriated Vince wearing a vandalised bush-hat – which on a previous occasion had also been superglued to Jack's head – Vince promptly removed it from Jim's head, but knew at that point that his potential Aussie star was up against it. Carrying little or no respect from the established stars or enhancement talent alike, Jack wasn't made to look good in the ring; any momentum created by the faux Paul Hogan gimmick was soon vanquished, and Jack was back in the bush by the spring of 1988.

Tom did like the company of a French-Canadian called Jos LeDuc, who joined the WWF in his forties in 1988 under the moniker the 'Headbanger' – which was appropriate as he was known for his craziness when under the influence of drink and drugs. With his drinking buddy Harley and his main source of bar-room entertainment Outback Jack both out of the picture, Tom latched on to Jos to fill both roles. Disgruntled that he was regularly the first one to drop whilst downing beers and pills with Jos, Tom resolved that he would, eventually, out-party the Headbanger. When he finally did, largely by spiking Jos's drinks even though they were taking dangerous amounts of pills willingly, Tom claimed victory by setting his lit cigarette atop Jos's comatose bald head. When the smouldering tab singed Jos's head, he sat up and stubbed it out against the seat of his chair before shuffling off to his room, leaving Tom laughing proudly. The next day, Vince fired Jos. Unlike Dynamite, Jos simply couldn't compensate for his wild and controversial antics outside the ring with his performances in it.

Whether Tom liked you or not, your livelihood was collateral damage when it came up against his ability to have his own dark fun.

* * *

Being locally honed stars and part of the Hart family, Dynamite and Davey were wrestling royalty in Calgary. When their fellow 'roided-up gym buddies fancied a shot at wrestling, or jobbers from the WWF that they liked wanted a higher place on a roster, they would send them Stampede's way and expect them to be trained appropriately and given jobs.

One such example was a champion bodybuilder named Jeff Beltzner, who became the butt of the age-old dinosaur-statue rib on his first trip to Drumheller, which sparked its traditional round of Stu Hart impressions from the boys – the most rousing of which was by the charismatic Brian Pillman.

Pillman had become a popular babyface, but as he was booker Bruce Hart's buddy and tag team partner in 'Bad Company', many in the locker room resented Pillman's swift rise through the ranks. This wasn't helped by his good looks and confidence, which could easily be perceived as arrogance and obnoxiousness. He had been known to flex his muscles and beam his smile at girls in bars, stealing them in a flash from under the nose of a colleague who had been buying them drinks all night. Despite barely knowing him, the Bulldogs – Tom especially – had built up a fierce dislike of Brian. When a disgruntled Beltzner told the Bulldogs about being the latest victim of the Stampede rib culture, and that it had given Pillman, of all people, the opportunity to ridicule him, Tom told him that he needed to take physical retribution on Pillman at the earliest opportunity. He said that he and Davey would go along to the Pavilion before the Friday night Stampede show, as it was their rare weekend off the WWF circuit, to ensure no one else would intervene if Beltzner – 6ft 3in and 270lb – challenged Pillman. Worshipping the Bulldogs as he did, Beltzner took the bait. In the early evening of the following Friday, flanked by Tom and Davey, Beltzner paced the locker room awaiting the arrival of the man who, later in his career, would become known as the 'Loose Cannon' – both in and out of the ring.

Pillman pulled into the car park at the back of the building and Bruce, riding shotgun, immediately raised an eyebrow when he saw both of the Bulldogs' expensive cars were already there – they'd very rarely been to any Stampede shows that they weren't booked on.

'Bad Company' used the back entrance and followed their usual routine, stopping at the coffee machine before making their way to the locker room.

Pillman felt the hot coffee burn his hand as he walked through the locker room door and was immediately confronted by the giant bodybuilder that Tom had stoked up like a children's wind-up toy. But Pillman didn't take one backward step, and the two went head-to-head like charging bulls. When Bruce – and others – tried to stop the inevitable violence that could only negatively affect the promotion, a wide-eyed Dynamite stepped toward them and screamed, 'Let them fuckin' fight!' Within seconds Beltzner swung first and the fight was on, with the Bulldogs acting as real-life wrestling *lumberjacks*.

After trading spirited and painful blows, Pillman began to get the better of the contest and was landing speedy combinations at will. Stu, then 73, burst into the locker room and forced himself between the two fighters: he was still the only man who carried more proverbial weight in the Stampede locker room than the Dynamite Kid. Beltzner's face was a gashed and bloody mess as he was torn apart from Pillman.

Terminally ill Hart brother Dean was in attendance and was irate that the Bulldogs had initiated such sickening violence within the family business that they weren't even formally aligned with anymore. He began tearing a strip off Tom, who bristled with anger. Ross stepped in, reminding Tom of Dean's kidney disease (Dean Hart would pass away in November 1990).

Stu stripped Bruce of his booking duties over the incident, and Keith Hart, who had been out of the business for some time and was employed as a fireman, was drafted in to throw water on the flames as temporary booker.

23

THE ONLY WAY IS DOWN

'By the time [Davey] was 25 he'd already put his body
through more punishment than anyone should have to go
through in a lifetime.'

Bruce Prichard

SummerSlam
29 August 1988
Madison Square Garden
New York
The British Bulldogs v The Fabulous Rougeau Brothers
Attendance: 20,000

'THE WWF: WHAT THE WORLD IS WATCHING!' boomed
the voiceover as the golden and glistening World Wrestling Federation
logo appeared on the TV screens of the subscribers to the inaugural
SummerSlam – a third annual pay-per-view event that had been added
to the calendar.

The statement was true, the WWF had become a valued part of
cable programming around the world, leaving age-old promotions in a
desperate position as the glitz and glamour was piped directly into their
customers' living rooms. British wrestling had slumped to an all-time
low, as Max Crabtree continued to roll out the Big Daddy roadshow,
even though his brother Shirley was in his late 50s and morbidly obese.

The cameras then panned across the New York skyline, Gorilla
Monsoon having to shout over the boisterous capacity crowd at the

historic home of the WWF to introduce the show. As Monsoon and his co-host, 'Superstar' Billy Graham, talked excitedly about the main event – the 'Megabucks' (the 'Million Dollar Man' Ted DiBiase and André the Giant) versus the 'Megapowers' (Hulk Hogan and Macho Man Randy Savage) – the crowd's excited roar turned into pantomime boos as Jacques and Raymond, now heels and going as the 'Fabulous Rougeau Brothers', made their way to the ring wearing blue jackets with silver sequins that shone and shimmered. They were now portraying arrogant French-Canadians who showed disingenuous adoration for America and its people, and were introduced as 'from Montreal, Quebec, Canada, but soon to relocate to the United States' whilst they over-enthusiastically waved tiny little Stars and Stripes flags.

The opponents were introduced with more fanfare as 'Rule Britannia' chimed around the Garden – the Bulldogs were opening the show. To make matters worse, they weren't even going over, as Vince and the booking team had ordered a 20-minute broadway. Only a matter of months earlier, there was clear daylight in the tag team division between the Bulldogs and the Rougeaus, but with Dynamite having lost a little from his extraordinary best, and with their English tea-drinking gentlemen gimmick growing tired and being so obviously phoney, they were slowly sinking down the roster. In need of another heel tag team to replace the Hart Foundation, Vince was giving the Rougeaus a push.

The match itself was excellent, although Dynamite may have shown the effects of recent excesses as he wore his tights quite literally arse-about-front, displaying the Union Jack to the fore rather than the rear. But the Bulldogs looked confident, strong, and quick, while the Rougeaus played the obnoxious but capable cheaters to perfection. With ten seconds remaining before the 20 minutes were up, Davey pressed Dynamite high over his head like he was still only 150lb and launched him high into the air. Dynamite crashed down heavily on to the legal man Jacques and the match was surely over, but Ray kept the referee distracted long enough for the time limit to expire. Whilst both teams looked good, the Bulldogs' team captain Tom took exception to them giving the lesser-talented French-Canadians a helping hand up the ladder.

Tom arranged a meeting with Vince to discuss the future direction of the Bulldogs. Both he and Davey stood opposite Vince, who was seated at his desk. 'We're not 'appy with the way things're goin' Vince,' Tom began. 'We've lost momentum. I've been thinking, maybe we should *turn*.'

Hoping to make the suggestion more enticing to Vince, Davey chimed in excitedly before his boss had a chance to answer, 'Yeah, we could shave us heads and 'ave bulldogs tattooed on the sides!'

Tom turned his head and looked at Davey, who appeared giddy and proud of his suggestion, his dimples lighting up his face. 'I'll tell ya what Dave, you shave your head and get a bulldog tattooed on each side, and I'll do mine after, eh?'

'Guys, guys – things are going great!' Vince began, his eyes and mouth opening wide with faux excitement. 'You guys are still my top team! We're just mixing it up at the top, keeping things fresh. Let's not rock the boat; you're making money, yeah?' The Bulldogs shrugged and nodded – Vince was right, after all. They were earning more money than they had thought possible just a few years earlier; their families were living in huge homes in the leafy suburbs of a scenic and beautiful city, while they got to live a wild lifestyle out on the road. But as Vince ushered them out of his office believing he had appeased their concerns, Tom still wasn't satisfied with his existence as a jolly babyface tumbling down the roster. The more disillusioned he became with his work in the ring, the wilder and more reckless he became out of it.

* * *

Despite wanting nothing more than to settle down and live a quiet life in Calgary with his high-school sweetheart and soon-to-be wife Martha, Owen and professional wrestling had embarked on a love affair of their own. He signed with Vince, who, rather than adding another Hart to the rising family name within the company, gave Owen the gimmick of the 'Blue Blazer' – a do-gooder who wore a blue and white superhero outfit complete with mask and sequined cape and lectured the heels on their dastardly ways.

Owen's journey had eerily continued to take the same turns as Dynamite's. He had become a revelation in Japan, reigniting New Japan's junior-heavyweight division alongside the likes of Jushin Liger and Kuniaki Kobayashi following a fallow period after the loss of both Tiger Mask and Dynamite, and he was also carrying the Stampede roster. He had been the North American heavyweight champion for almost the whole of 1987 – in the process setting the longest reign in the history of the title – and in the spring of 1988, he held New Japan's International Wrestling Grand Prix (IWGP) junior-heavyweight championship alongside it. Following the end of the WWF–New Japan partnership, as Vince McMahon continued to alienate all allies and go it alone, the WWF-sponsored title had been made defunct in 1985, and New Japan had unveiled the IWGP championship in its place. Owen had become only the fifth holder of the belt and the very first *gaijin* champion.

When Bret handed his double-continent, double-weight-class champion younger brother to Vince on a silver platter, Owen was snapped up. But after witnessing his extraordinary high-flying ability, Vince designated him a superhero gimmick – albeit a typically tacky and cartoonish one. But Owen's talent couldn't be restrained and by late summer he was wowing crowds even before the bell had rung, as he would sprint to the ring – cape flapping behind him – before hopping on to the ring apron, bouncing on o the top turnbuckle and executing the perfect backflip into the centre of the ring. Geeky gimmick or not, the baby Hart had arrived on the scene.

Joining Owen as a new recruit shot straight into the mid-card was Tom's in-ring nemesis and backstage partner in crime from his time in Portland, Curt Hennig. Hennig had honed his immense wrestling skills almost to perfection; his frame was suddenly now thick and muscular, his hair was wavy and peroxide blonde and he swaggered with an air of arrogance only a man who *knew* how good he was could. There is little wonder that Vince gave him the moniker of 'Mr Perfect'.

* * *

Verne Gagne and his AWA were forced to finally give up their valiant effort to compete with the WWF and the NWA, and were liquidated. The NWA however, operating under Jim Crockett Promotions, had appeared to be competing strongly with Vince as they lavishly bought up almost all of the remaining territories. Playing up to the persona of their top star Ric Flair, they had portrayed an image of Rolex-and-diamond-ring-wearing, limousine-riding, jet-flying, wheeling-dealing sons-of-a-gun – woooo!

In reality, their desperate attempt to display success and compete with the WWF had driven them to the brink of bankruptcy. But in the autumn of 1988, the NWA was bought out and rescued by the media conglomerate Turner Broadcasting System, owned by billionaire entrepreneur and media mogul Ted Turner. They were quickly rebranded as World Championship Wrestling (WCW) and ironically inherited a seemingly bottomless pit of money, like the one they had so desperately tried to convince the world they previously had. The professional wrestling war in the United States was firmly back on, as two super-rich empires were about to embark on the final battle for supremacy.

24

THE SUCKER PUNCH

'It was a sad surprise to most of the wrestlers when Tom, our legendary pit bull, basically had his balls cut. Those of us who really knew him realised that getting his teeth punched out was the beginning of the end for him.'

Bret Hart

10 October 1988. Fort Wayne, Indiana. 10am

'The next time there's a fight between wrestlers in my company, everyone involved is fired!' shouted Vince McMahon in the otherwise silent locker room. All the stars were there: Hulk Hogan, Randy Savage, André, the Bulldogs. 'I hope you're all listening good, consider this your last warning,' snarled Vince, before wiping the sweat from his brow and fixing his tie in order to return to his strait-laced on-screen persona.

Having decided that a recent incident meant the escalating nature of the rib-culture in the locker room had to stop before things got any more out of hand, Vince had called the meeting at the venue before the TV recordings started. He had chosen to do it there and then as the TV tapings were the only occasions, other than PPV events, where all the stars were together, before they jetted off in different directions across the country to fulfil the simultaneous shows the WWF were promoting. Two wrestlers not in the room for the meeting were Jacques and Raymond Rougeau.

It had all started a week earlier.

Raymond, the older Rougeau sibling, was a former Golden Gloves boxing champion and well respected as a tough guy, having been taught to fight by his father Jacques Sr. However, Jacques Jr never professed to being anything of the sort, although he was also the more loud-mouthed and obnoxious of the two. This combination made him a prime target for the pranksters.

Following his match, with the reign of pranking terror at its most relentless, Jacques suspected his card-playing buddy Curt Hennig had been in his bag and messed with his personal belongings while he had wrestled – as the cutting and slicing of ring-gear and clothing had become an epidemic. He only checked quickly as he was making a quick getaway from the venue in Syracuse to catch an early flight home to Montreal, but he saw evidence of shredded material. He looked angrily at devoted ribber Hennig and, having grown tired of being the victim, said, 'You'd better not have messed with my stuff, Curt.'

'I've been in the bathroom the whole time!' Curt declared his innocence. 'The Bulldogs were around, but I'm sure everything is fine, Jacques.'

'I'm telling you Curt, I've had enough of this,' continued a riled-up Jacques, who stood over 6ft tall with swept-back fair hair. 'If they've messed with my stuff, I'm telling Vince!' With that statement he left the building, oblivious to the consequences that were about to unfold because of it.

When Dynamite and Davey returned to the locker room after their match, Curt informed them that Jacques' bag had been messed with and that Jacques had blamed them and had immediately gone to Vince to rat on them. This was a clever prank, even by Curt's high standards, because Vince had recently given the whole roster a gentler warning regarding his concern over the increasing maliciousness of the pranks. Dynamite jumped to the conclusion that Jacques must've been ratting them out to Vince the whole time. To make matters worse, the Rougeaus had requested going on early so they could make an earlier flight home, bumping the Bulldogs' match later, which had angered Dynamite.

In Miami three nights later, Curt invited Jacques over to the corner of the locker room where he had set up their usual card table.

The Rougeaus had arrived early, as their father, Jacques Sr, lived locally, so they were staying with him for a couple of nights either side of the show. Jacques took his seat with his back to the rest of the room as the door continuously opened and closed with a conveyor of arriving wrestlers. When the Bulldogs walked inTom spotted Jacques and stormed over.

Suddenly, Jacques was picking himself up off the floor, his right ear ringing. Dynamite had given him an extremely stiff flat-handed slap around the side of his head. The locker room fell silent as all the stars stared over at the brewing situation. Needing to save face, Jacques lunged at Tom, who quickly showed his notorious shooting ability by taking him down to the floor and striking him twice in the face before letting him up. When Jacques lunged again, Tom clasped him in a front-face lock and took him down again, compounding the bigger man's humiliation by forcing him to submit.

'That's enough, Dynamite.' Raymond limped over on crutches, having badly injured his knee in the ring against the Hart Foundation earlier that week. 'He's had enough, let him up.'

'It's fuck all to do with you, Ray,' shot Tom as he climbed aggressively to his feet before taking a swing at the older brother too.

'Oh, you're gonna hit a guy on crutches, now, are you?' said Ray, calmly.

'I'll tell yer what Ray,' replied Tom, pointing his finger, 'come see me when yer knee's better. I'll be waitin' for yer.'

Raymond helped his brother to his feet.

Jacques Sr, a former wrestler and promoter himself, was a respected tough guy back in the 1960s and expected his sons to defend themselves amongst their peers as he would have. On the drive back to his Florida home, neither he nor his two sons said a word; Jacques couldn't even if he had wanted to, such was the swelling around his mouth and jaw, but his pride had taken a much more painful beating than his face.

On the flight to Chicago the next day, Jacques and Raymond sat quietly nursing their respective injuries whilst the boys laughed and joked, each one in their own personal place on the daily upper-downer scale.

'We'd like to welcome the WWF to Chicago,' the air stewardess announced over the tannoy to a ripple of applause from the regular passengers. 'And we'd like to congratulate Jacques Rougeau on his boxing match last night!'

With that, the gentle clapping was joined by the laughter of some of the main pranksters, including the Bulldogs, Perfect and Mr Fuji. Jacques' humiliation was complete, while Curt Hennig was the puppet-master pulling all of their strings.

For the next few days, Tom would make a point of asking Ray how his knee was, usually in front of a crowd of wrestlers.

The Hart Foundation were working with the Rougeaus nightly, and Bret could tell their minds were elsewhere, he knew they were simmering. Bret urged Tom to ease off the brothers, telling him he believed they were planning revenge. 'Fuckin' let them try,' was the typical Dynamite response.

On the flight home to Montreal for a break ahead of the TV taping day in Fort Wayne the following Monday, Jacques – having barely spoken a word since taking the beating from Tom – said to his brother, 'At Monday's TVs, I'm making my comeback. I'm doing it with Vince, Hulk, Macho Man all in the building, so that everyone knows about it.'

Over that weekend, former boxer Raymond spent hours studiously teaching his brother the technical aspect of throwing the perfect punch. Practising using pillows, Jacques learnt how to generate as much power as possible and the ideal distance he needed to be stood from his unguarded target.

Feeling stronger mentally and physically, Jacques called his father down in Florida on the Sunday night – they hadn't said a word to each other out of a sense of mutually-felt shame since Jacques Sr had dropped them off at the venue before the initial fight.

'How're you feeling, son?' Jacques Sr asked, sensing a reinvigorated spirit in his son's voice.

'Much better, Dad. That's why I'm calling. Listen, I just wanted to let you know that I'm making my comeback tomorrow. I just wanted you to know that.'

'You, err, you said this guy is a real tough guy, yeah?'

'I guess.'

'Then, let me give you some advice, son.'

Jacques Jr was a little taken aback, thinking his dad, who had never backed down from a fight in his life, was about to tell him to do just that.

Both Bulldogs' Grandad
Thomas Billington, with
his boxing sons Billy and
Eric [Michelle Billington]

Thomas with
his namesake
grandson on his
lap, alongside
Grandma 'Nell'
and young Tom's
eldest sister Julie
[Michelle
Billington]

Tom plays
with his
younger
sister Carol
[Michelle
Billington]

Ted Betley looks on as his teenage prodigy begins his training [Michelle Billington]

Tonight's all star Programme

DE MONTFORT HALL : LEICESTER
WEDNESDAY, 22nd MARCH, 1978
EUROPEAN LIGHTWEIGHT TITLE CONTEST
JEAN CORNE
CHAMPION—France
— versus —
DYNAMITE KID
CHALLENGER
BRITISH HEAVY/MIDDLEWEIGHT TITLE
ROLLERBALL ROCCO
CHAMPION
— versus —
BERT ROYAL
CHALLENGER
BIG DADDY
25 stone blond giant
— versus —
"KOJAK" KIRK
Bald headed Bull-neck Brute
MARTY JONES
British Light/Heavyweight champion
— versus —
KING BEN
SILSDEN
Eliminator for British Lightweight Title
JIM BREAKS
Bradford
JOHN NAYLOR
Wigan
STEVE GREY
Peckham
BOBBY RYAN
Hanley

Tonight's all star Programme

VICTORIA HALL : HANLEY
SATURDAY, 20th DECEMBER, 1980
British Light/Heavyweight Title
CHAMPION MARTY JONES
Northants
— versus —
DYNAMITE KID
Just returned from America and Japan
CHICK CULLEN
Scotland
JOHNNY SOUTH
Salford
JOHNNY SAINT
World Champion — Blackpool
— versus —
EDDIE RILEY
Burly master
JACKIE TURPIN
Leamington Spa
— versus —
JOHN WILKIE
Potteries
GOLDEN ACE JOHN NAYLOR
Wigan
— versus —
YOUNG DAVID
Teenage Wonder

Tonight's All star Programme

QUEEN ELIZABETH HALL, OLDHAM
WEDNESDAY, 18th NOV., 1981
£500 K.O. TOURNAMENT
GIANT HAYSTACKS
Europe's Biggest wrestler
— versus —
RAY STEELE
Morley
BIG PAT ROACH
Birmingham
— versus —
WILD ANGUS
6ft. 5ins. 23 stone Giant
'TIGER' DALIBAR SINGH
The star of India
— versus —
COWBOY BRETT HART
Calgary, Canada
VIC FAULKNER
Bolton
— versus —
JOHNNY SAINT
Manchester
JOHNNY 'MUSCLES' ENGLAND
Wolverhampton
— versus —
PAT PATTEN
Midlands battler
MARK "Rollerball" ROCCO
Wrestling's public enemy No. 1
— versus —
DYNAMITE KID
Recently returned from America & The Far East

Tonight's All star Programme

SPECTRUM ARENA, WARRINGTON
FRIDAY, 11th DECEMBER, 1981
Heavyweight Tag Team Challenge
BIG DADDY
Mans and Dads favourite—Colourful character
partnered by
PAT PATTEN
Midlands battler
— versus —
KING KONG KIRK
MARK "Rollerball" ROCCO
Wrestling's public enemy No. 1
— versus —
'WONDER BOY' WRIGHT
Wolverhampton
GOLDEN ACE JOHN NAYLOR
Wigan
— versus —
JOHNNY SAINT
Manchester
— versus —
JACKIE TURPIN
Leamington Spa
DYNAMITE KID
Recently returned from America & The Far East
— versus —
COWBOY BRETT HART
Calgary, Canada
JOHNNY 'MUSCLES' ENGLAND
Wolverhampton
— versus —
STEVE LOGAN
Birmingham

[Tony Earnshaw]

'Young David' bursts onto the British wrestling scene. His promotional shots gained attention from various members of the Hart family [Darren Ward]

As a heel under the direction of John Foley, the Dynamite Kid regularly cut a gruesome figure [Michelle Billington]

British wrestling veteran John Foley became a pioneering villainous manager as moneybags 'J.R. Foley' [Orest Zmyndak]

The Dynamite Kid heads to Japan as a unique sensation, supremely confident in his ability [AFLO Images]

Tom and Michelle were young when they fell in love [Michelle Billington]

The happy young couple on their wedding day [Michelle Billington]

The Dynamite Kid and Tiger Mask embark on a rivalry and series of matches that would change professional wrestling forever [AFLO Images]

Tom embraces the Japanese
culture [Michelle Billington]

Tom relaxes at Hart House with the family patriarch Stu
[Michelle Billington]

Nose-to-nose: Davey
and Tom would be
cousins, rivals, friends,
and enemies
[Michelle Billington]

Davey helps his stricken cousin celebrate his
most glorious victory
[AFLO Images]

New Japan's WWF World Junior-heavyweight
champion
[AFLO Images]

'You need to hit him like you wanna kill him,' Jacques Sr insisted. 'It has to be over with that one shot. In fact, I'll tell you what to do – in the morning, on your way to the show, you stop by the bank, and you pick up a roll of quarters that will fit nicely into your fist. Grip on tight to that when you hit him.'

Jacques stayed quiet on the end of the phone, the full reality of just what he was going to do beginning to dawn on him.

'Another tip,' his father continued, 'if you can, make it just after he's had lunch – it's difficult to fight on a full stomach.'

Jacques found out where the bank was in Fort Wayne, but it didn't open until 10am. The Rougeaus would be a little late to the venue. At the very time Vince was warning everyone in the locker room that they would be instantly dismissed the next time there was any backstage violence, Jacques Rougeau was standing opposite the bank clerk, exchanging a ten-dollar bill for the roll of quarters which he intended to use for maximum detonation on the Dynamite Kid.

10 October 1988. Fort Wayne, Indiana. 1pm

Jacques Rougeau stood in his wrestling trunks with his back against the corridor wall. Raymond stood opposite him. They tried to look casual. Jacques gripped the roll of quarters tightly in his right hand to relieve his tension. They knew the Bulldogs were in the canteen at the end of the corridor and would have to walk towards them to access the arena or the interview positions where they would be recording after lunch. They also knew the Bulldogs were not alone, they were eating with Muraco and Bad News – a fearsome crew – but Raymond was prepared to take a beating to give his brother his shot at Tom.

Muraco and Bad News emerged from the canteen and went their separate ways..

Booking agent Pat Patterson told Davey that the Bulldogs' travel tickets for their upcoming European tour were ready for collection from the office, so Davey headed in that direction, arranging to meet Tom at their filming spot shortly, and Pat made his way down the corridor towards Raymond and Jacques.

In the canteen, Tom finished his cigarette, picked up his and Davey's plastic coffee cups and walked out alone. In his Union Jack emblazoned trunks, he turned into the corridor and walked directly towards the Rougeaus. For the first time in his life, by chance or by design or by a little of both, without his friends and most importantly, without his cousin and partner, Tom Billington was vulnerable.

Jacques refused to make eye contact, instead he feigned being intimidated. Tom puffed out his chest and smiled at Jacques, who finally looked up and stared back at him, before unleashing a whole week of tension, anger and shame through his right hand into the exposed mouth of the Dynamite Kid.

The tranquil hallway instantly exploded into carnage upon the sickening sound of shattering teeth. Pat Patterson began shrieking hysterically; quarters and hot coffee rained down to the floor, shortly followed by a deluge of thick blood, which also spattered on to Jacques' face and torso as Tom's knees buckled – but he did not go down.

Jacques froze, praying the job was done, but Tom stumbled towards him, with his hands on his knees, and like an unstoppable horror-movie villain, looked up. His teeth were shattered; dark blood spewed out of his mouth, he snarled and grimaced as he tried to regain his balance and go on the offensive.

'Jab! Jab!' Raymond screamed over Pat Patterson's cries for help. Jacques did as his older brother and team captain instructed and began to thrust his left fist into Tom's face. Still, the Dynamite Kid would not fall.

With the noise and commotion echoing through the building, Bad News Brown and Don Muraco soon arrived on the scene and pulled Tom away. They dragged him into the locker room to give him medical attention, but Tom was still on his feet, spitting blood-laden profanities and threats at Jacques, and still wanting to fight. Jacques' adrenaline burst out as he yelled that if Dynamite followed through on any of his threats, he'd end up in a wheelchair – little did he know that fate was already sealed for his nemesis.

All of Tom's front teeth – two at the top and two at the bottom – were knocked out; the inside of his mouth and his palette were shredded and required extensive stitching.

The very next day, the Bulldogs were on a long-haul flight for a European tour. They put on shows in sold-out arenas in France and Italy, where Dynamite and Davey continued their nightly battles against the physical team of Demolition. 'No shots above Dynamite's neck' was

Family: Michelle (back) hosts Sunday dinner for her brother Mark, Tom, Bronwyne, Ted, Diana and Davey; and Tom, alongside Davey, welcomes his parents to Canada [Michelle Billington]

Friends and rivals: Tom, Bad News, and Bret [Michelle Billington]

WWF-bound Dynamite Kid and Bret Hart teamed up in bloody battles to send Stampede Wrestling out in style [Rachel Ling]

But a new generation of talent was emerging, led by Owen Hart and Brian Pillman (shown here either side of Bruce Hart) [Orest Zmyndak]

The British Bulldogs became the number one tag team in the world [AFLO Images]

The WWF tag team division hots up, with teams such as the Hart Foundation and the Fabulous Rougeau Brothers [Getty Images]

the only adjustment made for the devastating facial injuries, and Tom barely missed a beat. But in an ironic twist of fate, he had already made plans to spend a week at home in Golborne following the brief tour, so just like Jacques had been forced to do, he had to face his own proud fighting father with slurred speech, a swollen jaw and dented pride.

Vince had hoped that having the warring factions in separate continents would cool hostilities before he needed them to share the same locker room again – or even more worrying, the upcoming *Survivor Series* in which they would be on opposite sides of a ten-team elimination tag match. But with the men involved – Tom in particular – he knew intervention to prevent further escalation was required. Rumours were rife that both families had 'connections' in their respective Canadian cities and that the situation had the potential to get *truly* out of control as threats of broken legs began to emerge.

After studying the Bulldogs' and the Rougeaus' schedules, Vince calculated that the first time that he could arrange for them to meet in a controlled manner would be at San Francisco airport as their respective flights landed to begin the next tour, so he booked the 'Admirals Lounge' to chair a make-or-break summit.

Vince, already seated at the head of the table, invited all four men into the room. The two tag teams sat opposite each other as tensions grew. Tom already looked considerably less healthy since the incident; his face was gaunt and seemed to be sinking into the gaping hole where once there had been teeth. Davey sat quietly beside him, puffing out his chest and trying to gain the macho advantage. Jacques bristled, nervously expecting a vociferous argument to ensue. Raymond, despite still being on crutches, had a typically calm demeanour.

'Look, you guys are going to be working the same towns for the next few weeks,' began Vince. 'All this has already gone too far; I don't want anything else to happen. So, I'm telling you guys now, this is over.'

'I just don't appreciate being sucker punched, Vince,' Tom said, his words slurred and spluttered through his broken mouth.

'And what about your attack on my brother in Miami? That was uncalled for; that was uninvited; that was unjustified,' Ray calmly responded.

'I'll tell you what, you pay for these teeth to be fixed, then I'll leave it,' Tom said in Jacques' direction. When Jacques began to respond angrily, Ray cut him off in French, and offered to pay for the dentistry to bring it to an end.

But it wasn't over. Not in Tom's mind. He cut a more intimidating figure than ever backstage as his mood hit new dark depths. Jacques went to extreme lengths in a bid to avoid what he felt was an inevitable comeback.

'Tommy,' began French-Canadian mid-carder Dino Bravo in hushed tones, 'I've gotta tell you something.'

'What's up, Dino?' asked Tom in the otherwise empty locker room.

'Jacques flashed at me. He says he's making a call from his hotel every single night. If ever he doesn't call, they are to assume you have done something to him.'

Terrified for his family, Tom bought Michelle a 9mm handgun and began teaching her how to use it. She was scared and horrified and screamed at Tom to tell her what it was all about. He told her what Dino had told him. (In 2021, Jacques Rougeau admitted showing Dino Bravo the name of a fictitious mobster, but says it was only a ploy to frighten Tom and prevent any retaliation against him.)

With his ego as shattered as his mouth, his pride and respect in the locker room irreversibly damaged, his professional pride being dented by his descending ability and the Bulldogs' current standing on the roster, Tom only needed the smallest of excuses to walk out of the WWF.

That moment soon arrived when the Bulldogs were the victims of an apparent flight ticket mix-up which left them having to make their own way back to Calgary from Chicago. Even though the mistake seemed genuine, it pushed Tom's sensitive 'disrespect' button and on top of everything else, made him reach out to Giant Baba the first chance he got. All All Japan would jump at the chance to get back to him, who, once Dynamite told him he was interested in working for Baba again, simply said, 'When can you come?'

To leave the world's most prominent promotion was a life-changing decision. Tom was turning his back on fame, money and security. Davey had been his tag partner for six years, he was his loyal cousin and had followed Tom every step without question, and he did the same again.

They handed in their notice to Vince two weeks before *Survivor Series*, agreeing that the PPV would be their final appearance with the

WWF. There was very little protest from Vince, who possibly felt the troublesome and less dynamic Bulldogs weren't worth the investment that they had been in 1985.

Dynamite and Davey were professional enough to work well with the Rougeaus at the event that saw them pocket another $20,000 pay-cheque each. With four teams on each side, the match was scripted so that the Rougeaus were eliminated early, giving them over 30 minutes to get out of the building before the Bulldogs were finally eliminated.

In a far shorter time than it had taken to get their mainstream wrestling career underway, it was over. They turned the clock back five years on their careers, returning to an arduous schedule of alternating between Stampede and All Japan.

Vince gave Tom the $1,800 dentist quotation, but he chose to leave his teeth unfixed.

With guaranteed income down and the unspoken fact that his wrestling days may be numbered, and the lingering fear their address sat folded up in the wallet of a mobster somewhere in Montreal, Michelle convinced Tom that they should downsize. Tom initially refused, fearing it would look like he was running or that downsizing made him appear like a failure. But the Calgary housing market had boomed, and they were able to sell their huge acreage for more than double the $220,000 cash they had paid for it. They moved to a five-acre plot on the other side of town and could've been financially secure.

Davey, on the other hand, was trying but failing to get his young family financially settled. He and Diana had bought their house at a bad time, with Calgary real estate expensive and interest rates sky high, burdening them with a $3,000 per month mortgage. They were also honest and careful with their tax returns, with Davey paying an extortionate rate on his high income. Davey had been popular in the WWF locker room, becoming friendly with the likes of Hulk Hogan, Roddy Piper and Randy Savage. What he learnt was that many of them had trademarked their wrestling names and registered them as incorporated businesses, therefore getting tax relief on their business-related endeavours; for those based in the US, this meant a proportion of even their mortgage could be written off against their tax bill – such a loophole didn't apply in Canada. Trademarking their gimmick name also meant that they owned the intellectual property associated with it and could switch to any promotion at any time using that name. As part of Vince's master plan to dominate wrestling, he was actively trademarking WWF gimmicks that his creative team brought to life. As independent wrestlers, Dynamite and Davey still had the British Bulldogs in their own hands.

Davey and Diana discussed their options and decided that a move to the US was probably in their future, but in the meantime, all they could do to prepare themselves for a better and more secure financial future was to get 'British Bulldogs' trademarked. It would be an expensive and time-consuming investment, costing several thousand dollars and consisting of much paperwork.

Tom scoffed at the idea when Davey presented it to him. Moving to or working in the US wasn't something Tom saw in his future and he knew that the Dynamite Kid was worth more in Japan than the British Bulldogs anyway.

'I see tail wags t'dog in your house Dave,' Tom said mockingly when Davey told him that Diana was pushing to get this done too. No matter how Davey or Diana dressed up the idea, Tom was unwavering. Knowing how stubborn and proud his cousin was, Davey knew it was a lost battle, so he went ahead and registered the British Bulldogs trademark at his own expense and in his own name only. Davey knew by now that Tom's career, and therefore their iconic tag team, were on the slide and at some point in the future, he would have to go it alone.

Tom's shoulder was next to give out, yet he continued to pound it into the mat with the help of all the numbing agents he swallowed and injected. When he finally had a scan, it was confirmed that the ligament was no longer even attached to the bone. He had an operation, which left his arm in a sling on the family moving day. Michelle chatted to her friend Sandra, who was helping them move to their new house in Cochrane.

Drunk and irritable, Tom accused Michelle of ignoring him. He ripped off his sling and writhed his stitched-up shoulder around, trying to throw it back out in a temper.

'Stop it!' Michelle began to scream, 'you don't have to do this anymore, Tommy! We have money now! I'll get a job. You can stop wrestling!'

'I'll never quit!' he snarled back.

Michelle would begin every day by stripping off the sweat-soaked bed sheets after a night of listening to Tom wriggle and whimper. Only now he was home so much did she realise just what pain he was in.

Just weeks after the operation, Tom was back in the ring.

25

BACK TO THE FUTURE

'That skinny little kid who'd told me he was going to be a
wrestler like me, had done exactly that. He was still only
young, maybe 20 or 21, but he was looking very good in the
ring. He was a nice lad as well. Chris was a good listener and
a good learner. He listened to me in the dressing room and on
the one occasion that I wrestled him in the ring.'

Tom Billington

Friday, 3 March 1989. The Pavilion, Calgary

'I am still enraged,' began Ed Whalen as he stood beside the Dynamite
Kid and prepared for their interview. 'I don't know whether you saw it
Dynamite but Bulldog Bob Brown hit Benoit with a chair, cost him
the match. What else is new with this idiot?'

'Ed, Bulldog Bob Brown, first of all, he's disgusting, I'm sick and
tired about him,' Tom stumbled and slurred his words. He was wearing
his iconic black, white and red leather vest, his hair was greasy and
unkempt, he had a straggly moustache, his skin was an ashen tone and
his eyes narrow. Over his right shoulder hung his blue wrestling boots,
tied together by the laces. 'Ed, ya'know,' he continued, 'I've known
yourself for ten or almost 11 years now. I've been around the world
three, four different times. Now I'm back in Calgary, but I'd like all
these people out there in TV-land to know, I think it's right about time,
errm, I'm not sure whether I think it's time, for me to hang my boots up.
I've got too many injuries – my back, my knees, my shoulder, different
things. I think, well, I can't set a date, but anyway I'd like to dedicate

these boots to a young man who I believe will be the superstar of the nineties. Ed, that's Chris Benoit.' Tom handed the boots to Whalen, who appeared instantly emotional and overwhelmed and began to eulogise into the camera about the Dynamite Kid.

'He's been one of the great fighters,' Whalen said, 'I've seen him come through this territory; I've seen him at the point in time where he was so injured I feared that he might end up a cripple, and he continued on, he had a terrible knee injury first of all – came back too – it was right here in this arena, he hurt his back badly, went on to the WWF and suffered further injury and he's not kidding when he says he has a series of bad injuries and I'm rather stunned that he's about to retire but, er, when that time comes these boots go to Chris Benoit.'

Since returning to Stampede three months earlier, Tom had been so impressed with the work and dedication of Benoit, coupled with his own sense of career mortality, that he felt the need to deliver a rare emotional *promo*, symbolically and almost literally passing the Stampede star on to Benoit.

Benoit wasn't just a wrestling colleague of Tom's, he was actually working for Tom, who had been offered the role of booker by Stu almost instantaneously when he heard that the Bulldogs were walking out on the WWF.

Dynamite and Davey's return had caused a stir throughout Calgary and particularly amongst the old Stampede faithful, who had believed they would never see their homegrown world-renowned stars back on the full-time roster of their comparatively tiny promotion. Tom had continued to bill them as the British Bulldogs (and by definition, the cousins that they were, despite the Stampede fans having been told for five years that they were strangers and bitter enemies). Remaining a tag team naturally helped Davey do the majority of the dynamic work to cover over Tom's physical ailments.

To add to the turmoil involved in the return to Calgary and Stampede for Tom, his friend and mentor John Foley had died of throat cancer the previous summer. At the funeral, Foley's daughter had asked Tom to lift the lid from the casket and check that her dad was wearing his favourite wrestling boots. Tom did so, and silently shared a final moment with the man who had been his loyal father-figure for the last ten years.

Stu had asked Tom to take the book from Keith, whose six-month stint in charge had seen a slump in business, as he demanded the wrestling be a more realistic shoot-style which the fans found boring compared to the blood and drama they had become accustomed to. The locker room had become an ill-disciplined and tension-filled environment. It was hoped the respect held for Tom coupled with his fearsome no-nonsense reputation and legendary in-ring psychology would transfer healthily into the role.

It started quite brilliantly, the Bulldogs' return alone enough to pack out venues across the territory and reinvigorate the promotion. They quickly won the tag team championships on 7 December to huge fanfare and adulation in a cage match over champions the Cuban Commandos (Cuban Assassin and Gerry Morrow). Tom brought in his old friend Don Muraco, who had been fired by Vince following misbehaviour on the European tour. Muraco immediately embarked on a rivalry with the North American heavyweight champion Makhan Singh (Mike Shaw), and just two days after the tag title change, another world-renowned star was holding a Stampede championship, and the promotion appeared to be in the ascendancy.

The success continued through December, with audiences, locker-room morale and discipline all improved beyond recognition, but New Year's Day 1989 would bring about the Bulldogs' first All Japan tour in four years – they would be gone for the whole of January. Tom decided they should drop the belts to 'Karachi Vice' (Makhan and Vokhan Singh) to enhance the heel stable further still and to keep the tag titles active while they were gone. But this act of selflessness backfired – the loss, followed by the long hiatus, would take the gloss from their momentum. Veteran heel wrestler and manager 'Bulldog' Bob Brown stepped into the breach as temporary booker while they were gone.

In Japan that year, the Bulldogs were delighted to be reunited with their old running mates such as Abdullah the Butcher, Terry Gordy, Dan Spivey and Stan Hansen; although notably missing were Tom's previous drinking buddies Terry Funk and Harley Race, who were both in varying states of semi-retirement.

The Bulldogs won 16 out of their 17 matches on the tour, including an all-*gaijin* instant classic for the finale against the Malenko brothers

(Joe and Dean), but returned to Calgary to discover disarray in the ranks once again.

Tom's performances both behind the scenes and in the ring were becoming a concern. On his good days, Tom was still fun-loving and passionate. He had taken to turkey farming on the new smaller acreage at Cochrane and had become adept at killing and preparing the birds for Michelle to cook giant meals for family and friends. On bad days though, he cut a scary figure around his own household, drinking almost around the clock, starting the day with a huge vodka and orange and relaxing with his arsenal of guns pointed out over the acreage, shooting at anything that moved. Michelle implored him to go back on the road with the WWF, but that was something his pride would never allow him to do. He was turning up to work late and drunk, and his disillusionment with the business was becoming clear; his well of inspiration as booker appeared to have run dry as he continuously put on violent gimmick matches such as street fights, chain and cage matches. The fans became saturated with blood and gore without the necessary storyline or build-up to justify it, and the ticket sales began to descend once again.

The Bulldogs formed an unofficial faction with the other top babyfaces, including Brian Pillman and Chris Benoit, to battle the Karachi Vice nightly in various singles and multi-man tag matches, which enabled Tom to spend as little time in physical action as possible, therefore giving his broken body the chance to perform on the next arduous but lucrative All Japan tour in May.

With crowds diminishing and unrest reappearing amongst the wrestlers, Tom descended yet further into a lifestyle of drink and drugs and insane practical jokes. He began missing shows, especially those requiring ungodly road trips in the rusty old vans. When Stu held back his pay-cheques on these occasions because Tom was still primarily in-ring talent and one of the highest-paid wrestlers on the roster, Tom began to show the kind of dissent and disharmony he had been promoted to stamp out. With the spring Japan tour on the horizon, Tom appeared to have abdicated the booker role, with no desperate pleas coming from the Hart family for him to take back a hold of the reins. Once again it was Bruce that stepped into the breach.

Davey was now wrestling more singles matches than he had in six years and was in great form and shape. Ted Betley's nephew Johnny Smith had settled in Calgary and was always a solid performer for Stampede and had become close with the Bulldogs – Dynamite in particular. He was contracted with New Japan, but All Japan were interested in him joining and taking some of the workload from Tom by becoming a third Bulldog. Unfortunately, since the controversy with the Bulldogs five years earlier, transfer between the two promotions had become completely embargoed. But as a favour to Johnny, Tom called in some favours and made it happen. Despite Tom's star dimming in North America, it still shone as brightly as ever in Japan, where respect and status wasn't quite so fickle. Johnny travelled east with Dynamite and Davey that May as the third British Bulldog.

Japan continued to bring out the best in the Bulldogs as a team and in Tom, who found his god-like reception there a painkilling injection in itself. But that completed the cycle once again, as Dynamite would fly and bump around to delight the fans that adored him, only doing further damage to his already fragile physical well-being.

They tore the roof from the Nippon Budokan in front of over 15,000 vibrant fans as they battled Japanese mainstays and *gaijin* royalty in Stan Hansen and Terry Gordy, with Davey once again instigating gasps of amazement as he pressed the mountainous Gordy high into the air with apparent ease.

Bruce steadied the Stampede ship whilst the Bulldogs were in Japan. Despite them being the biggest names in the locker room, Bruce wasn't looking forward to their return. They had burnt out as a tag team and were a negative influence on the road, as their callous pranks were being carried out without fear of retribution, such was the respect and standing they held amongst the boys and the Hart family they were married into. Their decade-long reign of spiking drinks, cutting up clothes and defecating in bags continued; but Davey turned the reign of terror up a notch when he set fire to a hotel bed while a rookie wrestler slept inside it. Tom was rumoured to have attempted a similar act on Harley Race several years earlier.

Stampede was once more heading down the toilet. They needed the Bulldogs to begin earning their money again; they were meant to be the shining lights, the money drawers and the mentors to the potential stars of the future. Instead, in recent times they had been far more damaging than profitable. Bruce had one last throw of the dice and was pleasantly surprised when Stu gave it the green light. A mega-programme that would be make-or-break for Stampede: '*The Dogfight of the Decade*'.

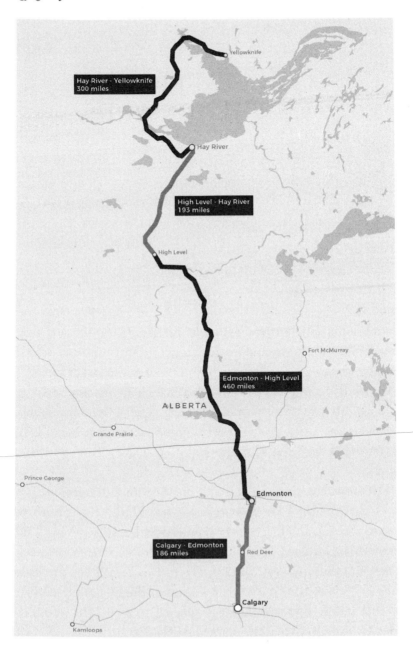

THE DOGFIGHT
OF THE DECADE

'I'm not proud to say it, but we were a bunch of junkies back then. [We took] pain pills, marijuana, cocaine, anything we could get our hands on. Tommy was into pill-popping. I can't even imagine all the pills him and Davey took.'

Milad Elzein (Abu Wizal)

June 1989

'There's some things you always take for granted in life and one of those things is the unity and friendship of the British Bulldogs,' began *Stampede Wrestling* roving reporter Jim Davies in the locker room. The Dynamite Kid stood next to him with a chain hanging around his neck and down his bare torso; a bandage was wrapped around his forehead.

'There was a terrible misunderstanding in that last bout,' Davies continued, 'Dynamite Kid thought that Davey Boy Smith had ambushed...'

Dynamite cut him off. 'Just wait one minute. I didn't *think* it was Davey Boy Smith; I know for a *fact* it was Davey Boy Smith who came to the ring and hit me over the head with a stick. Why? I don't know.' (It had indeed been Bulldog Bob Brown who had attacked Dynamite.) 'But my own belief is, Davey Boy Smith you are jealous of the Dynamite Kid, you've been jealous of the Dynamite Kid from day one! It was only two days ago when I spoke to the good Lord almighty himself,' Dynamite pointed stiffly skywards, 'the good Lord

John Foley, he said "Kid, never trust Davey Boy Smith!" He told me that seven, eight, nine years ago! Davey Boy, you tried to double-cross me! I was in that ring; I spilt my blood with Johnny Smith! He spilt his blood! The match had nothing whatsoever to do with you! But no, you had to come in and hit me over the head with a stick!'

At this point Davey entered the locker room and angrily protested his innocence. Johnny Smith followed in and insisted that Davey was indeed a family traitor, and he and Dynamite began to beat on Davey with a giant chain. Chris Benoit arrived to save his friend, but Dynamite and Johnny beat him into a corner as well. The battle lines were drawn; it was Bulldog versus Bulldog and both had their allies intact. Also jumping around amongst the carnage shouting 'Get him, get him, get him,' was evil manager Abu Wizal – which confirmed beyond doubt Dynamite's turn to the dark side.

Other than the odd word being muffled as the air whistled through the gaping hole at the front of his mouth, the promo was a dramatic improvement from Tom. He looked lean and comfortable in his own skin again as a heel. The best heel turns are those that are believable, and there is little doubt that Tom had been able to call upon some past legitimate feelings of resentment towards Davey, who had blazed a trail in Tom's red-hot slipstream for over a decade. Despite his physical and mental frailties and serious substance addiction, a fire was back in the eyes of the Dynamite Kid as he yelled into the camera lens; he was ready for one last serious singles run against his own flesh and blood and the man he had spent the most time in the ring and on the road with.

Dynamite and Johnny Smith became the 'British Bruisers' and began to battle Davey Boy and Chris Benoit nightly across the territory.

A few weeks later, the contract signing for the *Dogfight-of-the-Decade* was filmed at the Pavilion. Ed Whalen hosted alongside Jim Davies and first, he got the thoughts of an agitated Davey Boy on the recent turn of events, before Dynamite sauntered down the aisle, flanked by Abu Wizal in his Middle Eastern headdress and full body garment, to a chorus of boos. When Whalen finally turned to Dynamite, he started his opening question by speaking of his surprise and sadness at the breakdown of the legendary Bulldogs.

'Mr Whalen, why would you be surprised?' Dynamite responded. 'I took this man around the world three different times; I made him a world champion; I made him what he is today … he was riding my coattails from day one, I'm sick and tired of carrying this 265lb goof, it's as simple as that, 265lb goof. You can't beat me!' he pointed aggressively at Davey.

After much stalling and procrastinating by Dynamite, all to the successful annoyance of the audience, the contract was signed and with it, confirmation that the *Dogfight-of-the-Decade* would commence, and it would climax with a one-on-one match on 21 July at the Corral – the finale of Stampede Week 1989.

Booker Bruce had a problem though, in the form of Ed Whalen. Whalen was crucial to the Stampede TV show; he was the gel that knitted together the carnage and provided light humour and one-liners that made the show appeal to a wider audience. He was against much of the violence and shenanigans the promotion was known for, and so when Stu begged him to come back on board when Stampede reignited, knowing they needed him more than he needed them, Whalen had a level of creative control written into his contract. He loved the Bulldogs and hated the angle turning them on each other, believing that they, as the babyface heroes they were in the WWF, were the way forward for the promotion. The compromise was that the majority of the matches between them, particularly any bloodthirsty and gruesome ones, would take place on the non-televised events on the road. Most promos shot other than the contract-signing for TV, were hosted by the secondary commentator Jim Davies. The programme that was supposed to save the promotion quickly became a diluted version of what it was originally designed to be.

※ ※ ※

'Not while I'm driving, Dynamite,' said Bruce as yet another beaten-up Stampede wagon growled and spluttered its way across western Canada. Tom had just offered him an already open bottle of beer.

The level of frailty of the particular vans in use at the time was usually a clear indicator of the standard the promotion was working to, and in the summer of '89, that was certainly the case. There were several holes in the floor of this particular monstrosity, the rust around the edges of which flaked away as the vehicle vibrated and chugged hour after hour.

The regular week-long loop had started like any other. The opening show in Edmonton had been a solid one in front of a good crowd, and the tour was promising to be the same for the whole week, as fans had snapped up tickets to see a *Dogfight*.

However, morale within the group was operating about as well as the van's engine. They had seemingly all turned even more to their vice of choice and excesses were running wild, as were tempers. Even the strict kayfabe adherence was being flaunted, as babyfaces and heels swapped and changed which van they travelled in at every rest stop on the first marathon leg of the journey – the eight hours from Edmonton to High Level. Beers were being chugged regardless of the time of day and the stench of stale ale, cigarette smoke, urine and farts hung so heavy in the scorching, dry summer air it could almost be seen, even chewed on.

The further into the wilderness they got, the larger the monstrous bugs being splattered on the windscreen became and they stopped regularly to allow deer and antelope to casually saunter across the road.

Bruce was too long in the tooth to ever accept an already-open beer from Dynamite, but even he didn't believe Tom would be reckless enough to spike his drink while he drove hundreds of miles on the treacherous Canadian roads. But Tom wouldn't take no for an answer, so Bruce feigned having a swig and then gave it to Japanese wrestler Suma Hara, who was sat up front alongside him – hoping to remain safe from the pandemonium going on in the back.

When Bruce pulled into a gas station a little further up the road, all the boys clambered out of the back like a confusion of bandy-legged wildebeest lost on the Serengeti. When one of the boys opened the front door for Suma Hara to get out, he crawled nervously and slowly out of the van, before proceeding to dash around the gas station like a headless chicken, screaming and shouting from an apparent ongoing hallucination.

Just what was that beer laced with? Bruce thought, before launching a tirade at the Bulldogs. 'I'm driving, you imbeciles! We could've hit a semi head-on!' Dynamite denied the idiotic act, but no one believed him. He was drunk and pilled-up, and those around him knew that he was capable of anything while in that state – and had good form for it.

During this tour, Tom cut an angrier figure than ever, as the realisation that his body had failed him continued to dawn. When he had previously roamed western Canada, he was putting on one-hour non-stop action-packed masterpieces weekly, but now he was struggling to muster a decent ten-minute match. Davey had become the relentless top draw and Tom resented it, sniping and belittling his cousin at every opportunity. Davey, though, just continued to take Tom's abuse and follow and support him without question. The Jacques Rougeau incident also still haunted Tom, and in his darkest times he longed to prove he was the toughest guy in the locker room and he certainly didn't like Bruce tearing a strip off him in front of the boys.

Mercifully, they made it to High Level, and yet again, a full house was left satisfied.

But tensions were fraught, and a couple more days into the long, debilitating trip, as plumes of dust exhausted behind them from the dry, gravel roads, one of the vans broke down. In addition to the two vans, road agent Bob Johnson was part of the fleet in his own Ford, so Bruce and wrestler Ricky Rice climbed into that vehicle, leaving the remaining entourage to squash into one 16-seat bus, many with their luggage perched on their laps. The fun, games and partying were over, as were any remaining fumes of morale.

In the Ford, Bruce casually commented on the levels of despair this particular trip was driving the promotion to, which included a remark regarding the laughably stark and bitter contrast for the Bulldogs from 12 months earlier, when they had been jet-setting WWF superstars.

After another pitstop, Ricky Rice jumped back aboard the bus and sensationalised Bruce's comment, saying he had been getting a real kick out of Dynamite and Davey's plight. As Tom stared out of the window drunken, drug-crazed, tired and clammy, Bob Johnson's Ford appeared in view as it slowly overtook them on the dual carriageway, Bruce with his seat reclined and feet up on the dashboard. The ticking time bomb that was the Dynamite Kid was about to explode.

But despite everything, the *Dogfight-of-the-Decade* programme was filling the venues and when the disgruntled stars saw the packed crowds, they performed. That was the case at Yellowknife in the penultimate town of the tour and the furthest one away from home. Bruce and Bob Johnson left that same evening, as Bruce was on a promotional local radio show in Hay River the following morning before the show. Although he knew they would be crammed like hungover sardines in one van, it was 'only' a five-hour journey this time. He told them to be on the road by noon, believing he was leaving them in high spirits as the shows were going well; instead, there was mutiny afoot, as the tired and substance-abusing wrestlers concentrated their discussions on the abominable trip Bruce and Bob had arranged for them. If Bruce had just jumped from a sinking ship, there was little doubt the new skipper was Dynamite.

Bulldog Bob Brown and his wrestling nephew Kerry had made their own way around the loop, enabling them to squeeze in some fishing time on the Great Slave Lake. By 7pm in Hay River the following night, only Bruce, Bob Johnson and Bob and Kerry Brown had arrived at the show. Bruce had been meant to be working with 'Lethal' Larry Cameron, but instead, he and Kerry agreed to start the show with a completely improvised match with no backstory. Bob Brown put on his wrestling gear in case he too was required to fill time in the ring, where Bob Johnson was acting as the makeshift announcer.

After wrestling for 40 minutes, Bruce sent a message backstage via Johnson for Bulldog Bob to ready himself to take over from Kerry. As Bob and Kerry were family and part of the same heel stable, it was the only solution that made any kind of storyline sense. They created a context that Bob was out for revenge after Bruce had supposedly cheated to beat his nephew. The crowd looked on, confused and unimpressed.

Bruce had been wrestling continuously for almost 90 minutes when he finally got word that the boys had arrived – it was now past 9pm. He wrapped up his match with the elder Brown and stormed to the back. What he did not know was that the boys were in an even fouler mood than he was – their ill fortune, however, had been self-inflicted. Many of them had partied heavily in Yellowknife; the drink, pills and cocaine not only aimed at numbing their usual aches and pains, but now their fraught mental states too.

They had emerged from the sordid motel at various times throughout the day, like early man finding his way out of his cave

The timing of the whole fiasco couldn't have been worse, as it was Owen's eagerly anticipated wedding to childhood sweetheart Martha on Saturday 1 July – just a single day after the bruised and battered rabble landed back in Calgary. Bruce certainly wasn't going to be enjoying the prime-rib feast or giving his carefully prepared speech as the best man. He was furious and on arrival back at Hart House insisted that if either Tom or Davey attended the wedding, then he wouldn't. Little did he know, Tom hadn't actually been invited. Dynamite, in lieu of all of the Hart family, was instead expected to lead the promotion to their show in Edmonton that same evening. This was news to Tom, who made it clear to Ross he expected to be at the wedding. Ross, tactfully as ever, told Tom that in light of the recent events, it wouldn't be proper for him to attend the wedding; he implored him to go to the show in Edmonton instead.

Diana dashed to Hart House with a sheepish Davey in tow, who made a heartfelt apology to Bruce, being honest enough that his level of drunkenness multiplied by the severity of the road trip from hell were the reasons for his actions.

Tom didn't attend the wedding; nor did he go to Edmonton. Instead, he wallowed in yet another boozy session at a Calgary strip club and informed the Harts that he had quit their sinking ship of a promotion. The *Dogfight-of-the-Decade*, the programme that was supposed to save them, was over before it had properly begun.

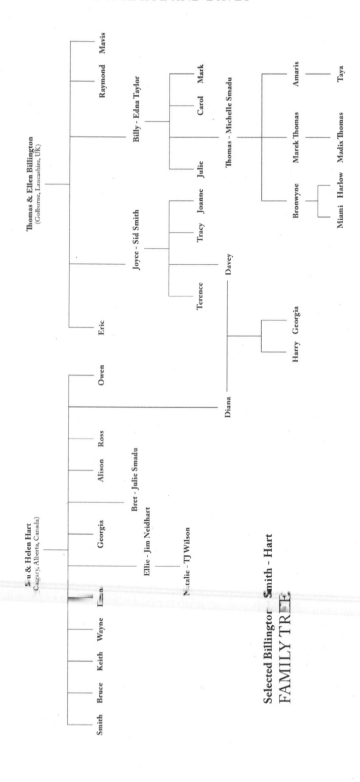

Selected Billington - Smith - Hart
FAMILY TREE

27

CRASH

'I've seen [Dynamite] go into the ring with a melon-sized
swelling on his lower back, barely able to walk. He would still
work the match and take some ungodly bump, then he'd get
on that bus with the rest of the boys. He really needed help to
get to his seat, but he wouldn't accept any; he'd make it all the
way to the back by himself because he was too damn tough
to take help. He'd get to one of those seats, get himself a beer
and do the same thing the next night.'

Terry Funk

4 July 1989

'Ya know, you really should be wearing your seatbelt on this road,'
driver Ross said to Davey, who was riding up front alongside him as
they sped west on the highway. They were mid-way through the 11-
hour trek to Prince George, British Columbia.

Ross sat forward to maximise his concentration as he was forced
to put the windscreen wipers to full velocity to clear his vision from
the driving rain; he was driving as quickly as possible as they had left
Calgary 90 minutes behind schedule and Ross needed to make up some
of that time if they were to make it to the show on time.

They had been so late setting off because the promotion had hit rock
bottom once again. Their beaten-down van needed repairs following
the previous seemingly never-ending road trip, therefore a van had to
be hired from Budget Rentals.

upstaging this one. They told their story perfectly as the long-reigning champion appeared to have finally met his match. Almost 20 minutes of fast-paced, hard-hitting action neared its dramatic climax, as the crowd willed their hero to finish the job, but Mr Perfect proved resilient.

The momentum changed and it looked as though the crowd were going to be disappointed, but as Hennig dropped a leg into Bret's groin, the Hitman caught an ankle in each hand and in an instant had them crossed over; he flipped on to his front, stood up and 20,000 people went crazy as they realised that he had smoothly locked in his sharpshooter finishing hold. Curt quit instantly and Bret Hart was the new Intercontinental champion.

* * *

The demise of British wrestling coincided not only with the stateside rise of the British Bulldog but also the rise of Sky TV in Britain. Sky did a deal to air regular WWF programming, which became a pop-culture sensation and the UK market opened up for Vince in a bigger way than he had ever imagined.

In early October the WWF embarked on another European tour to capitalise on the growing popularity. The tour opened with an emotional and memorable night at the Royal Albert Hall – the fabled home of UK wrestling – as Davey won a 20-man Battle Royal which featured the likes of the Undertaker and the WWF's newest megastar, Ric Flair.

Flair had been the NWA's and subsequently WCW's saviour throughout the '80s; their perennial champion and showstopping performer at every single one of their major events. He was their Hulk Hogan – but he was a masterful heel, as they traditionally ran with a charismatic rulebreaker at the top with underdog babyfaces chasing but just falling short – whereas Vince liked a hero champion who continuously overcame the seemingly insurmountable odds.

Since Turner Broadcasting had taken control of the company, the suits had taken over – and not the sharp and vibrant type worn by Flair. Non-wrestling businessmen had been placed in booking positions and Flair had rebelled against it. The fallout had led to him walking out with the NWA heavyweight championship belt and signing for Vince

– using the heritage of the NWA title to proclaim that he was the *real* world champion.

The Battle Royal was now becoming Davey's speciality, as he won yet another in Paris. For the remainder of the tour, he battled and beat the gargantuan Earthquake, leaving fans in awe as their idol hoisted the 400lb monster up on to his shoulder. In Davey's corner for the series of matches was an ashen-faced and crutch-dependent André the Giant. In the storyline, Earthquake had attacked André and severely injured his leg, but in reality, the legendary giant was growing old ahead of his time. Acromegaly had continued to deform him physically and he now lived in permanent agony and was almost completely immobile.

Romantically, André's appearance at Davey's side in Paris, in his home country, which saw him crack Earthquake with his crutch to assist a Bulldog victory, was his final ever appearance in the WWF. He died in that same city just 15 months later.

Machinations began to move the WWF on from what has since been labelled the 'Golden Era'. The timing of Flair's arrival was perfect. Whilst his ego and party lifestyle were a thing of legend within the industry, he was not a muscle-bound steroid abuser.

With Flair's assistance, the Undertaker defeated Hogan and won the WWF title at *Survivor Series*. Due to the controversial nature of the ending, an immediate rematch was booked for a one-off PPV the following week, *This Tuesday in Texas*. When that match also descended into chaos, WWF on-screen president Jack Tunney made the title vacant and declared that the 1992 *Royal Rumble* match, to take place six weeks later, would crown the new champion.

Davey had challenged for the WWF title for the first time at house shows during the Undertaker's brief spell as champion.

* * *

'For those of you that don't already know him, this is my brother Owen,' Bret said proudly to the boys in PT's, a San Antonio strip club that they'd organised to descend on following the successful Texas show. Hogan was hosting, with 'Road Warriors' Hawk and Animal, Sergeant Slaughter, Curt Hennig, a returning Brutus Beefcake, Big Boss Man, Hercules, Davey and Jim scattered around him. Everyone welcomed Owen back into the fold and Bret announced the beers were on him. Ric Flair was hosting a separate celebratory shindig – whilst the kayfabe rules had become blurred, Hogan and Flair schmoozing together would still be deemed one step too far.

The drinks and merriment flowed all night. At around midnight, a drunken and dishevelled Vince McMahon stumbled into the bar and declared the party was just getting started.

Wide-eyed and boisterous, Vince was suddenly the centrepiece, not Hogan, who subsequently dared the 'Legion of Doom' to perform their devastating 'Doomsday Device' finisher on the boss from the top of the bar. Whilst Animal walked over to Vince and casually crouched behind him and hoisted him up on to his shoulders, Hawk climbed up and held on to a stripper pole.

'I'm gonna take his fuckin' head off!' Hawk declared. The boys stared and goaded, cheered and chanted. Hawk took to the air, but just barely brushed Vince enough to send him backwards, where Hogan and Beefcake were waiting to catch him.

As Vince was gently placed back on to his feet, a smattering of applause came from some of his employees, as Vince grinned wide and toothily, for a second allowing himself to believe he was the wrestler he'd always dreamt of becoming. Some of the boys, though, directed disappointed boos at Hawk's lacklustre effort.

'The Hart Foundation would have had the balls to do it!' Jim gruffly boasted.

'You're damn right!' Bret confirmed.

Jim grabbed Vince and thrashed him around like he was a teddy bear, placing him in the bearhug set-up for their own 'Hart Attack' finisher. Davey and Owen chuckled with excitement as Bret gulped – Jim was serious, and he couldn't back down after scorning Hawk. He slammed his drink down and leapt into the air, clotheslining Vince hard and following through. The three of them laid in a heap, as howls of laughter and disbelief filled the room.

The noise quietened down as they all awkwardly watched Vince attempt to regain his footing. As he finally made it to a standing position, he glared at Bret and excitedly yelled, 'You owe me a drink, Hitman!'

'Yeah, don't worry, I'm buying again,' grinned a relieved Bret.

As the lights went up in the club shortly after, with the dancers long clocked off, Davey was running around with Vince McMahon slumped over his shoulder, looking for an open enough space to land his powerslam, but a call came from behind the bar that the police were on their way just in time to save Vince from another heavy bump. The gang had been oblivious to the procession of final calls and requests for them to leave.

The designated drivers swiftly got into their cockpits and the stragglers – semi-dressed strippers among them – clambered into whichever car they could fit. Sergeant Slaughter, with Vince on board, burned rubber as he led the getaway, pushing one squad car out of the way in order to make room for the convoy to follow. They headed to the Marriott where Ric Flair had vowed to host the after-party's after-party in his penthouse suite.

It was around 3am when the mob descended on the hotel reception and asked the clerk to call Flair's room. When there was no answer, they knew that meant Flair had run an even longer night of misdemeanour than they had. Vince took charge and demanded a key for the room.

'I'm Vince McMahon, dammit!' he said, and with that, Vince got the key.

The elevators were crammed with men of all shapes and sizes as they shot up to the 40th floor.

In the penthouse, they took it in turns to randomly shoot wrestle one-on-one, whilst raiding the minibar and taking turns to piss on Flair's bed – he'd been the enemy for so long, it was difficult for the boys to see him as an ally.

* * *

The most eagerly anticipated *Royal Rumble* match yet opened with 'Rule Britannia', as Davey Boy was given the seemingly impossible task of winning from the number one entry position. This was a clever way of protecting Davey's status in the upper echelons of the roster and as a Battle Royal specialist. He lasted a respectable 24 minutes before being eliminated by eventual winner and new champion Flair.

Owen's return had also been good for Jim, as they formed the 'New Foundation'. But the tag team's life was as short as Jim's hot-headed temper. On 16 February, when called for a random drug test as part of the new regime, he had refused on the basis he couldn't pee, but would try again after their match. He then refused to put over rookie team 'The Beverley Brothers' and left the building without taking the required piss. All this was on top of Jim having not paid back the legal fees Vince had paid on his behalf for his successful defence and subsequent awarding of substantial damages for wrongful arrest following a dispute aboard a US Airways flight. When he turned up to TV tapings in Tampa the following day, Vince summoned him to his office and told him, 'You're fired!'

As he stormed out of the building, Jim grabbed a TV monitor and hurled it at Chief Jay Strongbow's head, as it was Strongbow who had called him for the drug test.

Bret had briefly lost the Intercontinental title to, of all people, Jacques Rougeau's 'The Mountie' character, but regained it by defeating his friend Roddy Piper in another barnstorming classic at *WrestleMania VIII*. Owen was impressing – now as Koko B. Ware's partner in 'High Energy' – and Davey was going over strong in the upper-mid card against the likes of Rick Martel and Ted DiBiase.

Davey missed *WrestleMania VIII* largely out of pride. He had been due to face the Berzerker but when the producers realised they were overrunning for time, they asked him to keep it to a one-minute squash match. He refused, telling them he didn't short-change the fans like that, and so the match was pulled altogether. But the spring brought about yet another lucrative homecoming tour of Europe, where Davey headlined and defeated all-comers: former WWF champion Ric Flair (who had lost the belt to Randy Savage at *WrestleMania*) in Milan, Brighton and London; 'The Repo Man' in Dublin, Glasgow and Birmingham; Irwin R. Schyster in Sheffield; and had his arm raised after yet another dramatic Battle Royal victory in Munich.

Davey was still only 29, his career was riding the crest of a wave and momentum was still only driving it skyward. He and his young family were living in the Sunshine State, safely away from any Calgary troubles.

But the first in what would be a series of dominoes fell late in April 1992 when one of Davey's drug tests in the new regime tested positive for ecstasy. Davey explained that, whilst hanging out with other wrestlers in a hotel room, he believed he must've inhaled cannabis smoke that had been laced with crushed-up ecstasy. His suspension was upheld, and the failed test was on his record. Davey was disheartened and sunk low during his suspension.

Meanwhile, Vince was making major plans for *SummerSlam*. He was considering Washington DC as the venue but had been blown away by the popularity they now held in Europe, in particular in the UK, which was proving a goldmine with live tours selling out instantly and merchandise stands always left ransacked.

Feeling an itch developing that he needed to scratch, Vince enquired about the availability of London's iconic Wembley Stadium for his summer extravaganza.

30

AND WE'RE OFF TO WEMBLEY

'Hart versus Bulldog was a near-classic match, probably the
best WWF singles match on a major show since Savage-
Steamboat in 1987 ... 4½ stars.'

Dave Meltzer

May 1992

'I can promise you, nobody will be able to follow us,' Bret insisted to
Vince as they discussed the idea of a brother-in-law versus brother-in-
law match in front of 80,000 people. He sold him on his and Davey's
kinship, on the stellar all-babyface match they had put on for just a
few hundred people in Regina nearly a decade earlier, and on their
in-ring chemistry. Vince imagined the scene Bret had laid out and his
eyes widened.

'I've even got the finish in my head ...' Bret said mischievously.

'I don't wanna know, Hitman!' Vince replied, stopping Bret in his
tracks. 'Surprise me!'

It was on. Bret Hart versus Davey Boy Smith for the Intercontinental
title at a sold-out Wembley Stadium would main-event *SummerSlam*
– even over the WWF title match between Randy Savage and the
Ultimate Warrior.

Davey returned to the ring on 1 June, winning a 40-man Battle
Royal to relaunch himself back to the lofty position on the roster he
had previously held. But he wasn't quite in the same peak physical
condition he had been. His matches were short as he won nightly,

mostly working with Repo Man, yet he was gassed out by the end of them.

'Another one, Bret?' asked Davey in a Massachusetts hotel bar following a long day of TV tapings on 20 July.

'No. Early nights for me from now until Wembley,' replied Bret. 'I can't stop thinking about it. 80,000 people; the main event in an open-air stadium.'

'Yeah, I know,' Davey looked more nervous than excited. 'Another one, please,' he said to the waiter. He then winced as he stepped from his stool to get out his wallet, and put his hand down toward his knee.

'You okay, man?' Bret asked.

'Yeah. Blew the knee a little today,' Davey said as he popped a series of Demerol through their foil sleeve and chucked them back with the remainder of his beer. He'd beaten Iron Mike Sharpe in under three minutes earlier in the day.

'Well, you take it easy, Davey. Goodnight,' Bret said.

Davey tossed, turned and sweated out his toxins in bed, before waking up screaming in the early hours of the morning. The painkilling effect of the drugs had worn off, his knee was swollen and agonising. He couldn't continue with the tour and was sent home to Florida.

The verdict was that Davey should be able to wrestle by the time *SummerSlam* came around in five weeks' time, but not before, as he would be running the risk of the injury recurring. At best, he was going to be ring rusty for the biggest match of his life.

Over the next few weeks, the WWF filmed and ran various vignettes with Diana, Stu and Helen, who all spoke of a family being torn apart by Bret and Davey's wrestling competitiveness.

'It's a house divided. We're falling apart,' a tearful Helen said.

Diana spoke of the split loyalties she felt between her beloved brother and her husband. They all spoke of their desire for it to be settled, and that the Intercontinental title paled into insignificance when compared to family harmony. The seeds of a story where art met reality were being planted for the fans, and anticipation grew and grew.

Davey, Bret and the other WWF superstars arrived at the hotel in London as hordes of fans spilled out chanting 'Hitman! Hitman!' and 'Bulldog! Bulldog!'

WWF fanfare had taken over London, and Davey was mobbed as he took his family sightseeing.

He was still nursing his knee, which had developed a flesh-eating staph infection, through a long recovery and his lower back still required the copious amounts of strong painkillers he took daily. He hadn't wrestled in almost six weeks.

Finally, at the entrance rehearsal the day before the biggest matches of their lives, Bret and Davey got together and planned out their magnum opus.

SummerSlam
29 August 1992
Wembley Stadium
London
Intercontinental Championship
The British Bulldog v Bret 'Hitman' Hart
Official attendance: 80,355

The joyous fans had snapped up every ticket in a matter of hours of them going on sale so that they could get a rare in-the-flesh glimpse of the larger-than-life superstars from a world far away. But they had been somewhat taken for granted with a poor and predictable first two hours of the show, which had opened with the stadium bathed in glorious sunshine. They had played along with glee as the sun began to set over the iconic twin towers of the stadium and the Macho Man and the Ultimate Warrior title match ended in a disqualification melee involving Ric Flair and Mr Perfect. As darkness began to set in, they watched on as the Undertaker ominously took his long walk out to the ring, accompanied by Paul Bearer and a giant black hearse, before his short match against the 'Ugandan Giant', Kamala – which once again ended in a disqualification and a melee.

Immediately after that match, the broadcast cut to backstage reporter Sean Mooney, who stood beside a tanned and glistening British Bulldog, draped in a sequined Union Jack cape which sparkled into the camera. He smiled the smile of a nervous man trying his best to portray a confident one as he rubbed his palms together and spoke of this night being a dream, and the dream was going to come true when he would end it as the Intercontinental champion and having brought peace to his warring family.

Then it cut to Gene Okerlund with Bret, who spoke with genuine passion about how he had introduced Davey to Diana, of the help he had given Davey in getting his career to where it was, how Davey was ungrateful for that and how he was going to turn the British Bulldog's dream into a nightmare.

It was then back to Mooney, this time at ringside with Diana, who spoke emotionally of the healthy competitiveness that Bret and Davey had always held, but now she was scared that they were going to destroy each other and the family.

The floodlights provided the only illumination as 'Rule Britannia' suddenly chimed and the stadium erupted.

Walking ten paces ahead of Davey was then-British, European, Commonwealth and soon-to-be-world heavyweight boxing king Lennox Lewis, who waved a giant Union Jack high into the air. Davey stopped halfway down the long walkway and looked around, soaking in the sensational scene and emotionally-charged reception. Suddenly, he appeared steely-eyed as he shouted and gestured appreciatively.

Finally back where he belonged – in the ring – Davey's transformation back to a confident wrestling superstar was complete as he spread his arms wide to fully reveal the ultra-patriotic cape and took in a huge breath. They worshipped him. A tsunami of giant foam fingers, Bulldog signs and camera flashes crashed over him. 'Rule Britannia' had to restart, so long was Davey's introduction as he now strode with confidence and climbed the turnbuckles to salute the masses with his outstretched cape.

The unmistakable guitar riff echoed into the night sky, signalling the arrival of the Hitman. The crowd erupted into cheers once more for Bret, who had quickly become the most popular wrestling star in the world. But they soon corrected themselves, realising that, even if it was just for that one night, Bret Hart was the pantomime villain, intent on preventing their local hero from achieving his dream.

When the music stopped it was simply replaced with the constant reverberations and air-horns of a stadium that felt like a living, breathing giant. The crowd excitement reached fever pitch as Bret and

Davey went nose-to-nose. The camera continued to cut to a petrified-looking Diana to remind viewers of what was at stake.

The match got underway with some basic stuff, but the crowd really popped the first time Davey performed a gymnastic routine to counter a hold that even Dynamite would've been proud of, with a smooth flip and a handstand to achieve his own leverage.

The match built, layer upon layer, every move and routine executed perfectly. Davey's counters caused the crowd to erupt, with the boos for Bret slowly getting louder. When Bret ducked and sent a diving Davey Boy flailing to the outside in a heap, Bret began a constant onslaught. Minute piled upon minute as the crowd desperately willed Davey to make a comeback – they were utterly transfixed.

Davey instigated his comeback in spectacular fashion, pressing Bret above his head but stumbling backwards and crotching him on the ropes, before going through his own impressive attacking repertoire, culminating in the running powerslam. 'ONE, TWO' – the crowd yelled along with the count, assuming it was over – but Bret kicked out and Davey slumped helplessly, looking resigned to the fact he might not be able to beat his brother-in-law if his patented powerslam couldn't end it.

They continued, trading suplexes and clotheslines until they were strewn across the ring in exhaustion. Bret cleverly entwined their legs, and when he began to turn over on to his front, the crowd realised what was happening, and suddenly, the sharpshooter was locked in, right in the middle of the ring. No one had ever escaped. The crowd screamed at Davey to make it to the ropes.

'This is unbelievable!' referee Joey Morella – son of the legendary Gorilla Monsoon – yelled at Bret and Davey as he leant in supposedly to ask Davey if he was ready to quit.

The fans exploded once again as Davey finally made it to the ropes and the hold was broken. The camera then cut to a tearful Diana. Bret raised Davey to his feet, whispering, 'Let's go home,' into his ear. He attempted to whip him across the ring, but Davey reversed and it was Bret who bounced from the ropes before diving over a crouched Davey in a sunset flip attempt, but the local hero hooked his ankles and sat down into an impossible pinning position. One. Two. Three.

'Ladies and gentlemen, the winner of this bout, and the new Intercontinental champion, the British Bulldog!' yelled Howard Finkel as the overhead cameras swept across the crowd, creating unique celebratory scenes that would last a lifetime as 80,000 sets of limbs flailed uncontrollably.

'I can't believe it!' boomed Vince McMahon on commentary. 'One of the greatest wrestling matches of all time has just taken place!'

A dejected Bret sat solemnly in the ring, whilst Davey stood staring at his new belt in disbelief, before walking over to his friend and brother-in-law and offering out his hand. Bret climbed to his feet and turned his back, extracting more of the desired pantomime boos from the crowd that were so desperate to see the family reunited. He looked back and realised that they were right, before walking back over to Davey and shaking his hand and the pair warmly embraced. Diana joined them in the ring and the show ended with the three of them hugging tightly as fireworks filled the London skyline, 'Rule Britannia' played loudly and not a dry eye remained.

That evening, the WWF set a merchandise record that would stand for decades, selling almost $1.5 million worth of mostly British Bulldog products.

As a complete spectacle, the match is widely regarded as one of the greatest of all time.

31

THE BIGGER THEY ARE,
THE HARDER THEY FALL

'All our hearts went out to him. Dynamite was hard to love,
but we did, and it was heartbreaking to see the best worker I
ever knew finally reveal his inner agony at the mistakes he'd
made and how things had ended up for him.'

Bret Hart

JUST THREE days after *SummerSlam*, at a TV taping to be broadcast
two weeks later, Ric Flair won the WWF title from Randy Savage.
But it was clear that Flair just wasn't as over in the WWF as he had
been in WCW – he was *the* NWA man, after all. He looked every
day of his 43 years and needed to be the champion to carry off his
arrogant trope.

A long-term heel champion wasn't the WWF tradition, but it had
been the NWA's, and was now WCW's.

Flair and Vince soon agreed that his days were numbered, not just
with the belt, but with the company. When the time was right for him
and WCW, he could go back. As amicable and mutual as that decision
was, Vince knew he couldn't risk Flair doing to him what he had done
to WCW when he had jumped in Vince's direction, taking the belt
with him (how the WCW bosses would love to settle that score). So,
Vince assessed his options for his next champion: Hulk Hogan was
laying low and considering his career options following the steroid
scandal and the popularity of both Macho Man and Ultimate Warrior

were on the wane. He needed someone new to cut through into a new era, and he had the Hitman.

Vince flew Stu out to Saskatoon for a house show, where the Hart patriarch beamed with pride as his son slapped his sharpshooter on Flair, who duly banged his hands on the mat whilst squealing like a scalded cat. The crowd were almost as shocked and delirious as Bret had been earlier that day when Vince told him of the sudden plan.

Davey, meanwhile, was defending his own title with pride multiple times each week, mostly against Shawn Michaels. Shawn had turned heel at the beginning of the year by virtue of throwing his Rockers tag team partner Marty Jannetty through the window of Brutus Beefcake's barber shop set. His talent had made him stand out as a future top-tier star in the new era that was dawning, one where smaller men could reach the summit. He was now the 'Heartbreak Kid', a cocky upstart with a chip on his shoulder – the trouble was, that reputation was being earned both in and out of the ring.

Michaels had long been earmarked as the next heel Intercontinental champion and the obvious choice to win it from babyface Bret, but the opportunity for the Wembley extravaganza had been too good to pass up. With Bret now the WWF champion, to add balance to the roster, it was felt they needed a heel Intercontinental champion, and the Bulldog was about to get his heart broken.

Davey didn't take the news well and let it get him down. It was understandable; almost all of the previous champions had held the title for several months. With the exception of the Mountie's two-day reign as a transitional champion, Davey's 59 days would be the shortest stint with the belt in the 13-year history of the championship.

Dutifully, Davey allowed Shawn to pin him following a purposely mistimed superplex attempt at the taping of *Saturday Night's Main Event* on 27 October. The match was aired on 14 November and Davey was subsequently called into Vince's office and, to his astonishment, fired on the spot.

Growth hormone had been used by Olympic cheats as a substitute when testing for steroids had started and wrestlers had now discovered this loophole. Whilst they had been in England that summer, the Ultimate Warrior had asked Davey if he knew anyone who could get him some. Davey had pointed him in the direction of a gym manager.

Liking the product and the price on offer, Warrior proceeded to have large shipments sent over to him in the States. When one of these was confiscated by customs, the Drug Enforcement Agency got involved and tied it to Vince and the WWF, who were still under investigation.

Vince had to be seen to act fast and mercilessly. He had fired Warrior immediately, who sang like a canary and implicated Davey. After the recent positive test and suspension too, Vince had no choice, and fired Davey with a heavy heart. He liked Davey and saw him as one of his next generation of headliners and told him the door would be open once the heat of the ongoing investigation had gone away.

Davey had fallen so fast. He set about getting work elsewhere and talks inevitably began with WCW. In the meantime, he performed a couple of shows for the brand-new Philadelphia-based promotion Eastern Championship Wrestling (later to become Extreme Championship Wrestling). He also contacted Giant Baba and got himself booked on his first All Japan tour in three years for March 1993.

* * *

1 February 1993. Platt Bridge, Wigan

WWF champion Bret Hart sported the familiar double-denim he enjoyed off-camera as he stood in quiet contemplation in the small car park directly outside the ground-floor flat Tom now lived in. Many of the block's windows were boarded up; there was more graffiti than brick on view; kids ran feral outside and, most worrying of all, a lone blackened car smouldered ominously nearby.

He was with Nasty Boy Brian Knobbs and Chief Jay Strongbow. They were in Manchester for a show the following evening (Vince was pressing on with his UK invasion even without his local star attraction) and Knobbs, a Dynamite Kid worshipper, had tracked Tom down and arranged to swing by. He'd chosen to invite Bret because of his long and close relationship with Tom, and the Chief because he had always thought so highly of Dynamite. The fact they were the current champion and Vince's trusty road agent respectively meant that a good impression from Tom here could have led to a potential return.

Tom answered their knock and invited them in, his white T-shirt baggy on his slender frame. His skin was paler than ever, his hair greasy and swept back.

He lowered himself awkwardly and painfully on to a tatty old couch whilst the others fumbled around looking for a place to sit. Joanne looked shocked enough by Tom's arrogant, dismissive and aggressive behaviour towards her to convince Bret that he didn't usually treat her this way, and he was merely putting on a show to assert his alpha-male image – one that would ensure he didn't receive the only thing he truly feared: pity.

Whilst his guests didn't pity him, they quickly became embarrassed. Tom stubbed out another cigarette as the butts mounted up by his side, along with beer bottles and painkillers.

'Why don't you come back, Tom?' Bret asked.

'To the WWF? No chance,' Tom answered with predictable stubbornness.

'Bret's the champ now, Tommy, it's all changed,' Knobbs said.

'Yeah,' Tom nodded, taking a swig of his beer, 'Intercontinental, right?'

'No, Dyno. He's the world champion now. He's got the big belt,' Knobbs replied as Bret looked to the floor, feeling almost guilty at how their respective careers had gone in such starkly different directions in the last five years. After a pause, Tom grinned an all-knowing grin, as he realised that if Bret had made it to the very top, he certainly should have done too.

'Nah – even if I wanted to, I'd have to get back on the juice.'

'No, you wouldn't – it's banned – just ask Davey!' Knobbs added.

'Nah, I'm doing okay over 'ere, Bret. I'm in the main event with Dave Finlay at the moment – 130 quid a night.'

Objects crashed against the exterior of the flat every now and again during their stay. As Tom explained, that was why the windows were boarded up.

The trio left politely, inviting Tom for a drink at their hotel bar later that evening, an offer he accepted. Chief Jay broke the stoic silence on the drive back to the hotel to admit he wished he hadn't gone, as the experience had somewhat tarnished the memories he had of one of his all-time favourites.

Tom turned up at the hotel bar that night. Bret and both of the Nasty Boys lifted his spirits. Bret reiterated that he had planted seeds with both Vince and Chief Jay on his behalf.

'Nah. I'll never go back, Bret.' Tom's self-destructive pride could never be moved. Bret already knew that and he said goodbye to an emotional-looking Tom and wished him well. Bret looked back as he entered the elevator, and saw that Tom was sobbing into his beer, with only the Nasty Boys to comfort him.

* * *

That same February, Davey Boy made his debut for WCW – and Ric Flair made his inevitable return to the company. Davey had struck a deal with executive vice president Bill Watts on a $1,000 per night contract, and an unwritten understanding that he would get substantially more and a cut of the gate for European dates, being the main draw there, as WCW planned on using Davey to compete with the WWF for the UK market. They immediately promoted him for their upcoming UK tour, for which ticket sales rocketed when he was added to the line-up. They even went so far as to license an official magazine focusing entirely on the career, training methods and home life of Britain's most famous wrestler – Davey was the only talent that WCW produced such a dedicated magazine around.

On the tour, he defeated Rick Rude in London, Aberdeen and Belfast, and 'Vinnie Vegas' (Kevin Nash) in Birmingham, Manchester and Dublin. The show was a commercial juggernaut by WCW's usual standards, as they sold out almost every arena and sold masses of merchandise, as families queued for hours for their Bulldog T-shirts, mugs and posters.

A long unbeaten run shot Davey to the top of the roster alongside Sting as the premier babyface. Sting (Steve Borden), was WCW's answer to Hulk Hogan – the charismatic, inspirational hero. With spiked blond hair and colourful face paint, he constantly battled the bigger villains. The two dominating monster heels were Big Van Vader and Sid Vicious. Vader, real name Leon White, was a boulder-like behemoth standing 6ft 5in tall and weighing well over 400lb. He was an agile super-heavyweight who had already held major titles the world over when WCW installed him as their main heel and therefore their champion in the summer of '92. He was legitimately feared by opponents because of his unrelenting and mercilessly stiff style; he didn't stomp his foot to disguise the lack of impact on his punches, he wore MMA-style gloves and bludgeoned the face of his foe, forcing them to genuinely duck and weave, creating a unique realism and intensity.

Meanwhile, Sid Vicious had been 'Sid Justice' in a brief Hogan-challenging run in the WWF. With a statuesque 6ft 9in physique, curly blond hair and a natural wide-eyed, deranged face, he was a booker's dream as a monster heel.

With two top-tier bad guys and only Sting opposing them until now, Davey Boy was the perfect arrival. When he returned from Japan at the end of April, Davey and Vader began to square off weekly with the title on the line and Davey often won by disqualification as the champion and his ringside manager Harley Race realised they couldn't beat the Bulldog so would take their sheer brutality too far. Davey was looking sensational. More tanned and muscular than ever and with white and gold tassels bouncing from his forearms, legs and boots, he appeared more the superhero than even the WWF had ever made him. The crowds gasped with amazement as he delivered his full arsenal of power moves on the gargantuan Vader, holding him perfectly vertical in the air for several seconds during his patented suplex and thrusting him on to his shoulder with relative ease for the running powerslam.

WCW was where Davey was first introduced to faces that would play a big part in his future and was reacquainted with ones from his past. Chris Benoit was wrestling there after completing his education in the New Japan dojo, evolving into every bit the 'Dynamite Kid Mark II' he had dreamt of becoming, performing sensationally in Japan as the 'Pegasus Kid' and winning the IWGP junior-heavyweight championship.

'Flyin'' Brian Pillman was a tag team champion in WCW alongside 'Stunning' Steve Austin as they riled the fans as the arrogant and rule-breaking 'Hollywood Blonds'. Mick Foley had forged his way through the lowly independent promotions and started at the bottom with All Japan and finally made it to the North American big leagues as Cactus Jack.

Davey and Sting, suddenly wearing matching red, white and blue sequined overcoats, partnered to battle Vader and Sid the whole summer. WCW had gone through some dramatic changes as they sought the formula that might topple a weakened and scandal-stricken WWF. They replaced executive vice president Bill Watts with former AWA announcer Eric Bischoff and decided that, rather than be the traditional wrestling alternative for the more mature viewer, they would fight Vince at his own game and go for a cartoonish product. This would lead to Davey, through no fault of his own, being involved in two of the most laughably notorious moments in wrestling TV history.

WCW shot a short movie to promote July's PPV *Beach Blast*, which began with an evil dwarf snorkelling surreptitiously to shore to plant a bomb, which looked like it may have been provided by Wile E. Coyote, into a beached speedboat. Cut to Davey and Sting having a chance seaside high-noon showdown with Vader, Sid and Harley Race. They shouted at and goaded each other before agreeing to see one another at *Beach Blast*, to the delight of the children supporting their heroic Uncle Bulldog and Uncle Sting.

The acting really should have come with a public health warning for anyone with an overly sensitive cringe nerve, as Sting climbed aboard the booby-trapped speedboat and Davey did his finest David Hasselhoff after being tipped off by a suspicious eight-year-old girl. Davey then launched into the air like Shamu and tackled his buddy from the boat as a tacky explosion filled the TV screen and the boat suddenly reappeared, a little charred. The children all cried and mourned on shore, until Davey and Sting leapt out of the water hand-in-hand, the sight of which brought about screams of joy on the beach.

WCW created a series of similar movie-style vignettes, one of which saw Cactus Jack as an escapee from a mental hospital after he was severely concussed by Vader. Mick Foley would be forced to portray the depraved character he had nurtured for almost a decade as the leader of a homeless posse who believed he was a veteran sailor fallen on hard times.

Their most infamous TV gaffe though, was completely unintentional. WCW continued to woo WWF 'Golden Era' talent in a desperate attempt to recreate the phenomenon and attract the fans over to their side. They had Ric Flair back, but due to contract settlements with the WWF, he was temporarily disallowed from in-ring competition, so they had him appearing in his uniquely charismatic manner as the host of TV talk-show segment *A Flair for the Gold*.

Davey and Sting appeared full of smiles and babyface bluster on the live TV show to announce who would be their secret team member for the upcoming 'War Games' match, only to be confronted by agitated opponents Sid and 'Harlem Heat' (Booker T and Stevie Ray). Shouting ensued and veins popped out, before Davey and Sting announced that their partner was going to 'Shock the world, because he was … The Shockmaster!'

Hokey pyrotechnic flames erupted from the side of the set, and as they died down a fat body fell through the cardboard wall to the floor, his Stormtrooper helmet (sprayed with silver glitter) falling off his head. Fred Ottman – WCWs latest signing, formerly 'Tugboat' and 'Typhoon' in Vince's world – stumbled to his feet, dusted off his helmet and put it back on. He was supposed to have burst through the wall dramatically, not fallen through it. There was deathly silence as the stars desperately held in their laughter and the no-longer secret nor intimidating partner stood awkwardly panting. Davey broke the silence when he could be heard murmuring, in his thickest Lancastrian accent, 'He fell on his arse. He fell on his fuckin' arse!'

The autumn brought about another European tour, which had been hurriedly organised on the heels of the previous success. Davey's presence enabled WCW to sell out the Royal Albert Hall for both a matinee and an evening show on 30 October before a seven-day tour of Germany.

He had become a mainstream superstar in the UK, although somewhat fabled by his geographic absence from his homeland. When back on British shores, national media outlets scrambled for exclusive interviews and access to him, and he was invited as a guest on to prime-time TV chat shows and game shows. Within the wrestling business, he became known as the UK's answer to Hulk Hogan.

In singles or teaming with either Flair or Sting, Davey typically won all his matches in Europe against the likes of Vader, Rick Rude, 'Lord' Steven Regal and the Hollywood Blonds. But on his return to the US, Bischoff and the new hierarchy refused to honour the verbal agreement Davey had made with Bill Watts and paid him his standard

$1,000 per night with zero bonuses. When Davey no-showed for four house shows in protest, a standoff quickly turned into something more serious and Davey was fired for the second consecutive winter. In a final parting burial, the WCW announcers claimed on air that the Bulldog was in the building but was too cowardly to come out and face Rick Rude, his scheduled opponent before the firing had taken place.

Things were about to get much worse for Davey. A couple of weeks later, Bret called Davey and Diana in Florida for a pre-Christmas holiday chat but ended up being the one to break the news to them that Davey was a wanted man by the Calgary police.

32

SUMMERSLAMMER

'It was a case of a high-profile celebrity being in the wrong place at the wrong time. Although Davey did not initiate this conflict, he did what most men would do in such a situation, which was defend his wife from a belligerent drunk who was looking for a fight.'

Ross Hart

FIVE MONTHS earlier. 25 July 1993. The Back Alley nightclub, Calgary.

'When a beautiful chick like you and a geek like that are screwing, who's on top?' a young man slurred at Diana as she danced playfully with the teenage son of some friends. They were back in Calgary from Florida for Davey to see his doctor about his worsening back. Davey and Diana rarely went out while back in Calgary for weekends, due to fan attention, but had agreed to briefly swing by this particular bar to say hello to some friends, who wanted to impress other friends by their acquaintance with the wrestling superstar and the local beauty queen. Diana had invited the shy son of their friends on to the dance floor to alleviate his boredom.

'Ignore this idiot, Adam,' Diana said, turning away from the sleazy drunk, who moved closer to her. Davey happened to be walking over, patrons parting like the Red Sea to let his huge frame by. He raised his wrist and tapped his watch, indicating he thought it was time they left.

259

'Hey, I'm talking to the lady,' said the man – 20-year-old Kody Light.

'That's my husband!' Diana snapped.

'That's my wife!' Davey said, shocked at the cockiness of Light.

'Well you got a nice fucking wife,' Light goaded and grabbed Davey's hand. Davey gave Light a few seconds to let go, but the grip only got tighter. Suddenly, Davey used his free hand to force Light's head down into a front face-lock. Now it was Davey's grip that was getting tighter as he wrenched Light towards the doormen. Confident the bouncers were in a position to take over, Davey let go of his hold. A struggling Light shot upright, and when a combination of his excessive alcohol levels and the blood rushing back to his head caused him to collapse backward, his skull cracked like a dropped melon on the hard floor, with shards of broken glass piercing his head.

Light's friends came dashing over from one direction, the bouncers from the other. With an ambulance on its way, the doormen ushered Davey and Diana out of the back door before the situation escalated further.

Kody Light spent 47 days in hospital, much of it in a coma. He emerged with permanent brain injury, deafness in one ear and slurred speech – and he was pressing charges.

So, Davey returned to Calgary from Florida and turned himself in. He spent a weekend behind bars before bail was arranged. Diana put up $7,000 to get him out and then Stu put up $500,000 so that he could get his passport back and seek out wrestling work somewhere around the world; he couldn't work for the two North American giants and the independent Canadian territories were broke, so he would have to travel for reasonable employment.

In the UK, Shirley Crabtree had finally retired in 1993 at the age of 62. Until then he had still been the face of his brother Max's roadshow – still doing his belly-butts and one-minute cameos to wrap up the events in half-empty small venues. Max thought he had struck gold when he got the call from Davey declaring his availability. On 2 February 1994, Davey began an initial three-month tour of the UK in Gravesend, where he would play the former Big Daddy role – albeit performing for slightly longer and more impressively. He arranged with Max to have his own merchandise stall, where he would spend much of the shows posing for pictures and signing 8 x 10s.

On just the second show of the tour, Davey was to make his homecoming at Howe Bridge – just five miles from Wigan. His family came to the show, including one member that was not invited. Tom heard about the show and prepared himself to finally confront Davey. His father Billy was terminally ill with cancer, and about to die, having never spoken to his sister Joyce – Davey's mum – again after the breakdown of the Bulldogs.

Tom made his arrival at the venue known by tipping over the merchandise table, leaving picture cards of Davey strewn all over the hall. Tom was especially furious after hearing he could no longer legally wrestle as a British Bulldog, with Davey owning the trademark.

'All right, where is he?' Tom yelled at Davey's dad, who had just set up the table.

'He's not here yet, Tommy,' replied Sid.

'If you're here, he's here! Now, where is he?' Tom insisted, but before the situation had a chance to escalate any further, two police cars screeched to a halt outside. Someone had called them the moment they realised Tom was on his way; when they arrived, Tom was dragged out of the building in handcuffs.

Billy Billington would pass away two months later, at the age of just 59.

Despite the fact they all lived in the same streets, firm battle lines had been drawn between the Smiths and the Billingtons. Later in the year, Tom heard that Davey's brother Terrence had been telling people around the local pubs that the once great Dynamite Kid was 'only ten stone wet through these days' and so went to his house and gave him a Tommy Billington-speciality crack around the jaw for showing such disrespect.

On both occasions, Davey restrained himself from any personal confrontation with Tom as he couldn't risk being provoked into a physical altercation that would give the prosecution of his assault charge in Calgary further ammunition.

* * *

Owen's stellar work had seen him finally emerge as a singles star in the WWF. He had once again applied to the Calgary fire department in a bid to escape the business, but his wrestling talent continued to shine through, and with Bret a solid influence on him and within the WWF, he had agreed to continue. He now wore black wrestling gear with pink trim and sunglasses like Bret as the two formed a team to compete at the top of the roster. But, in character, Owen began to act petty and jealous of Bret's popularity and stardom. A brilliantly portrayed heel turn saw the brothers Hart ignite a long-running and ultimately thrilling feud. Owen beat Bret at *WrestleMania X*, but that didn't stop the older sibling winning the WWF championship from Yokozuna in the main event. As every babyface in the locker room celebrated wildly in the ring with Bret, for him having achieved the impossible in defeating Yoko, the show ended with Owen staring enviously at his brother and whispering, 'What about me?'

Davey sat watching Bret and Owen tear the house down from his mum and dad's in Golborne, and immediately turned to Diana and said, 'I need to get back there.' He had loved spending time back home with the parents he was so close to and had missed, enjoying his mum's full English breakfasts on a morning, going to his favourite Indian restaurant on an evening and catching up with old friends such as weightlifting mentor Walter O'Malley. The British tour was going quite well, as Diana set up office in the Smith family home, taking care of the bookings, paperwork and logistics. But seeing his friends and brothers-in-law in spectacular action on the grandest stage brought about a realisation.

Just days later, the telephone rang at the house and when Joyce answered, a deep, loud, American voice boomed down the receiver, 'Is Davey home ma'am?'

'Yes, who's calling please?'

'It's Terry.'

'David!' Joyce called out, 'Terry is on the phone!'

'Terry who?' Davey bellowed back.

'Terry who, sorry?' Joyce asked.

'Oh, just tell him it's Hulk.' Joyce's jaw dropped as she realised it was Hulk Hogan calling. She put down the receiver and dashed to Davey. 'It's Hulk bloody Hogan!' she said.

Hogan told Davey that he was now with WCW and was being paid a king's ransom. They had become good friends during their time as top babyfaces in the WWF and now Hulk wanted Davey to join him with the rival promotion so that they could work together at the top of the bill. Davey told Hulk what had happened with Eric Bischoff and that he didn't trust Bischoff enough to work for him again. Hulk assured Davey that he was as good as in charge, with creative control written into his contract.

The call ended with Davey confident that, one way or the other, he would be returning to work in the US; but he still longed to go back to his wrestling home of the WWF and re-join Bret and Owen. He would just have to wait patiently to see where the chips would fall.

Owen won the 1994 'King of the Ring' tournament in June and gave himself the moniker the 'King of the Harts'. Jim Neidhart had been rehired to join Owen on his envy-filled vendetta against Bret, which was booked to climax at *SummerSlam*.

The Hart family had appeared on TV in attendance multiple times during the programme – other than Jim they were all seemingly upset with Owen's actions and firmly behind golden boy Bret.

After a brief return to Calgary, Davey brought his family to the UK again in the summer for another tour throughout July and August. Whilst there, they got the news: Vince McMahon had finally been acquitted of his steroid trafficking charges. The heat had officially cooled. The British Bulldog was suddenly able to get involved in the family war.

SummerSlam
29 August 1994
United Center
Chicago, Illinois
WWF Championship
Owen Hart v Bret 'Hitman' Hart
Attendance: 23,000

With the iconic blue steel cage erected around the ring, Vince McMahon and Jerry 'The King' Lawler took a stroll from their commentary table to the corner of the ramp, where a huge area was filled with the brothers, sisters, in-laws and children from the Hart dynasty.

They began by asking the matriarch of the family what she thought of the current chaos. Helen told of the 'fever' that she believed had taken over Owen. Stu, sitting next to her, added that the better man would win on the night. The camera panned around and gave the TV audience a glimpse of an incredibly jacked-up and bronzed Davey with his frizzy hair resting on his huge shoulders. When Lawler dashed around to get his thoughts, Davey made it clear he was firmly in Bret's corner. Bruce and Ross were right behind him, both physically and with their support for Bret.

Jim Neidhart, however, looked on angrily, before getting his turn on the mic to bark his hatred towards the champion and his support for Owen.

Dave Meltzer awarded the match five stars, an unbelievable achievement given the inherent technical limitations of a cage match. For over 30 minutes the brothers put on a suspenseful masterclass of near-escapes and big bumps. The crowd, and the family, erupted with joy when Bret leapt down to the floor, leaving Owen dangling upside-down from the cage. While Davey and Diana celebrated, Jim cheap-shotted them from behind, sending both crashing over the railings before going on to attack Bret and drag him back inside and lock the cage.

The brothers frantically tried to scale the structure to save Bret, as Owen and Jim saw them off like they were playing a game of whack-a-mole. That was until Davey got to his feet, ripped off his shirt to reveal himself bigger than ever, a bespectacled Greek god, and climbed the cage. With that the crowd knew: the British Bulldog was back.

Just two weeks later, Davey was back in the UK as a key member of the 'Hart Attack Tour', which saw him and Bret team up to defeat Owen and Jim in tag matches to raucous crowds in London, Aberdeen, Hull and Birmingham. The Stampede boys were trampling their own furrow through the top of the wrestling world – all without their main inspiration and leader during their formative years: the Dynamite Kid.

Despite having a serious aggravated assault charge hanging over him, Davey was being pushed strongly as he went on a long unbeaten run, going over regularly against not only Jim and Owen but a range of other upper-mid-carders too.

But the WWF was struggling. Financially, they had cut their cloth accordingly, and with Ted Turner's billions being thrown at the veteran star names, many had joined Hogan and jumped to the opposition ship.

The dearth of top-tier talent led to Vince turning to an old but reliable name to fill a slot at the top of the card: Bob Backlund.

When Backlund had refused to drop the WWF championship to Hulk Hogan 11 years earlier, he agreed instead to lose it to the Iron Sheik, who would act as the transitional champion for Hogan to defeat. To help Backlund maintain his credentials after a five-year title reign, they had him refuse to submit whilst in the inescapable camel clutch. Mercifully, his manager Arnold Skaaland threw in the towel. The WWF bookers cleverly brought this storyline back to the fore, as 45-year-old Backlund snapped after more than a decade of resentment against not only Skaaland, but also current champion Bret, claiming he had never really lost the belt. A demented Backlund began attacking anyone and everyone with his cross-face chicken-wing submission hold and refusing to let go.

This led to a 'Throw-in-the-Towel' championship match at *Survivor Series*, in which Owen would be in the challenger's corner armed with a towel, and Davey Boy in Bret's as Stu and Helen sat ringside.

During the match, Owen and Davey clashed on the outside, which led to Bulldog being down-and-out following a head-on collision with the steel ring steps. Backlund synched the chicken-wing on a concerned and distracted Bret. Owen feigned brotherly concern and regret as the agonising minutes piled up with seemingly no one even able to throw in the towel for Bret. Owen then dragged Stu and Helen to ringside and handed them the towel; fighting man Stu refused but Helen's maternal instinct forced her to fall for the ruse, ending Bret's second championship reign after eight months.

Earlier in the show, Davey and Owen had been on opposite teams in a traditional *Survivor Series* elimination tag match, which saw the relationship between Shawn Michaels and his 'bodyguard' Diesel (Kevin Nash) terminally break down, as the handsome and smooth 'Big Daddy Cool', already a popular figure, turned babyface.

Just three days later, Diesel would squash Backlund in 18 seconds to win the title. All this was cunningly planned as the company worked the angles to culminate in their desired line-up for *WrestleMania XI*.

Diesel and Shawn Michaels had been the tag team champions but vacated the titles as they embarked on a feud against each other. Rumour had it that Owen and Jim were pencilled in to win the planned tournament to crown the next champions, but Jim's wild lifestyle continued, and he failed to turn up for some shows. As a result, they were instead eliminated in the opening round and Jim was fired again soon afterwards.

Behind the scenes, Davey was somewhat falling apart. The criminal case being built against him, which carried a seven- to 14-year prison sentence if he was to be found guilty, was now compounded with a simultaneous civil lawsuit for $1.3 million for Light's injury and medical expense compensation. Davey was also left heartbroken at the news that his beloved mum Joyce was terminally ill with stomach cancer, to add to sister Tracey's lifelong dignified battle with brain cancer. His perennial lower back problems were agonising. Davey added Carisoprodol (known by its brand name Soma) to his daily arsenal. Soma was used for musculoskeletal pain and worked by potently relaxing the muscles, with obvious side effects of dizziness and severe drowsiness. The drug quickly became popular amongst the wrestlers as a new antidote to their daily agonies.

Royal Rumble
22 January 1995
Sun Dome
Tampa, Florida
Attendance: 10,000

Glamour icon Pamela Anderson was showcased to the crowd and sat at ringside in her skin-tight dinner dress as part of the prize on offer for the winner, as she would chaperone them to the ring for their WWF championship main event match at *WrestleMania*.

As the camera finally zoomed out from Pamela's awkwardly seated body, Shawn Michaels' unmistakable 'Sexy Boy' entrance theme hit. He was the first of the 30 entrants. He pranced and grinded his hips in the ring in ways that would even make Pamela blush. His music was finally faded out and replaced with 'Rule Britannia'. Davey Boy was the number two entrant. Neither would surely have a chance of outlasting the 28 that were still to come at 60 second intervals.

Having wrestled countless times, Shawn and Davey began to work away in impressive fashion. But the current weak and gimmick-filled roster was soon exposed. Eli Blu was followed by Duke 'The Dumpster' Droese; Doink the Clown by Kwang; Bushwhacker Luke by Jacob Blu. Seemingly no entrant was a plausible winner other than the initial two. Mabel came and went, as did Mantaur. Bret had challenged Diesel for the championship earlier in the show with the match ending in a melee as Shawn, Owen and Backlund hit the ring to attack their nemeses; the Undertaker had also had a singles match, so all of them were not entrants in the Rumble match itself.

After 38 minutes of action only the sweatier versions of the opening two combatants remained, having seen off all of the competition.

Davey and Shawn went to war again, with the Bulldog immediately dominating. He had a jaded Shawn literally on the ropes as he energetically bounced off the opposite side of the ring and at full momentum, clotheslined HBK over the top rope. 'Rule Britannia' hit and an exhausted Davey climbed a turnbuckle to celebrate. But Spiderman-like, Michaels had clung on to the top rope and only one foot had touched the floor. He managed to roll legally back into the ring and simply shove Davey down from the turnbuckle to the floor to be declared the official winner. Pamela briefly got in the ring with HBK, but soon exited when he turned on his Chippendale routine to his self-sung theme tune.

With the Bret–Backlund programme running all the way to *WrestleMania*, where the main event would be Shawn challenging Diesel and the Undertaker taking on his annual monster heel – this time King Kong Bundy – others were left in limbo.

With his tag partner fired, this counted for Owen as well as Davey. Also, Yokozuna needed something to do now that he had been replaced by both Shawn and Backlund as the company's top heels. There was also another former main eventer at a loose end, even if his career at the top had been extraordinarily brief: Lex Luger.

Lawrence Wendell Pfohl had been a football prodigy, but when his gridiron career fell short he turned to pro wrestling and became Lex Luger. With the help of steroids and an addiction to bodybuilding, he sculpted himself a body that appeared to have been chiselled from stone. He took great delight in bronzing and oiling his muscles and, with a square jaw and blond bangs, he knew that his aesthetics covered up for his lack of top-level wrestling ability. Luger left WCW and joined the WWF as an arrogant heel in 'The Narcissist'. But Vince, still not convinced that the fans were correct in organically promoting Bret into the main babyface position, had turned Lex into an All-American boy with the tagline 'Made in the USA' and shoehorned him into all the main events to challenge Yokozuna for the title.

But the novelty had soon worn off; just like Hogan before him, Lex's matches were short, predictable and laden with the same lazy nationalism-based trope. Fans had become used to Bret's long-form dramatic in-ring storytelling. Bret was soon back in the top position and would not be ousted for many years, becoming the first pro wrestler since Hogan to transcend the business, as he appeared on TV chat shows, had a regular weekly column in the *Calgary Sun* and even made a famous guest appearance on *The Simpsons*.

With the experiment of him as *the man* failed, Lex was exposed and at a loose end. He and Davey initially tagged together by chance against teams made up of united adversaries, but with their similar physiques and almost identical red, white and blue ring attire, they soon became an official tag team as the 'Allied Powers'.

Owen – a rival of Davey's – and Yokozuna – a previous enemy of Lex's – were thrown together as odd-ball, comedic heel tag team champions and the two new teams were set on a collision course. By default, Owen became part of 'Camp Cornette' – the stable of spoilt brat and machine-gun mouthed manager Jim Cornette.

The Allied Powers versus Camp Cornette became an entertaining summer staple, with the heels always managing to sneak away with their titles intact.

CAMP CORNETTE

'I don't think anybody understands how great an athlete
that [Davey] really was … he could do everything and even
though he put on so much weight to have the body, he still
moved like a light-heavyweight and he had such flexibility
and he was so strong at the same time; he was just a special
athlete in the ring. He was like a big kid and him and Owen
together, it lightened up the mood because they were always
happier getting into the mischief.'

Jim Cornette

21 August 1995. *Monday Night Raw*

'My partner, Lex Luger, had to go home for a medical emergency,
back to Atlanta,' Davey began into Vince McMahon's microphone
in the middle of the ring as Diesel stood beside them carrying his
championship belt. 'And we've got Mo and Mabel earlier, challenging
the Allied Powers. Now if Lex was here and I wasn't, I know what he'd
do; he'd go to work and he'd find the best partner he could ever find
in the World Wrestling Federation. Would you people like to see the
British Bulldog and Big Daddy Cool take on Mo and Mabel?!'

With the crowd frenzied at the thought of two of their favourites
joining forces, the match was on. Diesel was due to be defending his
title the following week against the supposed 568lb 'King Mabel' at
SummerSlam. Diesel started the match by bouncing Mo from pillar to
post with Davey a merry cheerleader. With Mo unable to mount any

offence, Mabel stepped effortlessly over the top rope and Diesel turned to face him as Davey also climbed into the ring to keep the numbers even. The crowd roared at the thought of getting an early glimpse of the two giants going at it, but suddenly, the Bulldog charged into the back of Diesel with a huge clothesline, sending him into the arms and the patented sidewalk slam of Mabel. The crowd were aghast. They'd known Davey Boy Smith for more than a decade and he'd only ever being an upstanding and honourable member of society – for the first time in his career (save for being a *gaijin* in Japan), Davey had turned heel.

It was soon clear who was behind such treachery, as Jim Cornette, clad in a typically garish red and yellow suit and armed with his trusty squash racquet, joined the new members of his 'camp' as they took it in turns to slam and crush Diesel.

If it appeared to the world that Davey had deserted Lex in pursuit of bigger things when he literally abandoned him in their next tag match, behind the scenes the roles were reversed. Lex was in talks with Eric Bischoff about a return to WCW. Bischoff insisted on the deal remaining secret so that it made as big a splash as possible when he unveiled Luger on the opening edition of WCW's new flagship show *Monday Nitro* – which had been scheduled to go out live on TNT and head-to-head with *Monday Night Raw*. A new and recognised way of determining who was winning the wrestling war was established in the TV ratings of every Monday night.

Just three days after participating in a WWF match, to the shock of everyone – Vince McMahon included – Lex Luger strolled out on *Nitro* in what would be the first of many shots fired during the live simulcast over the next few years. Two Stampede luminaries and Dynamite Kid-inspired stars opened the first ever *Nitro*, as Brian Pillman and Jushin 'Thunder' Liger set the standard with a barnstorming fusion of high flying and hard hitting.

* * *

'I can't wait for us to work together again, now I've turned,' Davey said as he sat drinking beer in a bar with Bret. 'But the fuckin' Kliq's taking over,' he sighed. 'Fuckin' Shawn; he's barely 200lb sopping wet!'

'Shawn's a decent guy, but he's got his little hang-ups,' Bret replied. 'Unfortunately, one of them is being an asshole.'

Davey had shaved off his permed locks in favour of a military-style buzz-cut to match his new no-nonsense heel persona. As the evening wore on, Bret noticed Davey was laughing like he had in the old days as they reminisced. When Davey tried to grab the bartender's attention, Bret jabbed him in the ribs just after he'd reminded him of the time Jim had put fisheyes in the pockets of Davey's baggy pants. Davey missed his shot at getting served; his big dimples had been indented in his face so long that his cheeks had begun to ache.

The clique they were referring to was the powerful Shawn-led locker-room faction that had evolved containing Diesel (Kevin Nash), Razor Ramon (Scott Hall), 'the 1-2-3 Kid' (Sean Waltman) and a newcomer from WCW in Hunter Hearst Helmsley (Paul Levesque). They had become such an insular group that they nicknamed themselves 'the Kliq' in order to make their comradeship official. Shawn had long had the ear of Vince, declaring himself a WWF diehard soldier with unwavering loyalty as more stars began flirting with, or even jumping to the bitter opposition in WCW. He was an exceptional performer but was seen as arrogant and temperamental outside of his own select group.

The five of them travelled, roomed and partied together and also seemed to have gained a lot of creative control over their angles and therefore, over the whole roster by association. They manipulated their way to title reigns and main events and therefore, the higher-paying slots. Shawn, now a popular babyface, even began referring to his fanbase as the Kliq as an inside joke and insinuation that they had taken over the show.

Assholes or not, that didn't stop Davey partying with two-fifths of the group after he had battled Shawn for the Intercontinental title on 13 October in Binghampton, New York. Half of the roster was in Europe, including Diesel, Razor and Hunter, so Davey was travelling with Shawn and the 1-2-3 Kid. They decided to have a night on the tiles as they stopped over in Syracuse and found themselves blindly intoxicated in Club 37, situated in the Ponderosa Plaza.

Unable to get a taxi to take them back to their hotel at closing time on a Friday night, one of the bouncers asked his girlfriend to take them back – keen to get them out of there as Shawn had apparently managed to piss off a group of guys by flirting with their girls.

Another patron had tagged along with them for a free ride home too. As they drunkenly fumbled their way into the small two-door car, footsteps from behind them began to get ominously louder.

'Hey! Fag!' one of the pissed-off guys suddenly shouted. Davey found himself wedged in the back between Waltman and their guest (a Robert Jones) as Shawn was climbing into the passenger seat. Suddenly, Shawn was dragged to the ground and beaten mercilessly with fists and boots and slammed into the concrete floor and the car bumper. Davey frantically attempted to get his huge frame out of the car but was blocked in every direction by bodies and car seats. When he finally got out, he threw one of the attackers from a helpless and bloodied Michaels with ease. Davey was then leg-dived by another, who he soon had in a tight front face-lock, but yet another came around his back and eye-gouged him. Davey let go of his hold and spun around to engage his latest attacker.

In the meantime, their driver, Donna Jones, had dashed back to the club to get her bouncer boyfriend, who arrived back on the scene with a colleague in tow and the perpetrators scarpered in two white Ford Broncos, which sped off with a screech of their wheels, almost running down one of the doormen.

Shawn was rushed to hospital and treated for concussion and severe lacerations to his face; he would be out of action for three weeks and forced to forfeit the Intercontinental title. Davey, though, worked the very next night in Syracuse, walking out with a blackened and bloodshot eye. In keeping with the wrestling business, rumours of what had actually happened that night were quickly exaggerated, with the attackers soon becoming off-duty marines and as many as ten in number.

Just the following week, Davey challenged for the WWF championship in the main event of a pay-per-view for the very first time as he went up against Diesel.

Bret Hart was on commentary at *In Your House 4*, and he was drawn physically into the action when it spilled to the outside. After Davey lumped him one around the ear, Bret gave chase back into the ring and inflicted some ground-and-pound on his brother-in-law to the delight of the crowd. But the referee called a halt to the match, disqualifying the champion for Bret's interference. This resulted in a fracas between the disgruntled champion and the Hitman.

Diesel's popularity was running on fumes after almost a whole year of him carrying the belt nonchalantly by his side, and when Bret rolled him up to win his third championship at *Survivor Series*, the crowd popped wildly. That served to finally build the rematch that the world had waited more than three years to see, but this time, it would be the big belt on the line: Bret Hart versus the British Bulldog.

In Your House 5: *Seasons Beatings*
17 December 1995
Hersheypark Arena
Hershey, Pennsylvania
WWF Championship
The British Bulldog v Bret 'Hitman' Hart
Attendance: 7,289

'Bret Hart, you've been jealous of this man since the first day you laid eyes on him in 1981!' Jim Cornette screeched in Jim Ross's microphone as Davey flexed his oiled-up muscles and Diana stood behind him as the dutiful wife. 'Calgary Stampede Wrestling, he came in a fresh-faced hotshot kid from England; he stole your thunder, he stole your fans, he stole your father Stu Hart's respect; when Stu Hart came up and patted him on the back and said, "Davey, you're just like a son to me," that stuck a knife in your guts, punk! Then your sister fell in love with him and decided to get married. She used to be thinking that you were her hero, but all of a sudden, she had a new hero, Bret! Then he took your Intercontinental title; tonight, he's gonna make it a clean sweep, he's gonna give that knife another twist, punk, and Bret Hart, you're goin' down at the hands of the man you've never beaten – the British Bulldog!'

Even by pro wrestling and kayfabe standards, this was a stretch. Falsely claiming that someone had never been beaten, or beaten by a particular opponent, was commonplace, but almost never true. André the Giant, of course, had apparently never lost before his encounter with those 24-inch pythons at *WrestleMania III*, when he had in fact been beaten (and slammed) many, many times before. In pre-internet days and the easily forgettable results of house shows and dark matches, these claims were easy to make and difficult to disprove, and promotions were helpless to stop others booking their monster heel on a losing streak, so why shouldn't they make such claims?

On this occasion, however, Bret had not only beaten Davey several times, he'd actually pinned him in a successful title defence just two days prior, but at a non-WWF event. Rather, it was a Stampede show – of sorts. Bruce and Ross Hart had decided to put on a charity show to celebrate and commemorate Stu's 80th birthday. They had hoped to attract as many of the old Stampede stars as possible and, naturally, Bret, Owen and Davey wanted to be involved. Vince generously sanctioned his talent to be there and Razor Ramon defended his Intercontinental title against Owen, while Bret was booked to defend his world title against Davey in the main event. The fact that the WWF and WCW, in the midst of a bitter and ruthless ratings war, both allowed their stars to take part showed the immense respect the Hart family – Stu in particular – commanded within the industry. Bruce even booked their respective talents against each other in a 'WWF versus WCW' match, which saw Chris Benoit defeat Rad Radford (Davey's WWF running-mate Louie Spicolli). Bruce also revived his tag team 'Bad Company' alongside Brian Pillman, as they wrestled the Funk brothers for a raucous crowd that filled the Corral like the old days. Veteran Keith Hart squared off with young prodigy the 1-2-3 Kid. Bret and Davey wrestled a hearty 13-minute match which ended when Davey attempted to lock in Bret's own sharpshooter, but the plan backfired when he was rolled up for the one, two, three.

Like Dynamite, Davey's angry heel promos were better than his awkward babyface ones, and he garnered heat with his new trademark of ending interviews by growling the final words whilst pumping his muscles into the camera so vigorously he would turn red and veins would pop from beneath his skin.

Diana had become a staple part of the product, forever at one side of Davey, with Cornette at the other. She was a stabilising influence on her husband on- and off-screen as he prepared for the most important battles of his life, also both on- and off-screen. More than two-and-a-half years after the incident, Davey's assault trial would begin at the end of January 1996. The anxiety of the possible outcome and cost of his defence – already threatening to ruin him – had increased his substance abuse and reliance on drugs, especially Soma and other downers and relaxants.

Bret thought long and hard about how to make the match as good as Wembley; their names, when said in the same sentence, were synonymous with that magical chemistry and conjured up iconic memories in the fans' minds. Neither of them wanted to sully that with a poorer display. It called for something different, something the WWF fans hadn't seen in a long time, something their Calgary matches *always* had: blood.

After 15 minutes of fast-paced toing and froing, Bret set Davey up on the top turnbuckle for a superplex, but Davey called upon his superhuman strength and hurled Bret up towards him before launching and crotching him on the top rope. The crowd gasped in awe as colour commentator Jerry Lawler declared the match over and the British Bulldog must be the new champion. Whilst all eyes, and cameras, were on the impressive Davey as he paced the ring, Bret was face down on the outside, surreptitiously spitting up the shard of razor blade he had concealed in his mouth and digging it deep into his hairline. Davey climbed out of the ring as Bret stumbled to his feet with his long sweaty hair still hiding the blood. Davey then launched Bret head-first into the steel steps and soon, the blue mats and Bret's face were smeared with freely dripping claret – with the fans believing it was the impact with the steps that had caused the deep gash. With intentional bleeding embargoed as Vince tried to maintain a cleaner-cut image and keep network executives happy, the fans hadn't seen this level of bloodshed in a long time and reacted to it like hungry sharks. When Bret attempted to catapult himself on to Davey on the outside of the ring, Davey caught him on his shoulder with ease and running powerslammed him into a puddle of his own blood. Soon, both men, the mats on the outside and the ring canvas were all completely smeared red, and the fans were in a state of frenzy.

'Time to go home,' Bret whispered to Davey before applying a rare *la magistral* cradle on Davey for the one, two, three. But Davey had still never submitted to the sharpshooter and he rolled quietly out of the ring with no typical post-match heel shenanigans; he walked up the ramp solemnly, with respect and sympathy from not just his wife, but the audience too.

Just like for their Wembley classic, the *Wrestling Observer Newsletter* awarded the match four-and-a-half stars, and many purists believe they achieved the impossible in having an even better match more than three years on.

Davey's schedule was soon lightened as he was given time to prepare for the imminent trial. This was reflected in a lesser *Royal Rumble* involvement; whilst still in the final four, he entered in the penultimate position and lasted just four minutes. Shawn won the match for the second consecutive year, meaning he would challenge Bret for the title at *WrestleMania XII*.

34

THE TRIAL

'The trial, which was in its seventh day, was expected to go into closing arguments on 6 February after making headlines throughout Canada during the first week because the prosecutor forced Smith, on the witness stand, to admit pro wrestling was fake.'

Dave Meltzer

FROM THE opening statements, Crown Prosecutor Gary Belecki painted the picture of a muscle-bound professional fighter, performing wrestling manoeuvres in which he was highly trained on a much smaller, younger man. The victim and his witnesses spoke of Davey performing a jackknife powerbomb on Kody Light, lifting and launching him across the club, with a head-first landing causing the life-changing injuries. Peter MacKenzie, a friend of Light's, testified that Davey had punched Light in the face before applying the headlock and ramming his head into a wall.

Belecki, keen to add the successful prosecution of a local wrestling superstar to his resumé, animatedly pressed home his theories, theatrically building to dramatic climaxes so convincing, that Davey's two young children were forced to get up and leave the courtroom.

Of the 12 eyewitnesses called to testify, only three supported the prosecution's claim that Davey had been overly aggressive, and their accounts differed as to which wrestling move he had used. In contrast, the witness accounts of those called by the defence gave largely similar versions: that Davey had engaged Light in a tight headlock and walked him towards the bouncers, and when he let go, Light had stumbled backwards and fallen. A bouncer also testified that Light had been warned earlier in the evening about harassing female patrons.

Yet Belecki's blows regarding Davey being a super-strong trained combatant appeared to be landing when placed against the sympathetic backdrop of a brain-damaged victim. He attempted to discredit the defence eyewitnesses, including Diana as he intimated she could be lying to keep her husband out of jail so that he could continue to bring home the big pay-cheques that kept her in the lifestyle that she led.

When Davey himself took to the stand, nervous and uncomfortable in his oversized suit, Belecki pressed him on what excessive force he may have used in the alleged assault of the victim.

Davey, previously one of kayfabe's final bastions, countered by insisting that the types of move he was being accused of using could only be performed with the cooperation of his opponent, before stunning onlookers into silence by saying: 'Every single thing in wrestling is fake.'

Writing this just a quarter of a century later, in a social media age where wrestlers flow in and out of character in full view of the public, appear in 'shoot' interviews in which they speak of their desire to 'work' with someone because they are such good friends; a world in which kayfabe is long extinct, it feels slightly ludicrous that this bombshell should rock a courtroom. There had been numerous exposés by retired or bitter old wrestlers, but in the pre-internet age, they had been largely swept under the ring apron. Whilst almost everyone knew it was predetermined, no current top-level star had ever said so on public record, especially not in such an all-encompassing and matter-of-fact manner.

'To put it bluntly, you are a fraud to the public,' Belecki changed the direction of his attack.

'If you want to put it that way,' Davey responded.

'You are putting on a show for Calgary and the world now, aren't you?' Belecki teased, now using Davey's profession to bring his character into question.

Davey assured Judge Jack Waite, who would be making the verdict in the non-jury trial, that he was telling the truth.

Veteran Stampede heel Gama Singh (Gadabra Sahota) was called as an expert witness for the defence and reiterated that Davey Boy was correct in saying that he wouldn't have been able to perform the type of moves described by the prosecution on a non-consenting foe.

The trial was already big news in Calgary, but the pro wrestling revelations had led to it being splashed across front pages internationally. Reading all about the latest developments, which were making an acquittal seem inevitable, was a man with a long-standing grudge against the Hart family. The following day, the prosecution called a surprising new witness to the stand. Into the courtroom, still looking every bit the biker in his faded blue jeans and bandana, walked Karl Moffat. Davey cast glances to equally shocked members of his family as Moffat went on to claim that Davey was definitely strong enough to perform a powerbomb on someone even without their cooperation.

Belecki then called Calgary Police Officer Sydney Sutherland, who had witnessed the incident for which Davey had been charged back in 1983. Sutherland told Judge Waite how he saw the accused, as a much smaller man than he appeared now, toss his partner almost six feet across the street with relative ease.

Suddenly, the acquittal didn't look so assured.

The defence put Ross Hart on the stand in an attempt to discredit Moffat's testimony. Moffat had tried to sue the Harts and the insurance company of Budget Rentals, who had supplied the van that Ross had crashed, severely injuring Davey but seemingly ending Moffat's promising wrestling career by breaking his leg. According to Ross, around 12 months after the accident, the insurance company offered Moffat a large settlement figure, but it was declined as Moffat held out for more in long-term damages. Suspicious of his activities, the insurers hired an investigator to track Moffat to see if his injuries were genuine. They had apparently captured footage of him dirt-biking, wrestling training and working cash-in-hand for a moving company. Moffat was forced to accept a much smaller settlement, and immediately began wrestling again on the independent circuit, but never fulfilled the early promise he had shown. He held a grudge and felt bitter towards the Hart family.

With Ross's testimony and further evidence given by Davey, where he informed the judge that Moffat had once been fired by New Japan for slashing the tyres of a company bus when he had become disgruntled, Moffat's credibility as a character witness was brought into question.

Davey's excellent defence team, led by lawyer Alain Hepner, continued to thwart the prosecution's often wild and inconsistent theories and accusations by sticking to the simple facts that the most reliable witnesses were clear in their testimonies that Davey had acted in self-defence and that the wrestling manoeuvres it was being claimed Davey had used simply could not have been carried out in that environment.

The key witness turned out to be Dr John Butt, Alberta's former chief medical examiner. Dr Butt had been initially brought to the case by the prosecution, as they believed his expert testimony would attest to their theory that Light's skull fracture had been caused by him being manhandled and thrown. But they then had the trial delayed largely because of Dr Butt's report: that the fracture just above the neck, which had caused partial deafness, slurred speech and impairment of motor functions, intellect and memory, was consistent with someone who had simply fallen backwards.

When asked under oath if he thought the injury could've been sustained by the type of assault described by the prosecution, Dr Butt said, 'I find it difficult to see how somebody is going to land that low on their head, but I can't deny the possibility,' and also confirmed, 'It's a classic injury for people falling backwards on a hard surface.'

'The accused's conduct can be properly categorised as self-defence,' Judge Waite said as he summarised on 7 February. 'The rights of a professional wrestler are no different than those of an average citizen.' The judge confirmed he had sympathy with the plight of Kody Light, but acquitted Davey Boy of any wrongdoing.

The flood of relief for Davey and his young family was overwhelming, but the verdict didn't lift all of the agony caused by more than two years of hell. The defence had cost Davey and Diana half a million dollars and the stress and anxiety had increased his reliance on strong prescription drugs. Diana was homesick in Florida, and with the trial behind them they decided to return to Calgary and did so that summer.

One week after the verdict, Davey was back on the road with Camp Cornette, which was now made up of himself, Owen, and his former WCW nemesis Vader.

WCW continued to throw Ted Turner's billions at over-the-hill superstars such as Hulk Hogan and Randy Savage and acted like vultures around established WWF talent whose contracts were drawing to a close, regularly luring them away with vast sums on long guaranteed-money contracts.

Whilst WCW filled the top of their roster with high-profile names, the WWF began to recruit the disgruntled talent being held back by this policy. As well as Vader, they signed Mick Foley – who they repackaged as the deranged 'Mankind' – and, separately, both members of the Hollywood Blonds tag team – Steve Austin and Brian Pillman.

Camp Cornette beat Ahmed Johnson, Jake Roberts and Yokozuna at *WrestleMania XII*, the main event of which saw Shawn Michaels zip-wire down to the ring from the rooftop to win his first WWF championship. He beat Bret in overtime following a stalemate 60-minute ironman match. Shawn Michaels was finally *the man*. Other than the Undertaker, who continued to be booked as more of a special-attraction than belt-seeking competitor, Bret and Shawn were the top two superstars by a considerable distance. Bret had no problem in putting Shawn over for his big moment, as he prepared to lighten his schedule for the rest of the year, spending more time at home and pursuing acting opportunities.

35

GOLD RUSH

'"Look at Owen, look at Owen," Bulldog hooted in his thick
English accent. "Oh that's too much. That's too fuckin'
much." Now I understood. Owen was definitely stinking
up the place, but, unlike me, he was doing it on purpose …
simply to amuse the boys.'

Mick Foley

8 May 1996. Kuwait

The sun sparkled on the vast open ocean and beat down on the boat
from which brothers-in-arms Davey, Bret and Owen fished.

They were in the Middle East for a lucrative five-show tour
sponsored by a syndicate of wealthy locals, who had offered to take the
trio on a private sea-fishing excursion. As they relaxed, they discussed
the latest machinations backstage, which had become perennially more
interesting and scandalous than the on-screen antics.

The Kliq had decided to expand their horizons. Kevin Nash and
Scott Hall had agreed to jump to the opposition, taking up the eye-
watering cash on offer at WCW whilst Shawn Michaels and Hunter
Hearst Helmsley stayed with the WWF. The subplot was that the
Kliq were consciously working towards a scenario in which they held
the top money-earning and gold-laden positions at both companies,
effectively monopolising the whole industry.

Suddenly, attentions turned to Davey's whistling reel and straining
rod. An hour-long battle ensued between the British Bulldog and a 3ft
yellow shark. Davey sweated and struggled; veins popped from his huge

muscles. He beamed with delight as he finally pulled it aboard the boat. The defeated beast flipped and slithered all over the deck as Davey's hosts circled to kill it in order for it to be taken back to shore. But Davey was so in awe of its fight and inexhaustible energy he ordered them to back off and insisted it be returned to the ocean.

* * *

On 19 May, Hall and Nash made their final WWF appearances at a New York house show. Typically, they wrestled their running-buddies Helmsley and Michaels respectively. The main event was inside a steel cage and Shawn won by leaving Diesel seemingly unconscious in the ring after hitting his superkick and walking out of the open cage door. But he dashed back in and kissed the heel Diesel on the forehead, who then sprung back to life as though he had been a frog and Shawn a princess. Razor Ramon and Helmsley – bitter enemies earlier in the show – then hit the ring together and the four members of the behind-the-scenes faction hugged for the whole world to see, before climbing atop a turnbuckle each and performing the Kliq's sacred hand gesture to the crowd. This instantly became known as the 'Curtain Call' and many regard it as the moment kayfabe officially died. Wrestlers and staff, most of whom had spent their lives 'protecting the business', were apoplectic backstage. To add to the disrespect, all this had taken place inside the fabled home of the WWF – Madison Square Garden.

To counter the incessant offence of WCW, which was cutting through and beginning to win the ratings war, the WWF continued to turn more toward storylines of sleaze and scandal. This served to get Davey Boy back in the main event picture when, in storyline, Diana accused the boy-toy champion of making sexual advances towards her. An incensed Bulldog leapt to his wife's defence, and he and the Heartbreak Kid were set on a collision course. The twist that was set in motion by Jim Cornette and Bruce Prichard was that video footage would emerge of the incident that would in fact show Diana making advances on Shawn. But the whole Hart family were unhappy with this angle, worried how Diana would be perceived. Davey called Stu to update him and register his own concerns with the family patriarch so as to distance himself from any blame. Stu then called the office and spoke to Jim Cornette, who believed it was Owen pulling one of his notorious ribs using his perfect Stu impression, and so attempted to turn the prank back on Owen by launching into an X-rated tirade in which he described an orgy-like soft-porn scene they had planned for Diana. Cornette gulped with terror as Owen walked into the room with no telephone in sight.

'It's all that Bruce Prichard's idea anyway! Here he is now Stu,' Cornette motored as he handed a bewildered Prichard the phone.

'Hey Stu, how y'doing?'

'Errr, are you some kind of pervert or something?' Stu asked. 'You want my daughter to be in bed with Shawn Michaels! What the hell are you guys doin' down there?'

Despite Prichard's diplomatic intervention, it was clear that the storyline wasn't been bought into by the Hart-Smith family, so they attempted to wrap it up ahead of schedule at the upcoming pay-per-view.

In Your House 8: Beware of Dog
26 May 1996
Florence Civic Center
Florence, South Carolina
WWF Championship
The British Bulldog v Shawn Michaels
Attendance: 6,000

'Welcome back everyone to *In Your House: Beware of Dog*,' began Vince McMahon as 'Rule Britannia' echoed around the building. 'And the dog is on his way to the squared circle. We thank you very much for your patience – indeed what a storm on the outside of the building here, live from Florence, South Carolina.'

A thunderstorm was raging outside and the power had cut out after just the opening match. The building's emergency lighting meant that the arena had sufficient illumination for the matches to continue and fans just about had visibility. However, the television and vital communications signals were down. Panic ensued backstage as the power would intermittently come on but then be lost again. Bruce Prichard was running around prepping talent with alternative match endings depending on whether there was power or not, so that vital plot twists – such as Mankind emerging from under the ring he was now stuck beneath blissfully unaware of the pandemonium – weren't wasted on what may turn out to be dark matches. The power had returned by the time the main event came around, with Prichard having now armed them with three different potential endings.

With every change, Shawn bristled further. He was a perfectionist – and a temperamental one. During the match, he felt the need to communicate his displeasure with the audience, throwing his arms up in the air petulantly. A female fan heckled and screeched at him throughout and he began to unprofessionally retaliate, and soon the already unsettled crowd were more preoccupied by her than the distinctly average match in the ring.

The Bulldog was declared the winner and the new champion following a finish that saw both men's shoulders pressed to the mat for the three-count, before a confused cluster lasting several minutes and ending with the announcement of a draw served only to further dissatisfy the fans. There would be a rematch at the following pay-per-view, *King of the Ring*.

Davey actually gave notice to Vince the day after *Beware of Dog*, but only as a negotiating tactic. He wanted to stay, and Vince wanted to keep him.

'Davey, I don't want to lose you. Come on, you're family,' Vince told him. No longer a member of that family was Davey's friend Louie Spicolli, who was fired after he could no longer hide his drug problems. Spicolli would die soon after following an alcohol- and prescription drug-related overdose.

The 1996 King of the Ring would be the fourth edition of the tournament as an annual event, with Bret having won the crown in '93, Owen winning the following year and the giant Mabel becoming 'King' in '95. The coronation was used to give a younger star a huge boost to main-event level and Hunter Hearst Helmsley had long been the planned winner but was the fall-guy for the Curtain Call incident. With Hall and Nash having left and Shawn having manoeuvred himself into an untouchable position as the company's top man during Bret's hiatus, Helmsley was the only one that was punishable as McMahon needed to show some discipline to appease the angry locker room. In a move that would ultimately change the business forever, 'Stone Cold' Steve Austin was chosen to win the tournament in Milwaukee instead.

'You sit there, and you thump your Bible,' Austin began his coronation promo after beating born-again Christian Jake Roberts in the final, 'and you say your prayers and it didn't get you anywhere. Talk about your psalms, talk about John 3:16, well Austin 3:16 says I just whipped your ass!

'And as far as this championship match is considered, son, I don't give a damn if it's Davey Boy Smith or Shawn Michaels; Steve Austin's time has come and when I get that shot you're looking at the next WWF champion and that's the bottom line, 'cos Stone Cold said so!'

Just moments later, 'Rule Britannia' hit and out walked Davey, once again flanked by Diana and Jim Cornette. He and Shawn set about righting the wrongs of their previous encounter and put on a fast-paced thriller, won by Shawn after 25 exciting minutes, aided by the comedic commentary of Owen. Dave Meltzer awarded the match four-and-a-quarter stars in his *Observer*.

The pay-per-view also saw the live debut of a crutch-using Brian Pillman, whose arrival had been dramatic as he blurred the lines between kayfabe and reality. Following the breakup of the Hollywood Blonds, he had reinvented himself in WCW as the 'Loose Cannon', a motor-mouthed, untameable wildman. He regularly cut captivating promos in which he would openly break the fourth wall, using backstage politics and terminology to get the 'smart' fans genuinely questioning if he was acting out against the company. Even WCW talent and staff were left unsure, and it was becoming the talk of the industry. But Eric Bischoff was sanctioning it all – or so he thought. After Bischoff had seemingly released Pillman for his ongoing misdemeanours, they worked the angle so deep that, on Pillman's suggestion, they had his release legally and officially drawn up and processed, the idea being that he would appear for ECW in a similar deranged fashion then return as the hottest property in wrestling. But Pillman used his legitimate status as a free agent to play the WWF off against WCW. His wild antics were merely reflecting reality, though, and in April he fell asleep at the wheel of his Hummer and smashed it into a tree. He was in a coma for a week and his ankle was shattered. The WWF signed him regardless and when he emerged with his ankle in a cast at King of the Ring to cut a promo with Jim Ross, it was a very genuine injury – one that would prevent him from any actual in-ring action for almost another year. The injury was so bad that he too was developing an over-reliance on pain medication to add to his already wild lifestyle.

The signing had seemed like a rare victory for Vince, as WCW cleverly turned their bitter battle into a kayfabe storyline that would see them soar ahead in the ratings war in the summer of 1996. They billed Nash and Hall as 'The Outsiders', supposedly invading WCW programming on behalf of the enemy. When Hulk Hogan sensationally turned heel and joined them, the 'New World Order' (nWo) was born. With Davey still not re-signed and negotiations ongoing, WCW circled, hoping, and believing, that they were about to make the Bulldog the latest nWo member. But despite rumours of much larger money with the opposition, Davey finally signed a five-year contract with Vince for a minimum guarantee of $250,000 per year.

* * *

Further tragedy befell the Hart family that July when Matt, the 13-year-old son of Hart sister Georgia, died after being infected with a rare flesh-eating bacterium. Matt was the best friend of Davey's 11-year-old son Harry, and along with many of the other cousins – of which there were dozens – they would practise their wrestling moves every day, and even founded their own junior promotion. They had sworn they would become wrestlers like their fathers, uncles and Grandpa Stu before them. An additional boy amongst the ranks was Theodore James Wilson, a local boy befriended by Harry and Teddy Hart. 'TJ' was welcomed into the family and became a popular part of the furniture at Hart House. Naturally athletic, he became one of the most promising wrestlers of them all, and Davey would turn teacher for his blossoming son Harry and young TJ.

Matt's death devastated Davey. Harry, Matt, Teddy and TJ were like brothers and Matt and Davey shared a special uncle–nephew bond. Matt idolised his favourite uncle in Davey, and the feeling was mutual. The four youngsters had talked incessantly of one day having a tag team rivalry similar to that of the Bulldogs and the Hart Foundation.

* * *

Davey and Owen soon became an entertaining heel tag team and double-act, using underhand tactics to gain victories, interfering in each other's singles matches and engaging in a battle of one-upmanship – with Owen perfectly playing the part of the spoilt and jealous little brother that he had for so long opposite Bret. On 22 September, at *In Your House 10: Mind Games,* they beat 'The Smoking Gunns' (Billy and Bart) and won the WWF tag team championships to the type of crowd eruption that should be reserved only for a top babyface victory.

At that same pay-per-view, Brian Pillman, Owen and Stone Cold joined together in the ring to taunt the still absent Bret. Stone Cold was targeting a victory over the Hitman to confirm his arrival on the main stage.

'Are you trying to say Bret Hart's a chicken?' Pillman asked Austin.

'Bret Hart doesn't even qualify as being a chicken,' replied Stone Cold. 'He's the slimy substance that runs out of the south end of a chicken! If you put the letter "S" in front of Hitman, you've had my exact opinion of Bret Hart!'

Bret returned in November with the intention of working a programme with Austin before heading into the mega rematch with Shawn at *WrestleMania XIII;* which would invariably see Bret win to even up their rivalry and draw huge money and ratings with a trilogy decider down the line. While he had been away, WCW had offered Bret a mind-boggling $2.8 million per year for three years. Vince had been unable to match it, instead offering $1.5 million for the same period as part of a 20-year contract worth over $10 million in total. It offered security and played on the loyalty and relationship between the two parties. Bret signed the deal with the WWF which also contained a clause that, no matter when it was, he would have creative control over his results and storylines for the final 30 days he was with the company.

Bret beat Austin in a four-and-a-half-star classic at *Survivor Series,* an event that also saw the pay-per-view debut of 'Rocky Maivia'.

Royal Rumble
19 January 1997
Alamodrome
San Antonio, Texas
Attendance: 60,477

'He put me oot!' Bulldog raged as he charged past the cameraman on his way back to the locker room. In the ring, Owen was pleading

'Macho Man' Randy
Savage, Miss Elizabeth,
Bronwyne, Michelle,
Marek, and Tom
[Michelle Billington]

Despite their stardom, Davey and Bret headline a Stampede show, and, as ever, give their blood and sweat for the cause [Orest Zmyndak]

On their return to Stampede and with Tom ailing, Davey begins to emerge as a singles star [Orest Zmyndak]

Tom trained his close friend Joe Cimino, but to ensure Joe was fully initiated a week before he was to make his debut, Johnny Smith (John Hindley) stretched him. To Tom's great disappointment, Joe never stepped back through the ropes.
[Michelle Billington]

Good friends Davey, Don Muraco, Johnny Smith and Tom

Despite his physical troubles getting the better of him, Tom was still often fun-loving and family orientated. Here he plays with Marek in the ring, and tends to his turkeys to the amusement of his visiting little brother, Mark. [Michelle Billington]

Tom returns to Manchester to find a
friendly face at the airport
[Mark Billington]

Back where it all began [Mark Billington]

Meanwhile, the British Bulldog becomes a solo superstar [Getty Images]

Superfan and future wrestling historian Bradley Craig meets Davey in Aberdeen [Bradley Craig]

Tom was briefly reunited with Marek, as well as Bronwyne, in Wigan in 1995 [Michelle Billington]

With Satoru Sayama in Tokyo in 1996 [AFLO Images]

The Dynamite Kid prepares for his final match [AFLO Images]

'Davey Boy Smith Jr' – Harry – in action for WWE in 2006 [Getty Images]

When Bronwyne found Tom, they both found peace
[Bronwyne Billington]

Tom catches up with an old
friend in Bret Hart via Skype
[Bronwyne Billington]

An ageing Tom
and his niece Leah
[Leah Billington]

'The Billington Bulldogs' [Tony Knox]

Bronwyne, Marek, Michelle and Amaris celebrate their 'Tommy Day' at 'The Ship & Anchor' – a traditional British pub in Calgary [Michelle Billington]

Tom's grandchildren Miami, Harlow, Taya and Madix [Bronwyne Billington]

his innocence in Davey's direction. Davey had been attempting to eliminate Stone Cold when Owen clumsily tipped them both over the top; Austin managing to survive and roll back in, but Davey Boy crashing to the floor.

Austin went on to win the match, but only after the referees had missed Bret eliminating him. This would lead to weeks of Bret complaining about being screwed live on air, whereas Austin's redneck, no-nonsense persona was beginning to resonate with the fans.

On 13 February, Shawn suddenly forfeited the title, claiming that a knee injury, that no one had previously been aware of, was so serious that doctors had told him to quit. As he fought back tears, he also claimed that he had 'lost his smile' and needed to go home and find it. The locker room believed it was more likely that he would rather give up the belt and disappear for a couple of months than lose it in the middle of the ring to Bret at *WrestleMania*.

The extraordinary chemistry and rivalry between Bret and Austin meant their programme would be extended to climax at *'Mania*, and Sycho Sid and the Undertaker would contest the title match.

With backstage politics bringing down the mood, the boys were glad to be going on a nine-day tour of Germany. During this tour, a tournament would take place to crown a new European champion. Of course, Vince McMahon knew there was only one man who could possibly be that inaugural champion; the man who had been the company's flag-bearer in that continent for so many years, the man who had helped them build a lucrative European fanbase: the British Bulldog.

Davey beat Mankind in the quarter-finals and Vader in the semi-finals to qualify for the final in Berlin, where he would meet his brother-in-law and his tag team championship partner, the King of Harts, Owen Hart.

'You are going to see a wrestling match the likes of which you have never seen before,' Vince McMahon commentated on the match, which was replayed on the following *Monday Night Raw*. He was right. Whilst continually and subtly teasing dissention and jealousy between them as a secondary backstory, Davey and Owen put on a pure wrestling clinic. They flowed between acrobatic and unique routines; both of them countering with flips, rolls and handstands and landing on their feet from the most impossible of positions. They told the story of brothers-in-law outside the ring and brothers inside it who knew each other's styles perfectly. As a tertiary thread, they paid respect to Japanese, British and European wrestling, performing the whole match in a medley of those styles.

After a series of near falls that sent the crowd wild, the match ended when Davey reversed Owen's victory roll into his own pinning position. Davey raised his glistening new belt high in one hand and his tag team belt in the other; he was a double champion, and Europe's finest was officially recognised as being exactly that. He offered his hand to a frustrated Owen, who eventually shook it before hoisting his own belt high and taking one side of Davey's singles title and raising that too, subliminally communicating that they were the joint holders of the three belts. Bulldog cut Owen a suspicious glance.

The match was awarded four-and-a-half stars in the *Observer* and was widely regarded as the best match in *Raw*'s four-year history to date. And yet *Nitro*, whose main event was a tag team match which saw Lex Luger team with 'The Giant' (later known as 'Big Show') to take on the Steiner brothers, won the ratings war by a landslide. When those ratings were published, Vince finally accepted what some had been trying to convince him of for a while: today's audience didn't want technical wrestling, they wanted sleaze and scandal. The following week, unofficially at least, WWF's Attitude Era began.

36

ON THE SCRAPHEAP

'I'll be honest, when I started out wrestling as the
Dynamite Kid all those years ago, I had no idea things
would end up the way they did. But I'd do it all again. I
wouldn't change a thing. Which I know sounds strange
coming from a guy whose wrestling career put him in
a wheelchair, but it's true. Wrestling was my life, and I
loved it. No regrets. I had a blast.'

Tom Billington

These Days
7 October 1996
Ryōgoku Sumo Hall
Tokyo, Japan
The Great Sasuke, Mil Mascaras and Tiger Mask (Sayama) v Dos
Caras, Kuniaki Kobayashi and the Dynamite Kid
Attendance: 7,890

The Dynamite Kid, or the frail and skinny remains of him, pulled
on his Union Jack wrestling tights in the locker room. They bagged
on him the way the hand-me-downs he had first pulled on in Ted
Betley's gym over 20 years earlier had. He felt like a shell of himself;
an unrecognisable shadow of the Dynamite Kid.

His back, shoulders and knees were in particular agony following
the flight alone. He lived daily in the kind of pain most humans never
know. Nerve damage to his spine was now so severe that the whole left

side of his body was slow and unresponsive. Worst of all, he was seeing spots and feeling extremely light-headed – symptoms he had come to know were warnings another seizure was on its way. *Don't let it happen now. Please don't let it happen now,* he thought to himself. *Tommy, just hang on lad. Get the match over with and get your money.*

Yet worst of all for Tom, his pride hurt. He knew this was his last match; it simply had to be. But it was the first time in his career that he knew he had been booked because of who he was, rather than what he could do in the ring. Even as he had appeared in small shows for UK promotions for the previous few years, he was satisfied he was still worthy of his place at the top of the bill, and certainly of the small pay packets on offer. But here he was back in his beloved Japan, on a huge show, being paid a total of $1,400. He had resolved that his career was over after a small British event in Croydon, south London, earlier in 1996. After the show, he was approached by a Japanese gentleman who introduced himself as Hiroshi, a booking agent for upstart promotion Michinoku Pro – who had designs on breaking up the duopoly of Japanese pro wrestling.

The independent promotion had been founded in 1993 by ambitious young wrestling sensation 'The Great Sasuke'. To celebrate the third anniversary of its existence, Michinoku Pro was to hold a TV special broadcast from Tokyo called *These Days*, and as part of it Sasuke wanted the legends that had inspired him to take part and gain publicity to add to his promotion's momentum.

Tom was offered $700 each for two separate trips, one making a non-wrestling promotional appearance and the other competing in a nostalgia-filled six-man tag team match at the big show. He could not afford to turn the money down. Things had become so desperate for Tom that he had been taking part in a local bare-knuckle circuit, fighting violently and illegally in car parks and garages.

When he was brought out to the ring for an emotional reunion with Satoru Sayama, Tom looked every bit the scrapyard security guard he now was rather than the global sensation he had been a decade earlier, as he wore the baggiest of blue trousers and a scuffed leather jacket. A smartly dressed but now chubby Sayama gasped with amazement at the sight of his classic dance partner. The crowd popped with an outpouring of respect and emotion at seeing the two great warriors, friends and rivals share a ring once more, 13 years after the last time they had. A microphone was thrust at Tom, who did his best to recall the Japanese for 'number one' and shouted out 'Sayama, ichiban!' The crowd lapped it up. Tom and Sayama sat ringside together to watch the matches.

Sasuke, just 27 and still approaching his prime, cast himself in the legends match – on his team, 38-year-old Sayama and masked Mexican great Mil Mascaras. In the opposite corner alongside Tom would be Kuniaki Kobayashi and another legendary masked luchador in Dos Caras (behind their masks and behind the kayfabe curtain, Dos Caras and Mil Mascaras were brothers).

All six men received warm receptions, but the loudest cheers were reserved for Tom and Sayama. Tom looked stoic but emotional as he bit his bottom lip amid his thunderous reception.

Of course, the crowd were given their wish as the Dynamite Kid and the original and greatest Tiger Mask got the match underway, performing a classic routine of theirs, albeit akin to a veteran wedding band performing the Beatles' early hits.

Tom tagged into the match for short cameo appearances, yet each time he chose to take a bump or perform one of his classic high-impact moves – even snap-suplexing Sasuke on the hard floor on the outside of the ring.

His final time in the action as a legal competitor was, fittingly, with Tiger Mask, as he once again made himself a canvas for Sayama to paint his own final acrobatic masterpiece. When he tagged out on this occasion, he took a knee on the ring apron and held his head in one hand. He was a man struggling to cling on to himself – yet he wouldn't let the planned finish fail. With the match descending into chaos, Dynamite suddenly leapt into the ring, raised and twisted Sasuke in the air like he was a feather before dropping down with him for the perfect spiked piledriver, allowing legal man Caras to then sit-down powerbomb Sasuke for the one, two, three.

As he always had, despite the horrendous cost to his own well-being, Tom ensured every patron got value for their entrance fee out of the Dynamite Kid.

The next morning, as Tom made his way through Narita airport for what he assumed would be the final time, it happened. He suddenly felt warm and light-headed and began to see the stars again. He tried to shout for help, but no sound came from his mouth as he collapsed to the floor.

When Tom woke up in hospital, his whole body ached. Doctors medicated him and eventually discharged him – this time his promise to quit wrestling would be kept.

As 1997 arrived, wrestling and the relationships it forged weren't the only things Tom now had missing from his life; he had become completely estranged from his children in Canada. He had still never met his youngest daughter Amaris, but Bronwyne and Marek had visited him in the summer of 1995 – a trip funded by their uncle Bret, who kept Michelle and the kids close and often generously stepped in when the bills were becoming insurmountable.

Golborne was a gloomier place than ever following Margaret Thatcher's campaign to close down the mining industry. It was certainly a culture shock for an 11-year-old and a seven-year-old from the scenic and cosmopolitan city of Calgary, but the brave pair trekked alone to see the father who had left them over four years earlier.

Tom proudly showed Marek the new tattoo he had on his forearm. It was Looney Tunes' Tasmanian Devil, with 'Marek' written underneath. As a toddler, Marek had been a whirlwind of energy, causing Tom to nickname him 'Taz'. Bronwyne asked when he was going to get Tweety Bird tattooed after her (he had nicknamed her that due to her big blue eyes). Tom considered it, but decided that wasn't quite manly enough for him.

The highlight of that summer, for Tom, was going to be taking his kids to the iconic seaside fairground of Blackpool Pleasure Beach. They eagerly embarked on the hour-long drive, only for his beaten-up silver Ford Sierra to splutter to a halt on the M6 northbound. So rare was it that Tom used the vehicle, that he had mistakenly filled the tank with diesel rather than petrol. His frustration threatened to get the better of him at the roadside as he knew the day was ruined, until little Bronwyne assured him that it didn't matter where they were or what they were doing, so long as they were together. She told him the same after he scored her a spare ticket to go along to a Cranberries concert with some friends of his – as much as she liked the band, an evening without her dad was a wasted evening that summer. She and

Marek even joined him for some of his shifts, the three of them playing hide-and-seek along with Tom's two dogs, Thunder and Storm, in the scrapyard; eating food and sharing laughs together as they watched the monitors in his cabin.

But with international calls so expensive at the time and the households both sides of the Atlantic living on the breadline, little contact soon turned to none. When the children got a little older and began to question what had led to their dad's ultimate banishment from Calgary and their lives, they decided to move on without him.

Around the same time as his forced retirement from the ring, Tom split from long-term girlfriend Joanne and looked destined for a lifetime of lonely pain and anguish. That is why he was surprised when he met red-headed Dot, who had never heard of the Dynamite Kid, and romance blossomed. His wrestling persona had always preceded him in his few relationships and friendships, and that had since added to his suspicions about people who he thought were more interested in getting something from the Dynamite Kid than they were in spending time with Tom Billington.

Dot re-energised Tom and their whirlwind romance was sealed with a quick, low-key wedding. But Tom's past was always going to make any ride off into the sunset a bumpy one. His physical ailments continued to worsen; he still needed daily pain medication and the nerve damage in his spine was increasingly inhibiting his movement. With his staunch pride still his most potent foe, he continued to ignore the worsening pain and mobility, simply accepting that at just 38, he was an old man.

But then he collapsed while climbing some stairs and had to be taken to hospital. The damage rendered him unable to walk. A series of tests and X-rays were done and a date set with the specialist to follow up on the results, which Tom believed would probably be to determine which of the plethora of operations he surely needed should be done first.

Dot wheeled a bespectacled Tom into the consultant's room. When the doctor entered and sat down opposite, the look on his face told Tom it was going to be bad news. 'Mr Billington …'

'My name's Tommy, doctor. What's yours?' Tom tried to cushion the verbal blow he knew was coming his way by ensuring that it was delivered in a friendly manner.

'My name is Sam,' the doctor replied.

'Okay Sam,' Tom braced himself, 'can you just tell me what's wrong with me – altogether?'

'Basically, Tommy,' Sam sighed, 'the damage to your back is too extensive. There's nothing we can do for you.'

'But, will I walk again?' Tom asked hesitantly.

'I can't be absolutely certain, but no; probably not.' As requested, doctor Sam was telling Tom the bad news with little dressing. He told Tom that there was simply too much scar tissue.

'Thank you, Sam,' a shellshocked Tom said, before turning to Dot and saying, 'Get me out of 'ere.'

THE NEW HART FOUNDATION

'He had excruciating pain in his lower back from the 80s.
He was in agony and constantly seeing back specialists and
getting adjustments. He was living with pain for a long time
and couldn't get off the painkillers.'

Ross Hart

21 March 1997. Slammy Awards Ceremony, Westin Hotel, Chicago

'Ladies and gentlemen, our next presenter is the self-proclai...' host Todd Pettengill was then cut off as Owen stormed up to the podium.

The Slammys was a glitzy event that took place as part of *WrestleMania* week, where a mixture of serious and silly awards would be given out for the seasonal wrestling year coming to an end. All the superstars and their partners would appear in tuxedoes and glamorous gowns, whilst staying largely in character. Wholesome fun.

Owen had won a Slammy at a previous edition, but unlike the dozens of other winners, had taken to carrying the gold wrestling statue trophy to the ring as a symbol of achievement, referring to himself as 'Slammy-Award-winning Owen Hart'.

'Wooooooo! I did it again!' Owen gleefully announced to his peers.

'No. You're presenting this.' Pettengill placed the 'Best Bow-tie' award in front of Owen.

Owen took a second to think. 'Wooooooo. I did it again!' he repeated. 'And I have nobody to thank; once again, I did it all by my sweet little self!' The camera cut to a bespectacled Davey, displaying those big dimples as he beamed with pride and amusement at Owen's performance.

'Two-time Slammy Award-winner! I knew it! I'm a winner! I did it! Wooooooo!' Owen continued. 'Hey Bulldog, you may have two titles, but you don't have two Slammys!' he screamed as he took the opportunity to continue their ongoing one-upmanship. Again, Davey was shown barely able to contain his glee beside Owen's wife Martha, who also beamed with pride.

'Vader and Mankind,' Owen's attentions turned to their upcoming opponents, 'this Sunday at *WrestleMania*, you're gonna be in for the fight of your life, because myself and the Bulldog, we haven't been better ever! And you know what Vader, you don't have two Slammys like I do, because you're losers and we're winners – me and my Slammys! Wooooo!'

For a tag team championship match technically between two heel teams, when 'Rule Britannia' hit at *WrestleMania*, the crowd popped. Owen emerged from the curtain first, with his gold belt around his waist, his arms stretched high in the air and a Slammy trophy gripped in each hand. Davey strolled behind him, one belt strapped around his waist and the other casually held by his side.

'Hey Bulldog, I wanted to ask you,' Jim Ross interrupted Davey's walk-on for an impromptu interview, 'were you offended when Owen Hart said he was smarter than you and that he was the captain of the team?'

'You leave Bulldog alone!' Owen demanded. 'He's got two belts, and I've got two Slammys!'

'We're the champions!' insisted Davey, 'I've got two belts, he's got two Slammys, quit tryin' to stir it!'

The match ended in a double count-out when Mankind locked his mandible claw on Davey on the outside of the ring right in front of the onlooking Stu and Helen, who got to see their other son in one of the all-time classic matches immediately afterwards.

Bret and Stone Cold had a war for the ages, which ended when Austin refused to quit to the sharpshooter, but instead passed out as blood dripped from his nose and chin. They had executed their story so perfectly that Bret Hart, despite his victory, left as the heel and

Stone Cold left as the blue-collar babyface hero who refused to quit. The elusive double-turn had been accomplished.

The inevitable finally happened between Davey and Owen the following night on *Raw*. A miscommunication between them during a tag championship match escalated into an all-out brawl between the brothers-in-law. Once they had been separated by an army of officials, Owen grabbed a mic and launched into a tirade of Bulldog abuse, which culminated in a challenge for the European title. Following some choice words of his own, Davey agreed to the challenge.

The following week's episode began with Owen's unmistakably catchy entrance music. When 'Rule Britannia' drowned it out, the crowd cheered – they were desperate to love Davey.

Davey and Owen launched into stiff action, with Davey's nose becoming bloodied almost instantly. It was much more brawl than technical wrestling, as it appeared their relationship had broken down completely. When a steel chair brought into the ring by a desperate Owen ended up in Davey's hands, Bret screeched into the ring and tackled Davey to the ground. He frantically prevented the warring pair from getting at one another and, with some order restored, asked for a microphone.

'What are you fighting for?' Bret began. 'To satisfy a bunch of people who don't know the first thing about family values?!' he said as he pointed at the crowd, who began to boo. 'I'm asking ya ... I need ya.'

'USA, USA, USA,' the crowd began to chant.

'Yeah, USA,' Bret shrugged, 'you're talking about a country that's based its entire history on brother against brother.' The tone was set. Bitter Bret blamed the Americans that his family had lived and worked amongst all these years for them now being torn apart, and he would use America's hate to unify them again.

He spoke to Davey about their bond and about their Wembley hug, he reminded Owen that he had taken care of him as a kid and had got him into wrestling. Owen wiped away tears as his big brother told him he loved him, and the three shared a huge hug. The Hart Foundation was reborn, and they would wage war on Stone Cold Steve Austin.

The Legion of Doom had returned to the WWF and had come to Austin's aid to even up the numbers – but those numbers weren't even for very long. Being a Canadian heel synonymous with Stampede Wrestling and the Hart family, and with a common enemy in Stone Cold, Brian Pillman soon became the fourth member of the New Hart Foundation; and four become five at the end of April, when *Raw*'s main event saw Davey in singles action against current WWF champion the Undertaker. After Owen interfered and the match ended in disqualification, Undertaker and Stone Cold chased Bulldog and Owen out of the building, leaving an injured Bret at Austin's sinister mercy, only for Jim 'The Anvil' Neidhart to return and attack Austin from behind. Earlier that same night, Owen defeated Rocky Maivia for the Intercontinental title as he and Davey continued to collect almost all of the WWF's gold.

Pillman finally returned to in-ring action after 15 months out, as members of the group tagged together in shows up and down the USA, making more enemies as they rode like the outlaw heels that they were. Pillman's ring work was limited compared to the high-flying, high-impact style he had learned in the dungeon, but at least he was back.

The organic reaction in Canada and Europe to the Foundation's anti-American trope became that of cult hero worship. Bret, Owen and Davey were icons in their homelands and joining forces as a family, despite their often-dastardly antics, made them more popular than ever. The antiheroes all appeared in black leather jackets with personalised pink trim and draped in giant Canadian flags.

Despite his dependence on painkillers for his ongoing back and knee problems, Davey was happy and motivated as he travelled and worked with his oldest friends – his family.

* * *

Shawn Michaels returned to the ring at the end of May after less than four months out with the knee injury he had previously claimed may have ended his career. He had been making sporadic TV appearances in the meantime, mainly to run down Bret in a blatant non-kayfabe manner, claiming that Bret had shown no loyalty to the WWF and that he had held them to ransom during his time away; he also repeatedly claimed that Bret was obsessed with the WWF title and with staying above him in the roster hierarchy. Worst of all, he hinted that Bret had been having some 'Sunny days' – a not-so subtle suggestion that Bret had been sleeping with valet Sunny.

Shawn's first match back saw him team with Stone Cold to end Davey and Owen's brilliant eight-month reign as tag champions. But when Bret finally went home and discovered that both his wife Julie and his father Stu were upset about Shawn's 'Sunny days' comment, he was furious.

As he travelled with Davey to the next show, Bret confided about the heat he was getting at home and how upset Julie was. Davey told Bret that Shawn had gone too far and the only way to defend the family honour was for Bret to confront Shawn – physically. The next time he saw Shawn in the locker room Bret marched toward him and it quickly escalated into a scuffle. Bret landed a few blows before throwing Shawn across the room by his hair – a large clump of which came out by the root. Pat Patterson screamed for help to break it up, but a nearby Davey Boy was in no rush to assist. Shawn stormed into Vince's office and quit, claiming it was an unsafe working environment; Bret was suspended from appearing on the show. With the *Wrestling Observer* and other 'dirt sheets' now popular and more accessible via the internet, the fans knew all about the brawl and were as excited about the reality show backstage as they were with the product that was being scripted for them. The truth was, Shawn, like so many of his peers, had also developed a serious prescription drug problem. He used the situation to have some time away, with Vince's blessing. On-screen, Vince told the audience that Shawn had been suspended and stripped of his tag title.

Stone Cold versus the Hart Foundation, or 'Team Canada' as they became known, was dominating the majority of the WWF TV programming and had arrested the ratings lull that had seen WCW soar into the lead. It had countered the nWo storyline with their own alliance-based angle, one that enabled Americans and Canadians to justifiably and passionately cheer for their own. Fittingly, it would all come to a head not just in Canada, but in Calgary.

TEAM CANADA

'The peak was 6 July 1997 at the Saddledome in Calgary for
one of the greatest shows in WWF history ... The thunderous
ovation of the Hart family, several generations worth,
celebrating in mid-ring, was probably the biggest pop in a
North American wrestling ring in more than ten years ... What
was probably the second high point of Smith's career, turned
out just like the first one, a prelude to leaving the WWF.'

Dave Meltzer

In Your House 16: Canadian Stampede would see the whole of the New
Hart Foundation face off against Austin, the Legion of Doom, Goldust
(who had been feuding with Pillman) and former MMA superstar Ken
Shamrock.

The event turned into a Canadian *WrestleMania* – a weekend-
long festival to coincide with the famous rodeo saw the whole of
Calgary spill out on to the streets. Team Canada and the Hart clan
rode through the city on a float, including Diana, who was now 'Mrs
Calgary', as they waved at their adoring fans, who screamed support
and held up signs and waved giant flags. A queue more than a mile
long snaked through the buildings as people waited for their chance
to meet the men that represented their national pride against the
might of the USA. When an autograph session with Bret, Owen
and Davey was arranged, little did anyone know that 8,000 people
would turn up.

In Your House 16: Canadian Stampede
6 July 1997
Saddledome
Calgary, Alberta, Canada
The Hart Foundation v Stone Cold Steve Austin, the Legion of
Doom, Ken Shamrock and Goldust
Attendance: 12,151

Stone Cold's popularity was a phenomenon in the wrestling business. Rarely, if ever, has someone been as over as Steve Austin was in the summer of 1997. Yet when the sound of shattering glass pierced the home of the Calgary Flames, a chorus of boos shook the building. He joined the rest of his team in the ring and the boos turned to impatient cheers as the patrons knew what was next.

Howard Finkel was inaudible; his voice drowned out when he announced the Hart Foundation, starting with Brian Pillman. The Loose Cannon walked through the curtain on to the stage to be met by 12,000 equally wild-eyed crazies; he waved his hands to get them even further beyond the fevered peak they had already reached. He beamed his wide, contagious, genuine smile and he was supercharged. An equally loud greeting met Jim Neidhart, who screamed into the crowd to release the energy they had just stoked into him. 'Rule Britannia' hit to send the decibels soaring higher still, their adopted Davey Boy was home, with Mrs Calgary on his arm. His tanned face turned redder still, as he appeared almost emotional at the reception. The noise level continued for Owen, who waved both of his Slammy trophies high into the air before quietly joining his team-mates on the stage at the top of the ramp, all wearing their own versions of the now iconic leather jacket. For the first time, there was a pause between entrance themes, before Bret's electric guitar riff finally blew the roof off the building.

As Davey approached the ring, he passed his European belt to Diana and gave her a kiss on the cheek and a loving wink. Bret walked around the ring and put his sunglasses on his diminutive mom's head as 82-year-old Stu gave him a proud nod. They may have been heels, but not in Canada, and certainly never in Calgary. They were Stampede's soldiers and stampede they would. All the Hart family were there, multiple generations watching on proudly.

Bret and Austin finally got the match underway, and when Bret got the upper hand in the opening exchanges and was stomping away at his nemesis in the corner, the arena lost control.

'This building is shaking!' screamed Jerry Lawler.

'You've gotta be here to feel this!' added good ol' Jim Ross.

The commentary team had to yell to make themselves heard to the TV audience. The crowd pops were raucous, and they were frequent. With every tag introducing a new hero: pop! For every sticky situation broken up by Pillman, which he followed up by cackling in the opposition's faces and celebrating wildly: pop! With every offensive move and every counter move: pop!

Davey's introductory cheer was extended as he raised 275lb Hawk up into the air like he was a child and held him there for an eternity before crashing him down to the mat. The crowd had injected them with an overdose of adrenaline, and they were being repaid in kind.

When the match broke down into a melee, Austin attacked Owen's knee with a steel chair. Bruce Hart dragged Austin from his baby brother from behind the barricade, before Bret got retribution with a similar attack.

Owen had to be carried out of the fray but would later limp back out and roll Austin up from behind for the one, two, three and the biggest reaction of his career – the perennial pesky younger brother becoming the biggest of all heroes.

But Team USA didn't take the loss well and continued to assault the winners, causing the Hart brothers in the audience to storm the ring and make the save. The 'police' had to drag Austin out of the ring in handcuffs to stop the carnage, but when the Harts finally had the ring to themselves, the whole family joined the celebration.

Bret and Pillman supported a frail Stu into the ring whilst Owen helped Helen. Davey hugged Diana and when he turned around, he caught Harry dashing towards him and raised him high into the air. Bret's children beamed with pride as Owen carried his young son Oje before putting him down to give tiny daughter Athena a turn.

'This is a very special moment in our business,' screamed Jim Ross over Bret's music and 12,000 pairs of clapping hands, 'a very special moment in this industry!'

More kids scaled the ring, including future stars Teddy Hart, TJ Wilson and Natalya Neidhart, which was soon filled with dozens of family members spanning an 80-year age range.

Like a cruise liner slowly heading for an iceberg, the WWF was taking some turning around. *Nitro* was still winning the ratings war, but the quality of the WWF programming was cutting through and they were heading for calmer seas, thanks to stormy angles and ground-breaking TV events.

In Your House 16: Canadian Stampede is one of the most iconic events in wrestling history. For the five men that made up the Hart Foundation, it would be a night they would remember above almost all others for the rest of their lives. Unfortunately, for so many of them, that time would be tragically short.

Davey had already been to the WWF office staff to warn them of his concern for Pillman. Davey could see in Brian what he couldn't see in himself: a dangerous cocktail of over-medication, painkiller addiction and alcohol taking hold. Owen and Bret were equally worried about Davey, especially when he fell in the bathroom of his hotel room and cracked his face on the side of the bath, requiring 16 stitches.

Davey's friend Robert 'Jeep' Swenson died of a heart attack at the age of 40 in August 1997. Swenson was a giant part-time wrestler who Davey had met whilst picking up some independent shows in 1993. The two gentle giants hit it off immediately, sharing the same sense of humour and interests. They already had a close mutual friend in Hulk Hogan, as Jeep, also an actor and stuntman, had appeared alongside Hogan in the movie *No Holds Barred*. At that time in the late-80s, Swenson's steroid use had helped him enter the *Guinness Book of World Records* for having the largest biceps on the planet. Jeep landed the role as Bane in *Batman & Robin* in 1996. He invited Davey and Diana to the set to watch the filming, where they rubbed shoulders with Chris O'Donnell and Uma Thurman.

Both Hogan and Davey gave eulogies at Jeep's funeral.

39

THE THANKS YOU GET

'I saw the light die in Davey's eyes that day, darkness seeping
into a heart that was giving out.'

Bret Hart

One Night Only UK
20 September 1997
NEC Arena
Birmingham, England
WWF European Championship
The British Bulldog v Shawn Michaels
Attendance: 11,000

'Davey, how special is this homecoming going to be tonight, defending
your European title in front of your countrymen?' Jim Ross asked in
the locker room as a relaxed Davey sat open-shirted, his giant sequined
Union Jack flag and his European belt hung behind him.

'It's gonna be very special,' a sombre-looking Bulldog began, 'I
got my sister who's sitting out in the crowd who's battled with cancer
twice – once when she was a year old and just a few months ago, she
was in hospital in Manchester and they didn't think she was gonna pull
through. They've taken almost everything out of her that they possibly
can take, and she pulled through it. So, to me, she's a champion in my
eyes so I'm dedicating this match tonight to my sister Tracey.' Davey
stopped short, on this occasion, of promising to win for Tracey. That
was because he now knew that wasn't the case – he was going to lose.

Davey wasn't just the current European champion; he was *the* champion of Europe. He had been awarded the new title so that he could defend the belt in the main event on every leg of every European tour for the foreseeable future. This was his first defence of the title in Europe, and it was in front of his fanatical UK supporters. He had been told, not that he needed to be, that he would be successfully defending the title throughout Europe. This wasn't even a tour, it was, as the title of the event would suggest, a one-night-only pay-per-view in the UK.

Shawn had returned from his mutually agreed hiatus after two months, as the special guest referee in the WWF championship match at *SummerSlam* between Bret and the Undertaker. He had taken a swing at Bret with a steel chair, inadvertently knocked out 'Taker, and been forced to count one, two, three. Bret became a five-time champion and subsequently, Shawn turned heel (with Stone Cold the undoubted number one babyface, he had little option). Hunter Hearst Helmsley was moving up the roster nicely and, with his bodyguard Chyna, joined forces with Shawn on screen as well as off it to form what would become 'D-Generation X'. The group would also have an enforcer in the shape of a returning Rick Rude, who was a welcome sight for Davey behind the curtain as an old pal.

With their history of such great matches and with his new heel status, Shawn had been picked as the perfect man to put Davey over in a UK main event. He and Hunter had muscled their way on to the booking committee and Shawn had apparently been heard saying that he would be doing no more jobs as he worked his way back to the top.

In the promotional events and in the UK media frenzy, Davey had promised to win for his dying sister. Little did he know then, that on the day of the event, Shawn would convince McMahon that in just his fourth match back and only his ninth match in four months, he should beat Bulldog in the UK and take his title from him in order for him to gain as much heat as possible following his heel turn. Vince bought it and a switch in the result was sanctioned. Davey was left devastated when they told him before the show.

Thrusting his crotch all the way, Shawn danced his way down the ramp. He threw himself at some swooning teenagers and while the girls hugged him, a boy rubbed his British Bulldog action figure in

Shawn's face; Shawn snatched the toy, pulled out the front of his tights and dropped it down into his ever-gyrating genitals, before delving deep to retrieve it and tossing it back.

Davey entered to predictable adulation with his tiny, frail sister Tracey by his side. As they reached ringside, he put his arm around her and guided her to Diana and the rest of the family. He then got in the ring and paraded his Union Jack cape to the crowd that worshipped him.

The British Bulldog dominated the opening ten minutes of the match, displaying his awesome strength by pressing Shawn and throwing him around like he was a tiny doll. Shawn sold outrageously, allowing the fans to celebrate Davey's power moves to the maximum. Then Rude, Hunter and Chyna arrived to offer assistance to their struggling stable leader and the match quickly descended into a four-on-one handicap match. Davey was wearing a very visible brace to support his legitimately shot right knee. This was soon worked into the story of the match, as Michaels inside the ring and his dastardly pals on the outside worked the injury to the vociferous disgust of the crowd. Shawn ripped off the knee brace and threw it at Davey's family before applying a figure-four leglock on him. A bloody-mouthed Bulldog screamed in agony as he tried to break the hold or make it to the ropes, only for Shawn's allies to prevent him at every turn as the crowd chanted for their British Bulldog. When Davey went limp in the middle of the ring, with no fight left, referee Earl Hebner called for the bell. Missiles of food and drinks began to fly into the ring as boos echoed around the arena.

When the assault continued after the bell, Diana hit the ring, shortly followed by Bret and Owen and the soon-to-be-christened 'DX' scarpered.

The worked attack on the knee had genuinely caused further damage, and when a grimacing Davey rolled out of the ring, he was forced to limp slowly past a sobbing Tracey.

Just two days later, the WWF crew were back in New York to film *Monday Night Raw* at Madison Square Garden. Davey wasn't there, stressing that he needed a lighter schedule to enable his knee to recover. Whilst that was true, he was also down about how things had played out in England, and was becoming disillusioned.

Vince summoned Bret to his office at MSG and told him outright that he couldn't afford to pay him the amount they had agreed in his new contract. He told him he was free to go to WCW if he could still get a similar deal out of them to the one they were offering before. With Austin the hottest babyface in the business – largely down to his feud with Bret and the Hart Foundation – and Shawn now the heel at the top of the card and earning half the money that Bret was on, Bret was suddenly an expendable luxury.

Despite his knee being in horrendous condition, Davey returned to action at a house show a further two days later. He had now added ultra-addictive morphine to his painkilling arsenal. Bret allowed the Undertaker to beat him senseless in the main event, so much so that a child with a learning disability charged the ring to protect him. As Bret returned backstage, the kid shook off the security that had removed him from the ring and chased after his hero behind the curtain. When he reached Bret, he hugged him and told him that he loved him. When Bret looked up, he saw Davey walking away in a flood of tears – the scene just too much for Bulldog's fragile heart and mind.

The next pay-per-view was *In Your House 18: Badd Blood*, on 5 October from St Louis. Bret and Pillman were late; it was assumed they were on the same flight, so no one thought much of it. Concern arose when Bret arrived and told them he had travelled alone and had no idea where Brian was. Some of the boys confirmed he was at their hotel the night before, but no one had seen him that morning or since. Jim Cornette called the Budgetel Inn in Bloomington, Minnesota, to ask what time Brian had checked out of the hotel. The call was soon passed to a police officer who confirmed that 35-year-old Pillman had been found dead in his hotel room earlier in the day. Brian left behind five children and a pregnant wife.

In the wrestling business, 'the show must go on' message is taught as early as the sleeper hold. A zombie-like Bret and Davey partnered as Team Canada to beat the American team of 'The Patriot' and Vader. Bret was still the champion but was also inevitably leaving for WCW after being given little option by McMahon. The title didn't need to be on the line at this event as the main event was mouth-watering enough: the first ever 'Hell in a Cell' match. It would be Shawn Michaels against the Undertaker inside the inescapable steel structure with the winner to get a shot at Bret's title at *Survivor Series* five weeks later in Montreal, Canada. The Undertaker's long-presumed-dead 'brother' Kane would make his debut, rip the door from the cage and tombstone piledrive his sibling, allowing a bloodied Heartbreak Kid to steal a victory.

Vince wanted Stone Cold to reach the top of the mountain at *WrestleMania XIV* by beating his current top heel and champion at the time – who he now intended to be Shawn Michaels.

Bret agreed a $2.5 million per year contract with Eric Bischoff and was due to start with WCW in mid-November. He tried to make amends with Shawn by telling him that he would be in safe hands when they would meet in the ring at *Survivor Series* and that he would have no problem dropping the belt to him. But Shawn told Bret that he didn't feel the same way and that he would not do the same for him if the shoe was on the other foot. Bret retracted his olive branch and an impasse emerged.

When Vince told Bret of his desire for him to lose the belt to Shawn at the pay-per-view in Canada, Bret refused, causing Vince to envisage the death knell in his company's war with WCW: his champion and his title belt suddenly appearing on the live broadcast of the enemy – he had, of course, used the same spot himself with Ric Flair seven years earlier.

It was the day before the event, at the arena, when a compromise was seemingly agreed upon. Bret, continuously reminding Vince that he had creative control of his character for the final 30 days he was with the company, suggested he win the match in front of his compatriots – finally forcing Shawn to put him over – and then he would return the favour, and the belt, the following night on *Raw* in the USA. Knowing Shawn would not agree to this, Vince's compromise was that DX interfere, resulting in a disqualification win for Bret, who then could simply forfeit the title before leaving. Vince explained that they would capitalise on the fact that the smart fans knew of the genuine hatred between the two competitors; he himself and some security would be at ringside to create the illusion that the match and subsequent melee – which Bulldog, Jim and Owen would also run in on – had descended into a shoot.

Survivor Series
9 November 1997
Molson Centre
Montreal, Quebec, Canada
WWF Championship
Shawn Michaels v Bret 'Hitman' Hart
Attendance: 20,593

Davey and Jim walked behind Bret the whole way through the building. Alongside them was Bret's seven-year-old son Blade, who proudly carried the giant Canadian flag his dad would soon carry out to the ring. They were still in their ring gear from their match earlier in the show, having teamed with Doug Furnas and Phil Lafon as Team Canada to defeat another variation of Team USA. Owen had just lost his Intercontinental title match against Stone Cold moments earlier.

When they reached the *Gorilla position*, Shawn Michaels' 'Sexy Boy' music was suddenly drowned out by a chorus of boos. What they didn't know was that Shawn was in the ring blowing his nose and dry humping a Maple Leaf flag.

A suited Rick Rude marched towards the Foundation boys on their arrival, voicing his suspicions that Hunter hadn't hung around with him in Gorilla ready for the run in. 'I'll watch your back in case they try to jump you or try anything funny out there,' he whispered to Bret, who nodded in appreciation and took the flag from his proud son before disappearing through the curtain to an explosion of screeching guitar strings and roaring support.

Bruce Prichard sat in Gorilla watching the match on a monitor, communicating with the ringside commentators through his headset as Bret and Shawn tore the house down. Davey and Jim, now joined by Owen, paced the corridor, peeking through the curtain every so often as they awaited the cue from Prichard to dash to the ring. There was still no sign of Hunter.

After 20 minutes of hard-hitting action, designed to convince the crowd that the pair were genuinely inflicting pain on each other, the sound of the ring bell surprised everyone. It had come just seconds after Shawn had applied Bret's own sharpshooter on him, when referee Earl Hebner immediately signalled that Bret had submitted.

'What the hell!' said Prichard. 'Why've you rung the bell?' he screamed into the earpiece of timekeeper Mark Yeaton, who was stunned himself at the orders Vince McMahon had barked at him at ringside.

'What happened? What happened?' Owen asked frantically.

'They fucked 'im,' Davey said, peering through the curtain. 'They just fucked Bret; they screwed 'im.'

Whilst Earl Hebner sprinted out of the ring, Shawn untangled his legs from Bret's and rolled out of the ring into the waiting arms of Hunter, who had miraculously appeared at ringside and was feigning shock and surprise. Shawn's acting performance was hardly going to get him a role in the next Scorsese epic, as he stomped and cussed in apparent disgust – but still ensured he collected the belt. It would be several years before he finally admitted he was in on the plot all along.

Bret stared down at Vince for a few seconds before landing a huge goblet of spit right between his eyes.

'Bullshit! Bullshit!' the crowd chanted. They weren't fooled.

Owen, Davey and Jim swung around and stared at a bemused Prichard.

'What do we do?' asked Davey.

'I don't know guys,' replied Prichard, 'go out there as planned I guess.'

Bret's bottom lip quivered as his eyes met those of Owen, Davey and Jim. They still all rode together after all these years, but he felt he had let them down; he had been their leader since Dynamite's self-destruction. He felt he had let his fans down, his country and his stellar body of work down. He felt the Hitman character he had nurtured first with Jim as a tag partner, later with Owen and Davey as adversaries, and then all together alongside tragic Brian Pillman, had just been murdered.

Bret mimed the letters WCW into the air to leave the crowd in no doubt of his destination, or what had just gone down. Then he proceeded to smash up the ringside monitors before being led to the back by security.

In the locker room, Shawn sobbed as he begged Bret to believe he wasn't involved in the deception, throwing the belt he'd just beelined to collect from the side of the ring on to the floor and claiming he didn't want it.

The boys were angry, especially Ken Shamrock, Mick Foley and locker-room leader the Undertaker, as well as the Foundation boys and Rick Rude. Bret undressed and turned to get his towel to head into the shower and afforded himself a wry smile; some things never change – his towel was damp and screwed up: Davey had, as usual when he forgot his own, used Bret's.

The Undertaker persuaded Vince and his makeshift bodyguards – Sergeant Slaughter, Jerry Brisco and his son Shane – that they needed to face Bret to save themselves from a mutiny.

'Vince is 'ere Bret,' Davey called into the shower, 'says he wants to talk to ya.'

'Tell Vince to get the hell out of here before he gets hurt,' Bret replied.

'Bret says you should leav...'

'I heard him Davey!' said Vince. 'But I'm staying.'

'Says he's staying, Bret.'

Bret walked out of the shower sopping wet and sat down. As he reached over to pick up the Bulldog-used towel, Vince said, 'It's the first time I ever lied to one of my talent.'

'Who are you kidding, you lying piece of shit!' Bret snapped back.

'You left me no choice Bret, what was I supposed to do?'

Davey, Owen, Jim and Rick sat calmly beside Bret, with Vince, Shane, Slaughter and Brisco standing across the room; the Undertaker was overseeing as the battle lines were drawn, and Shawn held his head in his hands in the corner.

'If you're still here when I've finished getting dressed, I'll have no choice but to punch you out,' Bret said.

The tension built with each item of clothing. Vince was too proud to run and knew he owed Bret the opportunity to at least leave the locker room, if not the WWF, with his head held high.

'Okay,' said Bret when he finished tying his shoelaces and stood up, and all members of the stand-off braced for the collision.

Shane made a dash to intervene but was grabbed by Davey, who stumbled to the floor on to his already injured knee. Vince bowed his head to minimise the impact he knew was coming, but Bret's uppercut lifted him clean off his feet, so much so that an unconscious and limp Vince sprained his ankle as he landed like a starfish on the cold, hard floor.

Davey, Owen and Mick Foley flew home instead of to Ottawa for the following night's *Raw* in principled support of Bret, with Ken Shamrock, Jim Neidhart and Rick Rude offering to do the same. But Bret urged them to think long and hard about their futures. Shamrock stayed with the WWF and Foley backed down too and re-joined the tour midweek. Disgruntled Rick Rude and Jim Neidhart left shortly afterwards.

Owen was left in a deep dilemma. Not only had he been content in the WWF, he had a great contract with just two years left on it and had promised his wife Martha that he would retire when it finished at the end of 1999. He had behaved sensibly and frugally with his money; they were in the process of building their dream home in Calgary where they were raising their two young children. Owen had grown to hate life on the road more than ever and was counting down the days until his financial security meant he no longer needed to carry on with the wrestling lifestyle to support his family. To compound the financial aspect, Vince refused to let him or Davey out of their contracts, meaning they were obliged to buy themselves out if they wanted to leave. This didn't apply to Rick or Jim, who weren't under guaranteed contracts but pay-on-appearance type deals.

On the 17 November edition of *Raw*, Vince McMahon, still sporting a shadowy bruise under his left eye, was interviewed formally by Jim Ross to address what had already become known as the 'Montreal Screwjob'. He insisted that neither the referee nor Shawn Michaels bore any responsibility for the incident, in an interview which saw the often-blurred lines of professional wrestling find some clarity firmly in a reality-based narrative. Vince went on to say that he too felt no guilt, and that in fact 'Bret Hart screwed Bret Hart.'

That statement would go down in wrestling folklore, not merely for the words but for the cold and clinical fashion in which they were delivered. Jim Ross and other WWF bookers such as Bruce Prichard, saw the character that could, and would, become the biggest and most hated heel of the Attitude Era and bitter enemy of their blue-collar hero Steve Austin: 'Mr McMahon'.

Davey had re-injured his bad knee in the fracas that had ensued in the Montreal locker room – his lawyer citing this as the reason for Davey's ongoing absence from the shows. Davey took the opportunity to finally have surgery on the knee, which bought him time to negotiate with WCW; but it also meant more painkillers and time away from the ring and the life on the road he was so used to.

Despite being unhappy with Vince, the Kliq and WWF as a whole, Owen decided to stay. Unwilling to cost himself and his family their early retirement plans out of blind loyalty to his brother, Owen accepted a pay rise and the promise of a strong push and a programme with Shawn and was back in a WWF ring before the end of 1997. He didn't trust WCW with his career, so haphazard and poorly written were their shows and booking techniques.

Davey, however, just like he had twice before with Tom, was determined to show that loyalty. Davey and Diana had more to lose, too. They had spent an initial $60,000 producing a home workout video on the agreement that Vince and the WWF would help with the final production and marketing. Without the WWF affiliation, the project was left nowhere.

Davey agreed to pay the WWF the $150,000 penalty to terminate his contract and signed a three-year deal with Eric Bischoff worth an average of $383,000 per year.

On the 26 January 1998 edition of *Nitro,* Davey strolled out to only a little fanfare as he answered former NFL star and pro wrestling rookie Steve 'Mongo' McMichael's open challenge. Davey's face appeared chubbier than it had last time he had appeared on TV 14 weeks earlier. Later in the show he wrestled to a three-minute victory over the lesser-skilled McMichael. This would be an early indicator of what was to come.

40

RESCUE DOG

'Rarely, if ever, had someone with that much talent
fallen that far in the wrestling business.'

Dave Meltzer

Fall Brawl
13 September 1998
Lawrence Joel Veterans Memorial Coliseum
Winston-Salem, North Carolina
Alex Wright and Disco Inferno v British Bulldog and Jim Neidhart
Attendance: 11,528

The crowd appeared to have no idea who to cheer for. Alex Wright
– ironically the son of Dynamite's former sparring partner Steve and
nephew of Bernie, who both Dynamite and Davey had made their pro
debuts against – attempted to make the best of the match, but Bulldog and
Anvil appeared almost unrecognisable from their glory days. Towards the
end of the match, it took three attempts for Davey to get 'Disco Inferno'
up on to his shoulder for the powerslam to finish it.

On 13 April 1998, with Stone Cold Steve Austin now their
champion, *Raw* had finally ended *Nitro*'s 83 consecutive weeks on
top of the Monday night ratings war. Harnessing the controversy of
the Montreal Screwjob, the momentum of the WWF was propelling
it to becoming a mainstream cultural icon of its time similar to Hulk
Hogan's 'Golden Era' a decade before. WCW's lavish short-termism
had left them with outlandish salaries to pay to over-the-hill stars,

viewers were switching channels en masse, quickly followed by advertisers and sponsors.

Possibly the most baffling mercenary to be added to Eric Bischoff's roster was the Ultimate Warrior. In the main event of *Fall Brawl*, which also featured the likes of Bret, Hogan, Roddy Piper, Kevin Nash and Lex Luger, Warrior was to emerge randomly in the ring as smoke that had blasted from the turnbuckles cleared. In reality, he was climbing from a trap door fitted to the ring canvas.

The following night on *Nitro*, Davey wrestled a three-minute match against 'Barbarian'. Davey finished the match with a barely recognisable powerslam, as he hardly got his opponent off the floor before collapsing sideways on top of him for the three-count. Davey limped up the ramp grimacing heavily, his darkened eyes sinking into his pale face; he reached around to support the lower back that had troubled him for so many years. Even the morphine and excessive painkillers were not enough to dampen this pain. Davey had actually fractured his spine at *Fall Brawl* by taking a bump on the hidden trap door. It was a miracle he'd managed to finish the pay-per-view match at all, let alone have another match on live TV the following night. Davey was proving as stubborn as his cousin.

Even more artificial painkilling continued to numb the extraordinary anguish enough for Davey to wrestle a few more matches as he engaged in a programme against Alex Wright based around them both claiming to be Europe's number one star. With his father Steve having settled in Germany as a young man, Alex was actually a German native.

In a backstage promo, Davey was asked his thoughts on Wright claiming to be their home continent's finest. The minute-long answer was incoherent as Davey slurred his words and lost his way repeatedly.

On the road, a clearly troubled Davey told Bret of his woes. It was clear to Bret that Davey was in deep with his substance abuse – Davey would admit to needing help, but also admitted to not being ready to reach out for it. Bret was more surprised to hear that Davey and Diana's marriage was on the rocks.

After braving his way through a few more matches, he finally removed himself from the circuit, citing the back injury that had been caused by the trap door, which had been kept secret even from the stars that would be wrestling on it to prevent any leaks of the main event angle appearing in the dirt sheets. That main event was so ludicrously bad that it has gone down in wrestling infamy, and it only served to make more fans switch back to the WWF.

WCW cut Davey's pay by 30 per cent whilst he was out of action.

In November, Davey got news from his family back home in England that Tracey's long and brave battle with cancer was nearing an end. He flew home but didn't make it in time; his little sister passed away before he could see her one last time.

Body, mind, heart and soul; all of Davey was breaking and he finally accepted the help he knew he desperately needed. It took Diana to join Davey at rock bottom for him to accept help as she began divorce proceedings and told Davey it was over unless he turned things around.

On Boxing Day Davey took a two-hour flight north to Grand Prairie from Calgary, where he checked into the Alberta rehab facility. Diana dropped the divorce proceedings as hope appeared on the horizon. Clients at the facility were detoxified, and it usually took around five days before the system was clean; the same process took around three weeks for Davey – a hellish period of pain, bouts of psychosis and hallucinations.

Without the painkilling substances coursing through his system, his back and knees ached terribly, and his kidneys agonised as they struggled to cope with the sudden change in workload. He was taken from the facility to hospital for tests to check his kidneys weren't failing, and when the results came back, it was simply put down to withdrawal.

He started a business course that was on offer at the facility, as he began to look towards life after wrestling, but the severity of the pain ultimately made it impossible for him to attend the classes. He collapsed on 3 February and was again rushed to hospital, where once again his organs were given the all-clear. Frustrated, miserable and in agony, Davey discharged himself after seven weeks in rehab, one week short of completing the scheduled two-month programme, and he flew home to Calgary.

Davey's beloved mother Joyce was now dying of cancer too, and with so much of the disease running in his family, Davey became convinced that his own pain and suffering, particularly in his kidneys, must be cancer.

Harry broke his arm while amateur wrestling and Davey spent a whole night in the hospital by his bedside. He then got the call he had been dreading: he needed to fly home to England to say a final goodbye to his mother.

He was in agony for the whole trip and flew back an even more broken man immediately after the funeral, when he was hospitalised yet again. The doctors suspected he was feigning the severity of his symptoms to get some of the painkilling medication he was so addicted to on prescription, but when the results of his white blood cell count came through six weeks after they had done the test, they realised he had a severe staph infection in his spine that was getting worse, and was now life-threatening.

News spread fast and the media and wrestling dirt sheets began reporting that, at worst, Davey might die; at best, his career was over, but the most likely outcome was that he would be wheelchair-bound just like Dynamite. In the eyes of the wrestling world, the British Bulldog was put down.

The full extent of his back injuries were revealed: crushed C-9 and C-10 discs and a further four fractured discs.

One afternoon as Diana prepared to visit her husband, a FedEx package arrived at the door addressed to Davey. As it looked important and he wasn't in a fit state to deal with things, Diana opened it. It was details of the termination of his WCW contract which they were enacting under the inactivity clause. She took it to the hospital and explained to Davey that to compound matters, they now had no income. His plight was carrying much sympathy in the media and when this latest news came out, WCW and Eric Bischoff came under fire as a callous and cruel organisation. On 16 April Bischoff finally contacted Davey personally in a bid to arrest the escalating bad publicity, insisting that he had been left with little option but to release him as WCW continued to haemorrhage money and was a business in turmoil. In truth, Davey's high salary and lack of appearances had left Bischoff with little option.

41

ONE MORE RUN

'Davey [had been] one of the top wrestlers in the world ... He
was well liked by all of the guys and had several close friends
that he travelled and trained with. He had an infectious laugh
and a great sense of humour, often pulling elaborate pranks
that eased the monotony of the road, but really hurt no one.'

Mick Foley

17 April 1999. Calgary Hospital

Davey, now in a full body cast, managed to smile for the first time in
as long as he could remember when two of the friendliest faces in his
life, Owen and Mick Foley, visited him in the hospital (the WWF were
back in Calgary for a house show).

Owen had excitedly given Mick directions from the airport as
Mick wanted to visit Davey the moment they landed in Calgary for
the evening's house show. He assumed there would be a crowd of burly
wrestlers there eager to take the same opportunity. But he was saddened
when he found not one other single member of the WWF roster had
bothered to visit Davey. He would later write that it was the saddest
day of his whole career; the day he realised that the so-called 'wrestling
family' was not that at all, and no matter how popular or respected you
appeared to be in the locker room, once the business had used you up
and spat you out, even the majority of the boys would forget about you.

Davey told Mick of his shoddy treatment at the hands of WCW,
allowing Mick to give Davey the good news: he was now a two-
time WWF champion and they had effectively seen off the WCW

competition. The WWF's ratings and value were suddenly amongst the highest in its history and WCW had become a comparative laughing stock.

Later, a pained Davey had to restrain his laughter as Owen told him that he was once again the Blue Blazer – a decade after the gimmick had bombed previously. Owen told Davey that when they had suggested a typically sordid storyline in which he had an affair with Jeff Jarrett's valet Debra, he had shunned the idea and told them he wanted nothing to do with their sleazy new angles. That had led to them suggesting reprising the Blue Blazer as a sanctimonious do-gooder, lecturing the likes of Val Venis and 'The Godfather' for their womanising ways.

The conversation escalated quickly, and soon Owen was holding a phone to Davey's ear with Vince McMahon on the end of the line.

'You know, pal … we'd like you to finish your career off here, with your family,' Vince told Davey.

'You know me Vince, I've come back from worse things,' Davey said as he lay in a full body cast on a morphine drip. 'I'll be back in the ring before you know it, as long as you've got a place for me.'

'If you can get yourself healthy, there's always a home for you here,' Vince assured him.

And with that, Davey was given the hope he needed. He began to tell people that he had one more run left and a dream to fulfil in wrestling before he retired – to tag team with his son Harry, who was showing real promise as he continued his training in the dungeon.

With the infection a little under control, Davey insisted on being discharged from hospital on 21 April, when he heard that yet another good friend, Rick Rude, had suddenly died at just 40 years of age.

Despite returning home in a full body cast, with a nurse having to visit each morning to clean him and replace his catheter, Davey actually refused the morphine prescription that the doctors had offered him and opted for less potent and less addictive pain relief. He was determined that the British Bulldog would have one last run around his old park, with Owen as his partner in mischief once again; but little did he know that the biggest tragedy yet was just around the corner.

42

OWEN

'Owen saw humour in everything. He had a big,
easy laugh, and an even bigger heart.'

Dwayne 'The Rock' Johnson

Over the Edge
23 May 1999
Kemper Arena
Kansas City, Missouri
Intercontinental Championship
Blue Blazer v Godfather
Attendance: 16,472

The sweat dripping from Owen's chin was a combination of both heat and nerves as he balanced 80ft above the ring, about to make his entrance.

It was always hot under the Blue Blazer mask and feathered cape, but high in the rafters in the humid building, anxiously waiting to perform a dangerous stunt he wasn't comfortable with, it was stifling.

Six months earlier, the WWF had had Owen descend from the rafters with a locking carabiner, with no intention of him having to release himself. On that occasion, to add to the hapless comedy superhero gimmick they had devised for one of the world's top and most respected performers, they had his stunt purposely fail, to leave him dangling above the ring helpless to stop the foes he had been lecturing from taking shots at him; eventually having to retreat back up to where he had descended from.

At *Over the Edge*, he would have to land in the ring and unclip himself, so between the bookers and the third-party stunt coordinators, they had opted for a less-safe quick-release clip. Once in the ring, Owen was to immediately pull a cord so that his landing would look smooth for the pay-per-view audience, and the rigging team could quickly pull the line back up out of view.

Owen had performed a dress rehearsal test-drop a few hours earlier, but with the ring looking so tiny from the steel maintenance walkway they were perched upon, it did little to ease his anxieties.

'As long as you don't put your hands on this, nothing's going to happen,' rigger Bobby Talbert assured Owen during the rehearsal, showing him the release cord. 'When you get to the floor, you grab it and give it a deliberate pull upwards, so it gives me a visual cue to pull the rope back up.'

'Got it,' Owen quickly responded, nervously ensuring the flapping cape didn't interfere with the release cord.

The practice drop went well, but Owen didn't release himself quickly enough for the liking of some watching WWF officials, who audibly groaned.

Owen hadn't been his usual upbeat, humorous self as the wrestlers had joked in the locker room; he had been deeply concerned about his safety and had told some of them so. He had changed into his blue singlet and tights and white boots but stuffed the mask and cape into a rucksack and pulled on some overalls and a baseball cap to make himself appear as a maintenance guy as he trekked through the fans and up the steel steps. He had bumped into an old friend in Harley Race as he left the locker room, and soon found himself telling Harley how uncomfortable he was with the upcoming stunt. Harley tried to put Owen at ease the only way he knew how, with a light-hearted joke: 'Be careful the rope doesn't break.'

A rickety wooden ladder in the nosebleeds of the arena connected the stairs to the walkway Owen needed to be on. How ironic, he had been thinking, the only reason he was back as the Blue Blazer was because of his refusal to get involved in the sleaze and sex-motivated storylines of this new Attitude Era, and yet here he now was having to do this. Just being a great wrestler, talker and entertainer wasn't enough anymore. Owen had shot down so many zany and sleazy angles already, he just needed to get this one out of the way, he thought. The whole stunt was just yet another shot at WCW, who had their hero Sting drop from the roof superhero-like, week-in, week-out.

The WWF had also introduced a 'Hardcore' title as they tilted towards the extreme style in a bid to regain some viewers lost to ECW. Owen watched the Hardcore title match between Al Snow and Hardcore Holly from his perilous position 80 feet high, as the rigging team helped him into his mask and cape before fitting his harness.

Talbert told Owen it was time for him to climb on to the outside of the railings, where he tensioned up the equipment so that it was holding Owen's weight. He was now simply hanging there. On the giant screen, a 40-second promo-video of the Blue Blazer began, informing the audience who was coming next. Knowing the moment was upon him, Owen stretched out his arms for maximum comfort and to ensure the cape wasn't obstructing him. It was then the riggers heard a slight click and they knew instantly what it was. The snap release clip had opened. They looked over the edge in horror to see Owen hurtling towards the ring.

Referee Jimmy Korderas was still clearing some of the weapons and debris from the hardcore match from the ring. Owen, now knowing his fate, yelled 'Look out!' between his screams to warn Korderas that he was plummeting straight toward him. Owen crashed on to the turnbuckle at nearly 50 miles per hour, shattering his left arm and tearing his aorta, which left his lungs filling with blood.

Despite frantic attempts by paramedics to save him, Owen Hart was pronounced dead at the Truman Medical Center four miles away from the arena. He was just 34 years old.

* * *

Denial. Anger. Bargaining. Depression. Acceptance

The recognised stages of a grieving process can be difficult to manage for anyone, but for the already splintered Hart family, who had suffered loss and hurt in the preceding months, Owen's shocking and easily avoidable death proved simply impossible.

All at different stages of the journey, and each seemingly with an additional motivation or underlying loyalty guiding their thoughts, their feelings and the direction of anger, they mercilessly tore each other apart and in full public gaze.

Bret and widowed Martha wanted McMahon blood, or at the very least to see Vince held to account in a court of law for the unnecessary tragedy. The fact that he had made the decision to go ahead and complete the final two hours of the live show had convinced them beyond any doubt that the chairman of the company needed punishing for his callous handling of the situation both before and after the fall.

Bruce, Ellie and Diana actively sought to have any charges brought by the family against the WWF dropped in favour of a quick settlement. Bret and Martha accused them of looking after their own (or their husbands') potential employment opportunities with the promotion and the man responsible, certainly in their minds, for their little brother's and husband's death ahead of the justice Owen deserved. Both sides of the argument were soon actively trying to recruit the heartbroken Stu and Helen into league with them, knowing that their signatures on any legal papers would carry weight.

Poor Davey now had Owen's death to add to his own personal misery and so many other recent bereavements. But he continued to work hard on his own rehabilitation and physiotherapy in a bid to regain the job Vince had promised him so that he could provide for his own household once again. The truth was, Davey had come to regret leaving the WWF after Montreal – what he saw as one of the main instigators for his current hell – so given that the opportunity to return had been granted to him before Owen's death, assisted by Owen, no less, he had little motivation to once again turn down Vince's employment out of loyalty or duty to others.

Jim Neidhart was soon hired by the WWF as a talent trainer. Bret knew that Jim and Davey had just been fired by WCW and therefore could only realistically work for the WWF. He was therefore not against them working for Vince again, but he did expect them to remain neutral on the subject of Owen's death whilst the police continued their investigation into whether charges, up to and including manslaughter, should be brought. But Davey appeared on a news programme stating that Owen's death was merely an accident and that he was going to return to the WWF and win a title in Owen's honour, and he officially signed a three-year contract on 12 August, worth $450,000 per year. Feeling betrayed, Bret took a scathing shot at Davey in his regular column in the *Calgary Sun*, providing the analogy of a dog rolling in faeces. Davey then did an interview with the same publication, stating that he had shown Bret unending loyalty in following him out of the WWF and to WCW after Montreal, but that Bret had done nothing to help him in return just months later when his own career lay in tatters. Suddenly, even the strong bond between Davey and Bret was breaking.

On the 4 October episode of *Nitro*, Bret and Chris Benoit would put on a 30-minute classic in tribute to Owen in the very same arena the tragedy had happened. They hugged after Benoit tapped out to the sharpshooter, forcing the crowd to join them in tears. The final storytelling masterpiece of Bret's career had happened with a fellow Stampede Wrestling graduate.

Bret had always been determined not to become yet another tragic wrestling statistic. But he was WCW champion in the December of 1999, when inexperienced wrecking-machine Bill Goldberg challenged him at *Starrcade*. An overly stiff thrust kick to the head would leave Bret with a severe concussion. He continued to wrestle with terrible headaches into the new year, until his doctor diagnosed the true extent of his problems and ordered him to stop immediately. He made sporadic TV appearances to honour his hefty contract, until WCW terminated it in their usual classy way in October 2000: a letter sent via FedEx.

During the two years that WCW had dominated the ratings, they had attempted to further establish themselves as the dominant player in the wrestling industry by producing a second two-hour weekly show in *Thunder*, which would air on Thursday evenings. Vince knew he had to rival this or else lose fans on Mondays who had watched a cliffhanger ending the previous Thursday.

On 26 August 1999, the first episode of the new show *Smackdown* aired. Two weeks later the show was opened by the then Hardcore champion the Big Boss Man, who announced an open challenge for his title to be held there and then. The crowd were shocked to hear a typically 90s remixed version of 'Rule Britannia' hit, followed by a typically 90s dressed British Bulldog. Clad in extremely faded jeans and looking lean and motivated, Davey Boy took a matter of minutes to pin Boss Man before casually gifting his new belt to popular former Hardcore champion Al Snow. The following week on *Raw*, Davey explained to Jim Ross that he hadn't returned to the WWF to win any other championship than the only one that had eluded him during his long career, the big belt: the WWF championship.

With his intentions made clear and with an injury to the Undertaker creating an opening in the main event, Bulldog was placed into a six-man challenge match at the upcoming *Unforgiven* pay-per-view for the vacant title, alongside Big Show, Kane, Mankind, Triple H and The Rock, with Stone Cold Steve Austin serving as special enforcer. Just months after his career was completely written off, Davey was back in the main event of a WWF pay-per-view.

The match was won by Triple H (the main event moniker of the former Hunter Hearst Helmsley), but Davey appeared fit and strong, once again able to raise the giant men he shared the ring with high into the air with ease.

The following week on *Smackdown*, Davey was given a one-on-one title shot with Triple H, this time with The Rock as the special referee. The match would end in a melee when The Rock decided to lay the smack down on both competitors.

Davey would go one-on-one with The Rock at *No Mercy*, but his momentum, his brief run at the top and his self-respect were ended when he was slammed into a giant trough of 'dog poop' by Rocky, seemingly a shot across the bow to Bret following his newspaper remarks just weeks earlier.

It seemed that Davey Boy had been firmly back in the big time – but his demons still lurked under the surface. Davey missed Owen terribly. Owen had been his comfort and his support on the road. Not only was Davey grieving, he was without any of his Stampede brethren and was becoming a lonely and rudderless ship in the night.

In the coming weeks, Davey's eyes narrowed; his gait appeared less easy; his matches were shorter; his power less impressive. He trundled down the roster quickly and was soon appearing on tertiary shows *Jakked* and *Sunday Night Heat* as the leader of a random heel stable alongside Greenwich snobs the 'Mean Street Posse'. He regained his European title by defeating D'Lo Brown, but the belt had been devalued so badly in the two years since his first reign that it did more to confirm his demotion to the lower-mid card than it did to serve him any real glory. His six-week run with the title was ended when he lost it to Val Venis at the December pay-per-view *Armageddon*, before taking five weeks off for Christmas.

Davey continued to wrestle sporadically. He played a minor role as Kurt Angle's tag team partner against Chris Jericho and Chyna on the 21 February edition of *Raw* in Atlanta, Georgia, before flying to Tennessee, for the following day's *Smackdown* taping. Bulldog showed up at the Nashville Arena in an alarming state. Bruce Prichard and Jim Ross sat Davey down in private in the locker room. Davey drooled and slurred his words as he denied having a problem, but Bruce had been there himself and could see the signs easily, and Jim still carried the weight of his final conversations with Brian Pillman around with him, in which Pillman had vehemently denied having problems. They had seen and heard it all before in their combined decades in this poisoned industry.

Speaking on behalf of Vince, Bruce and Jim assured Davey that his job would be there waiting for him if and when he returned healthy.

'Okay,' accepted Davey, 'I'll go t' rehab back in Canada after this tour is done.'

'No,' Bruce answered sternly, 'you gotta go tonight; you gotta go right now.'

They got Davey to the airport and on to a flight directly back to Atlanta, from where he was taken straight to the Talbott Recovery Center. He was admitted into a four-month treatment for addiction to painkillers, sleeping pills, morphine and muscle relaxers.

43

CRIPPLED

'At that point in my life, when I first saw the
Dynamite Kid, the way he influenced me, the way
he inspired me to become a wrestler at that point in
my life, if I hadn't have seen him, I'd be somewhere
else and living in some other part of the world and
I may not be wrestling today because he was such a
strong influence on me ... to such an extent that I
pattern myself around him in terms of my training,
bodybuilding, wrestling – everything.'

Chris Benoit

25 March 2000

'YOU'RE TUNED IN TO CRIPPLER RADIO,' boomed the
introductory voice over the show's grungy theme music, 'BROADCAST
TO THE WORLD AT WWW DOT CHRIS BENOIT DOT
COM AND AT WWW DOT LIVE AUDIO WRESTLING
DOT COM, THIS IS YOUR WEEKLY AUDIO CHECK-IN
WITH WWF SUPERSTAR CHRIS BENOIT.'

'Welcome wrestling fans to a very, very special edition of Crippler
Radio,' began host Jeff Marek as the music faded out. 'Joining us this
week will not only be the one and only Chris Benoit of the World
Wrestling Federation, but as well, a little later on in the programme,
we're going to have both Chris Benoit and the Dynamite Kid talking
together for the first time in a very long time. But let's start off with
Chris. Chris, how you doing today?'

Following several years in his self-imposed wilderness, Tom had burst back into the mainstream wrestling scene with the release of his autobiography *Pure Dynamite*, in which he had spoken of his admiration for former protégé Benoit. He had subsequently been invited on to this weekly recording, posted on Benoit's own website long before the podcast era began.

'Very good Jeff, how you doing?' replied the man then known as 'The Crippler' in the WWF.

'I'm pretty excited I got to say,' said Jeff, 'I'm a big fan of both you guys, so this is gonna be a special one for me. Let's talk a little bit about you growing up in Edmonton watching Stampede Wrestling. Take us back to when you first saw wrestling in Edmonton.'

'Yeah, the first time I went to a live event I was 12 years old,' said Chris, 'and it was just one of these great wrestling atmospheres where the light hung over the ring and everything around the whole rest of the building was totally dark. I'll never forget the first time I saw the Dynamite Kid, his charisma and aggressiveness and the look that he had in the ring; from the first time I saw him, I not only knew that I wanted to be a pro wrestler, but I wanted to be just like him.'

'Obviously you've certainly emulated his style,' said Jeff, hoping to tease more of the lineage from Benoit.

'Oh totally, totally. Everything about him just always impressed me; his wrestling ability, his style, his aggressiveness, his execution.'

'How old were you when you first saw the Dynamite Kid?' asked Jeff.

'I was 12 years old the first time I saw him live,' said Chris. 'I'd seen him on TV a few times but the first time that I saw him live it really struck me.'

'Do any conversations you had with Dynamite stand out?' probed Jeff.

'They all stand out, really,' said Chris, 'from the first bit of small talk about training and then going up to him and showing him my arms and saying "I wanna be just like you; I wanna be a wrestler," and the time Tom gave me his boots in Stampede Wrestling. All those moments mean so much to me.'

'You still have the boots?'

'Yeah. Sure do.'

'You talked about training and Stampede, where you consciously tried to emulate the Dynamite Kid's style in the ring,' said Jeff. 'Do you still think about him now when you're putting matches together and when you're in the ring in the WWF?'

'Oh yeah, a lot of times,' Chris replied quickly. 'Sometimes, to get myself psyched up, I think about who I am and where I came from and what it means to me to be where I am today, and what I represent. And then a lot of times I'm out there and I feel like I'm representing a part of the Dynamite Kid; a part of Stampede Wrestling, that's where I came from. Those are my roots.'

'I can't help but remember when you won the title in WCW at the pay-per-view,' said Jeff, 'and you cut that promo at the end. One of the people you mentioned was the Dynamite Kid and how much he meant to you; was that always a dream of yours to one day win the world title and be able to talk about how much the Dynamite Kid meant to Chris Benoit?'

'I always talk about how much it means to me,' replied Chris, 'because he's such a big influence in my career. So much of what I do, it comes from me trying to be like the Dynamite Kid.'

'Let's talk a little bit about Dynamite's work in Japan,' Jeff changed the subject slightly. 'He had some outstanding matches with a lot of key people, but probably the most important programme he worked there was with Satoru Sayama; the original Tiger Mask. Do you remember when you first saw the Dynamite Kid in there with Tiger Mask; what were your feelings?'

'Unbelievable,' gasped Chris, 'watching those matches with him and the original Tiger Mask just cemented everything I ever believed in.'

'Do you think that that programme with Tiger Mask allowed guys like you to excel, ten years later?'

'Yeah, without a doubt, I think Tiger Mask and Dynamite were ten, 15 years ahead of their time back then; they definitely paved the way.'

Jeff and Chris then talked about their mutual admiration for Tom's memoir. In *Pure Dynamite*, Tom had been honest about some of his misdemeanours and the extent of his substance abuse, something that had garnered praise as many from the era of rampant violence and drug abuse were still adamantly denying any wrongdoing whilst their peers continued to die and suffer around them. He had, however, also taken every opportunity to lash out at his cousin and former world tag team championship partner Davey, as well as being blunt in his honest thoughts about many members of the Hart family.

To help promote the book, Tom had launched a website, run by Live Audio Wrestling – the same team that produced Benoit's website and audio show, and the reunion was made.

'Well, let's bring him on,' Jeff said excitedly. 'It's a pleasure to welcome to Chris Benoit dot com, one of the most outstanding wrestlers ever to put on the trunks and lace up the boots; Tom Billington; the Dynamite Kid. Tom, how you doing today?'

'Not too bad Jeff, yourself?' Tom's Lancastrian accent was thicker than ever as he connected into the call from his home in Wigan.

'I'm doing fine,' said Jeff, 'say hi to Chris Benoit – your old-time friend.'

Rather than say hello, Tom gave his verdict on Chris's career: 'Well, I'm very proud of what he's achieved. From WCW – which I don't rate – but now he's gone to the WWF and he's still achieving there, still doing a good strong job and he's still doing the dives from the top of the cage.'

'How would you rate Chris as a worker?' Jeff asked.

'Well, from one to ten, a very strong nine. He makes it very solid and believable in that ring. And it is believable when he comes off the top of that cage and lands, because you cannot break your landing. He will go in there with 100 per cent and even more, get in with anybody, even if it's that Rikishi, or that what's his name, Triple T ...'

'Triple H,' Jeff corrected.

'Triple H, sorry. But I'd rate Chris at the top of the WWF, but not the biggest man,' Tom said.

'I've known Chris for a while now and I know that he's probably his own worst critic,' said Jeff. 'He never feels 100 per cent comfortable about any of the matches that he's in. You've seen Chris work, Tom; what kind of advice could you give him?'

'Right now, I can't give him no advice,' said Tom abruptly, 'because I believe what I was doing in those days, like you said earlier, about working with Tiger Mask – we worked very hard, very dangerous, and after a while, people just loved to see them matches. But Chris, he can work with anyone; he could make a match with a wooden mop in that ring. He could make a mop look good, that's how good Chris is, and I'll give him credit for that. The thing is, with Chris, he is too shy to come out and say he is one of the best. I know how he thinks; deep down I think he knows he is, but he won't come out and say it. I remember one time, we were on a show and Chris asked me if he could do my diving headbutt off the top rope and I said, "Chris, you can do what you want." And Chris went in and did the flying headbutt; and ever since then, he's never looked back. He's one of the best. Where I left off, he carried on, and it ends up he's doing a better bleeding job!'

'How'd you feel about that, Chris?' the host turned back to Benoit.

'That's a great compliment, thank you very much, Tommy,' said Chris, even more softly spoken than he had been before. 'It's always been an honour to hear a compliment or a criticism from you, because you know I admire you so much and I admire your ability and your style so much, and I think that you've done so much for the business of professional wrestling throughout the world. I mean, in Canada and Japan, in the United States, to me you're, like, you know, what Wayne Gretzky was to hockey. I'm not the only one that said that, I mean Bret Hart has said that; a number of people have said that. And it's always an honour to hear from you, whether you think it's good or bad, because I take it to heart.'

'Tom, earlier on in this programme,' Jeff jumped in, 'Chris and I spoke a little bit about your matches with Tiger Mask; the date April 23, 1981, at the Sumo Hall, is a very important date in wrestling history. The first time the Dynamite Kid and Tiger Mask ever worked; the programme would change the face of wrestling history forever. Going into those matches Tom, did you have any idea how important they'd be in the grand scheme of things and how influential they'd be?'

'I didn't know it was going to carry on like it did, for a few years,' replied Tom, 'Tiger Mask, over there; Sayama, he'd become quite a big name and I think my name went up there with him for the wrestling ability and the high-flying dives and all that. It's hard to understand or say what I thought, but we did so many matches over there and the people didn't care if I won or lost. They just enjoyed seeing the action in that ring. We wrestled that many times, doing a lot of dangerous things – just like Chris would do right now – and that's why if Chris said to me, "Do you have any advice?", all I would say is that I can't give you no advice because you come off that top rope or top of that cage, I mean, if someone had said that to me 20 years ago, I would still do it, and that's why I'm in a wheelchair right now. But I would still do it all over again and I'm sure Chris would agree with that.'

'Chris, how about the dangers inherent in the business that Tom speaks about; you have any concerns about your health?' Jeff asked.

'Yeah, I do. But as Tommy said, I love what I do. I never look back and I'd do it all over again. I'm in love with what I do; I love being in the ring, I love wrestling. I love being a part of it. It's what I've always wanted to do, and it's all worthwhile to me.'

'Tom, Chris mentioned life on the road, but what was life on the road like in the World Wrestling Federation when you were there?'

'I enjoyed life on the road,' Tom answered, 'what passed time [on the road] for me, which was very good, and I never hurt nobody, but I do miss my pranks.'

'Oh yeah?' Jeff said, chasing further information.

'Sure I do. I had some good times with my pranks, like blowing people's suitcases up and things like that.'

'And cutting people's pants?' Jeff let Tom know that his reputation as a ribber preceded him as much as his wrestling.

'Yes, things like that, y'know, very mild things. But apart from that, in the ring, I was very professional; I worked as hard as I could. I think the majority of the wrestlers, when I was on the card, they weren't scared to go in the ring, they were scared to get back in the dressing room, just to see what had been blown up or cut up!'

'Did you have any favourite targets you kept going back to?'

'Oh, I always had a few favourite types, especially if I didn't like 'em. But even the people I did like, I'd still have a little prank with 'em. But, anyway, if I could just say something about Sid Vicious – he's a big man, looks the part, and he's a piece a shit. But anyway, I'm not talking about that idiot. Oh, one more thing before I go, I would just like to congratulate Chris and his wife on the baby boy or girl, whatever it was.'

'Thank you very much, Tommy,' Benoit said, his voice slightly breaking with emotion.

'You're welcome,' Tom said sincerely.

'Yeah, how is Daniel doing, Chris?' asked Jeff.

'Very good, very good. He's keeping us up at night still but I'm sure he'll grow out of that.'

'Last time we spoke, you said Daniel was growing bigger and bigger every week – he's gonna be a football player?' Jeff joked.

'I'll encourage him to do whatever he wants to do,' said Chris.

'We have a couple of emails here before we wrap up,' Jeff said. 'This comes in from a gentleman by the name of Dankind in Ontario: "My question for Tom Billington, the Dynamite Kid, is: who was the best tag team you faced in your WWF days and who do you feel the best tag team in the business is today or has the most potential?'

'Well, in the mid-80s,' Tom began, but he had misheard the question, 'I would say, and I don't like Davey Boy Smith anymore, you know that, but in the mid-80s, I would say the British Bulldogs. Because at that time he was a little bit agile, but I must admit he was a follower, not a leader. In other words, I was the captain of the team and I had to tell him what to do. He could work; he was agile; he was good, and we always got the people going. It's just a shame that he ended up on the morphine.'

'Yeah, it's an unfortunate situation,' Jeff said.

'By the way, Jeff, is he still in the clinic?'

'I believe so; he won't be out for another, I believe, 30 or 45 days.'

'That's what I don't understand, Jeff,' said Tom. 'How come Vince is paying $75,000 for that? Yet when I broke my back, he wouldn't give me $50?'

'Well, there's certainly a lot of politics surrounding this,' Jeff said sensitively.

'Exactly. I just thought I'd say that, Jeff.'

'Well, it's out there. Chris,' Jeff turned back to Benoit. 'Who would you rank as some of the greatest tag teams of all time?

'I guess I'd have to say the Bulldogs are one of my favourite teams of all time. The match that I've got on tape that I watch from time to time that I really like a lot is the Bulldogs in Japan, working against the Malenko brothers. It was a 30-minute draw, and it was one of the greatest tag team matches that I've ever seen. Great, great match.'

'We have another email here,' began Jeff, 'comes in from Spring Lake; the gentleman's name is Brian: "Let me start by saying it's an honour to hear my two favourite wrestlers of all time on the air together.

My question is, would the Dynamite Kid ever consider being a special one-time-only manager, or anything like that, for Chris?" Tom, would you ever consider doing anything like that?'

'No, not really,' Tom said with certainty, 'because I wouldn't like to get in Chris's way. He doesn't need no gimmick, nothing; he can go in the ring by himself and get the job done. I wouldn't go there, in a wheelchair, sat there like an idiot and show Chris up. Chris doesn't need a gimmick. If I was going to see Chris, I'd rather it be at my home, or his home, or at a hotel. I would love to see him sometime.'

'Chris, how would you respond to that?' asked Jeff.

'You know I'd love to have him, more than a one-time appearance. I'd love to have Tommy at ringside with me all the time. I look up to the guy so much and he's given so much and done so much, set some new standards in this business. It would be an honour to have him manage me at ringside, but that would have to be his choice.'

'Tom, do you ever get itchy to get back, obviously not getting back in the ring, but back in the wrestling environment and to be back with the boys?'

'Oh sure,' Tom replied to Jeff, 'I think about that a lot, but I wouldn't want to embarrass myself being pushed into an arena or dressing room in a wheelchair.'

'I don't think that'd be embarrassing yourself at all.'

'Well, that's the way I feel Jeff. I would love to see some lads; some wrestlers. But I do feel a little bit embarrassed sometimes in a wheelchair. I wouldn't feel ready for that at this moment in time. But I would like Chris to give me a call in private, if you wouldn't mind doing that sometime, Chris?'

'Actually,' Benoit replied, 'I wanted to give you a call and talk to you. We're going to be in London, on May 6th, where we have a pay-per-view and I'd love to have you over to the show. And, you know, I'll even fly in a couple days early to spend some time with you, because right after the show we have to fly back because we're in New York on Monday night, but it is on a Saturday and I'd fly in a couple of days early and spend some time with you; I'd love to have you over to the show as my guest.'

'When is it, May 6th?' Tom asked hesitantly. It was six weeks away, almost exactly the amount of time he had just heard that Davey had remaining in rehab.

'Yes, it is,' Chris confirmed.

'Well, like I say, give me a call in the next few days and we can talk it over and see what happens, how about that?'

'That'd be great, Tommy.'

'Okay. All right. Anyway, it was good talking to you.'

'Okay, Tommy.'

'Keep doing well for yourself and don't let nobody take advantage of you in that ring,' came Tom's firm and final words to his younger self, 'and you know what I mean by that!'

'I never do.'

'Well, don't.'

'Gentlemen,' Jeff interceded, 'I'd like to thank both of you for your time. Chris Benoit, any closing thoughts on the Dynamite Kid before we wrap up?'

'Well, as I said before, he's a major influence in my career and a big part of who Chris Benoit is as a wrestler today. I can't thank him enough for what he's done for professional wrestling and in terms of paving the road for the way I make a living, because I make a good living nowadays from professional wrestling and he definitely helped pave that road that I ride on nowadays.'

'More fitting words couldn't have been spoken. Tom Billington; the Dynamite Kid, thanks for joining us today,' Jeff said, bringing the interview to an end.

'Thanks very much Jeff and thank you Chris, and I'll talk to you later Chris.'

'Okay Tommy!'

* * *

In the agony of withdrawal and unable to process the latest emotional blow – the news that his marriage was over and Diana was moving on, dating rookie Stampede wrestler James Trimble, Davey checked himself out of the rehab centre in April after six weeks of treatment and flew home to Calgary.

The doctors' report read that, whilst they didn't recommend him leaving early, he did so for family reasons, and he had been progressing well up to that point. This was deemed good enough for him to return on the WWF tour.

337

The timing was great for him to cross the Atlantic to see his family and stay at his family home with his sick father, as part of the WWF going to England to hold pay-per-view *Insurrextion* at Earl's Court in London on 6 May. Suddenly, Tom's potential appearance at the show was cancelled, citing Benoit's busy schedule. The narrow northern streets would once again remain the minimum distance between the once inseparable Bulldogs.

The British Bulldog was brought out as the 'surprise' opponent for Hardcore champion Crash Holly, but the reception when he ran down the ramp in his jeans and Doc Martens was muted at best. Since the European title loss to Shawn Michaels in Birmingham, his drifting in-and-out of WWF television, the poor and confused booking as he had turned from heel to babyface and somewhere in between, depending on who he was facing, meant that even a UK audience didn't know how to react to their former superman anymore.

The British Bulldog's final televised match was a fitting one. It was for the European title against then-champion and legend-in-waiting Eddie Guerrero. It aired on *Sunday Night Heat* but was taped on Tuesday 22 May at the Roberts Municipal Stadium in Indiana. They wrestled to a decent five-minute double disqualification. Davey then flew home to Calgary, where he had a house show four days later to kick off a tour of western Canada.

Davey's final WWF match was, of course, in Calgary. He stumbled to victory over mixed martial artist and former Stampede comrade Steve Blackman at a house show on 27 May. It was painful for the Calgary wrestling-goers to watch one of their favourite sons in such disarray, with Davey continually failing to get Blackman off the ground for his signature power moves.

A wired and incoherent Davey turned up late in Edmonton for the following night's show. Agents Jack Lanza and Tony Garea removed him from the card and sent him home. His 'last run' was over, and he had failed to get to the dream of sharing a ring with Harry.

* * *

In November 2000, Martha Hart settled out of court with Vince McMahon over the wrongful death of her husband for around $18 million. Vince then bought out WCW for just $3 million in March

2001, finally accomplishing what he had set out to do 20 years earlier: eliminate all his competition and hold a complete monopoly over the wrestling industry. But in the wake of the WWF's billion-dollar success story, there lay too many wrestling tragedies to count.

A year later, following a lawsuit by the World Wildlife Fund over usage of its initials, the WWF was renamed and rebranded as WWE (World Wrestling Entertainment).

The quality of the show quickly deteriorated, but with no competition, this was seemingly of little concern as the WWE moved back to a more family-friendly product and attempted to distance itself from the sordid past that had gone before and show the world a clean-cut image. But Terry Gordy became the latest of wrestling's casualties when he died at just 40 in July 2001 – and yet the industry's darkest days were still to come.

* * *

Bruce Hart's wife Andrea had introduced Davey to some homeopathic remedies to help him with his recovery. Davey, feeling scorned by Diana's new relationship and knowing of the ill-feeling between his estranged wife and Andrea, allowed the situation to escalate and soon found himself romantically involved with his sister-in-law, plunging the family into more chaos and conflict.

Andrea left Bruce and their severely disabled son Rhett to be with Davey, taking their other four children with her. Arguments, fracas, threats, arrests and court cases followed as Davey's life spiralled out of control. After one blazing row between him and Andrea and Bruce, Davey climbed aboard his motorcycle and crashed it, almost fatally, setting his physical recovery back once again and furthering his reliance on pain medication.

On 4 November 2001, Helen Hart, the matriarch of the Hart family, passed away following complications with diabetes.

Stu's health dramatically declined in dealing with the loss of Helen, whom he had been married to for 53 years (he would pass away on 16 October 2003).

Out of loyalty to Davey and proving to be a classier employer than WCW, WWE continued to pay Davey his full salary. Davey attempted to ease his pain by spending big on motorcycles, vacations with Andrea and the substances he was once again hooked on. Then, the contract expired, and a heavy tax burden came to light.

Davey borrowed $20,000 from Stu and his father Sid also sent him money, as Davey rejected the option to return home to England and get a job as a local doorman, wanting to stay and fight for yet another wrestling comeback and for his kids, with his ultimate dream being a combination of the two: to form the 'New British Bulldogs' with Harry, who was already a solid and experienced Stampede wrestler at the age of 16 and stood over 6ft tall. But it seemed impossible for Davey to achieve that goal from this lowest ebb.

Davey was charged with breaking and entering and theft early in 2002, having let himself into Diana's townhouse and taken the wedding ring he had given her all those years before. With his recent record, it appeared inevitable that this time Davey would be sent to prison, but Diana dropped the charges to save him from that fate.

As the Hart family gathered for their traditional giant Sunday dinner on 5 May, they were shocked when Diana and Davey arrived together. Before they all tucked in, Davey stood up and asked for everyone's attention. He made an emotional plea for forgiveness for all the pain and embarrassment he had caused, before announcing that he and Diana were getting back together.

Diana then proudly interjected, adding that Davey and Harry had a couple of independent bookings coming up as the New British Bulldogs. Davey Boy was making another comeback, and Harry's career was on the move. WWE had always said the door was open for a clean and healthy Davey, who grinned proudly as the family discussed him and Harry teaming together – everyone was delighted to see those iconic dimples back on show after so much heartache. Seeing the happiness around the table, Davey became emotional and sobbed, 'I just want my life back.'

After dinner, Davey asked Bruce if they could have a chat in private. They stepped down into the dungeon, where an embarrassed Davey made a deeper and more personal apology for his affair with Andrea. He explained that he had only begun the flirtation as revenge on Diana for the divorce and what he saw as her own betrayal with one of Bruce's wrestling students, but things had gotten out of hand as genuine feelings had developed. The conversation ended with a firm handshake.

The new father-and-son tag team then hit the road, eastbound. They competed in two matches for Top Rope Championship Wrestling in Manitoba: in the Friday show they defeated Rob Stardom and Ryan Wood at the Keystone Centre in Brandon. The following night they won a six-man tag match with Zack Mercury lined up alongside them at a small community centre in Winnipeg, where just dozens of fans saw the British Bulldog, back in his traditional Union Jack tights, emerge from behind a curtain as 'Rule Britannia' played once more.

'It was a dream come true for both of us,' Harry would say proudly.

* * *

A few days later, Diana came home to find Davey sitting on her sofa. 'You look great', he told her with a smile. He himself looked the healthiest he had in some time, his eyes were clear, and the reddish-purple tone was gone from his skin as he appeared relaxed in the living room with Harry and Georgia.

The blaring sound of a car horn ended the serenity. Davey rolled his eyes, knowing he had to leave. He kissed Diana and told the kids he'd call them in a couple of days. He cast them a smile, those famous dimples piercing his cheeks as he walked away.

EPILOGUE

'Everybody, at some point in their life, must look back and wonder what they did with it. Did they do all the things they planned to do? Did they see all the places they wanted to see? I was 40 years old when I found myself in that position; not a great age, I know, for reflecting on your life's achievements, but that's because I was a wrestler, and in wrestling, depending on how dedicated you are to the job, careers don't last forever … Now I see it for what it was. We were living life in the fast lane – some of us faster than others.'

Tom Billington

DAVID SMITH
27/11/1962 – 18/05/2002

'I loved Davey like a brother. His biggest mistake was letting bad people influence his innocent heart. I spoke of how I remembered him best as that shy, handsome kid with big dimples … which left both Harry and his baby sister Georgia smiling with tears in their eyes.'

Bret Hart

ANDREA HART was the person honking the horn outside Diana's house that day. Davey had clearly still been conflicted when he returned from that 1,500-mile round trip with Harry, as he had repacked his bag for a pre-arranged weekend getaway with Andrea at the mountain resort of Fairmont in Invermere, British Columbia. He had apparently told his father Sid in their final conversation that he was going to break up with Andrea over the weekend. But on Sunday 18 May, Andrea had woken next to a lifeless Davey.

To those who weren't aware of his recent struggles, the death of the once great British Bulldog at the age of just 39 was truly shocking. He had competed in pay-per-view main events just two years earlier. Even with wrestling's recent death rates, this was major news. It shone a spotlight on the industry, and Davey was already the eighth wrestler under the age of 40 that had died in the year 2002 – a year less than five months old at that stage. It had become an epidemic.

Diana had loved Davey from the moment she found that picture of 'Young David' when she was just 17 years old. She immediately set about organising his service in Calgary, at which Bret spoke of the epic matches he and Davey had in Stampede and, of course, their fabled clash at Wembley Stadium.

Georgia and Harry, just 14 and 16 respectively, spoke with poise, dignity and strength in front of hundreds of tearful guests, including Chris Benoit, Chris Jericho, Hulk Hogan, Vince McMahon and many more wrestling luminaries. Harry spoke of teaming with his father, and that they were memories no one could ever take away. Diana and TJ Wilson also spoke heart-warmingly.

Andrea held a separate, smaller service which Bret also attended.

Davey's body was flown home to England, where a post-mortem and inquest also recorded a verdict of death by natural causes. The trace amounts of morphine and steroids in his system were not close to a lethal amount, but the inquest also heard that he had an enlarged heart.

Davey was then buried beside his mother Joyce and his sister Tracey in the graveyard of the Golborne Catholic Church, just yards from the family home in which Sid still lives, as of the spring of 2021. Joanne lives on the same street and is the only remaining sibling to care for her elderly father, following the death of Terrence in December 2020.

'I'd like to focus on the good memories,' Ross Hart would say. 'He had a lot of good qualities. He got caught up with painkillers and other addictions to fight his pain. He was caught in the middle of relationships. We wanted him to get his life together and make a comeback.'

Selected championships and accomplishments

- **All Japan Pro Wrestling**
  - Korakuen Hall Heavyweight Battle Royal (1989)
  - World's Strongest Tag Determination League Fighting Spirit Award (1984, 1985) – with the Dynamite Kid
  - World's Strongest Tag Determination League Skills Award (1989) – with the Dynamite Kid
- **Canadian Wrestling Hall of Fame (2 times)**
  - Individually and with the Hart family
- **Pro Wrestling Illustrated**
  - Match of the Year (1992) v Bret Hart at *SummerSlam*
- **Stampede Wrestling**
  - Stampede International Tag Team Championship (3 times) – with Bruce Hart and twice with the Dynamite Kid
  - Stampede North American Heavyweight Championship (2 times)
  - Stampede World Mid-Heavyweight Championship
  - Stampede Wrestling Hall of Fame (Class of 1995)
- **Wrestling Observer Newsletter**
  - Best Wrestling Manoeuvre (1984) – Power clean dropkick
  - Feud of the Year (1997) with the Hart Foundation v Stone Cold Steve Austin
  - Tag Team of the Year (1985) with the Dynamite Kid
- **World Wrestling Entertainment/Federation**
  - WWF European Championship (2 times)
  - WWF Intercontinental Championship
  - WWF Hardcore Championship (2 times)
  - WWF Tag Team Championship (2 times) – with the Dynamite Kid and Owen Hart

o   WWF Rookie of the Year (1985)

o   Battle Royal at the Albert Hall (1991)

o   WWF European Championship tournament (1997)

o   WWF World Tag Team Championship Tournament (1997) – with Owen Hart

o   WWE Hall of Fame (Class of 2020)

Legacy

'Even though he'd caused me a lot of stress, I still considered Davey to be more of a victim than a perpetrator,' Bruce Hart would write in his book, *Straight From the Hart.*

David Smith was a victim of many things. He was a victim of his own success, having battled and fought to be regarded as equal to both the Dynamite Kid and Bret Hart. For a decade between the mid-80s to the mid-90s he was one of wrestling's true top talents, but he is now largely judged only against the two legends with whom he is most closely associated.

He was mostly referred to and utilised as a 'powerhouse' performer, yet he retained almost all of the cat-like agility that had seen him as a trailblazing young acrobat alongside his cousin. It is still a mystery how both the WWF and WCW world titles evaded him; maybe it was his lack of mic skills or a missing charismatic edge that cannot be taught.

For me, he is the true forgotten victim of the Montreal Screwjob. At a time when his demons were showing signs of getting the better of him, he needed stability. The loyalty he showed to Bret is a typical measure of the man, but the upheaval caused personally and professionally no doubt led to further reliance on his destructive self-medication.

In Davey's case, history is proving to be an even-handed judge: almost 20 years after his death, he is remembered firstly as the most highly-decorated WWE wrestler to never win the world title; as one half of the most influential tag team of all time; and for being the winner of one of wrestling's greatest matches and spectacles inside Wembley Stadium at *SummerSlam '92.* That event, alongside the *In Your House 16: Canadian Stampede,* are possibly the two most electrifying sporting crowds I have ever seen.

In the year 2020, Drew McIntyre became the first ever British WWE champion. In that same year, it was announced that the British Bulldog Davey Boy Smith would finally take his rightful place in the WWE Hall of Fame. 'I grew up watching him,' McIntyre told *Sports Illustrated*. 'He made me think that this was something that was possible. For so long I heard, "Wrestling: that's an American thing." Seeing the Bulldog and the Union Jack, that gave me hope … The Bulldog was ahead of his time, extremely athletic, and he looked like a superhero.'

Davey, also the boyhood hero and inspiration of fellow Lancastrian Wade Barrett, almost single-handedly kept wrestling hugely popular in the UK during the 1990s. A generation of British wrestling talent would follow and headline pay-per-views all around the world, and still do today. The independent scene is thriving, and the WWE even has its own brand based here in 'NXT UK'.

Scotland's premier pro wrestling historian Bradley Craig warmly remembers the British Bulldog as one of the major figures who sustained his interest in the sport.

'I can still clearly remember the day I met Davey Boy Smith as an 11-year-old wrestling fan,' reminisces Craig, who has since become a close friend of Diana, Harry and Georgia. 'WCW were in the middle of the *Real Event* tour of the UK and Ireland, and a show in my hometown at the Aberdeen Exhibition and Conference Centre was set for Sunday 14 March. I was incredibly lucky, as my parents knew how much I loved wrestling and wanted to meet my childhood heroes. The tour had been in Manchester the previous evening and, after figuring out the time of the early afternoon Manchester–Aberdeen flight, my mum and dad drove my baby sister and me to Aberdeen International Airport in the hope of meeting some of the stars as they stepped out of the arrivals lounge. We timed it right and I met the entire roster of talent who were there.

'When I met Davey Boy Smith, it was like being in the presence of a superhero. He had an absolutely solid frame that made him stand out from the roster, even among ring giants like Big Van Vader and Vinnie Vegas. To this young fan, the British Bulldog couldn't have been nicer and, after Smith kindly signed an autograph and posed for a picture with me, I wished him well in his match later that evening.

'Although the card was stacked that night, many in attendance felt that the fourth match on the card stole the show. As spectators clamoured to return to their seats after the intermission, the Tina Turner-esque "Simply Ravishing" theme bellowed throughout the arena, as 'Ravishing' Rick Rude marched towards the ring. Rude was such a great heel and could incite hatred from a crowd better than almost any other ring villain at the time. After making fun of the legions of Scottish fans that jam-packed the AECC to a chorus of boos, the crowd soon erupted with a frenzy as "Rule Britannia" started blaring over the speaker system. Representing the very best of British, the emerging Davey Boy Smith got an unforgettable hero's welcome, as he was clad in his trademark Union Jack sequin cape.

'Rude was the perfect foil for the heroic Smith, and the two engaged in crowd-pleasing antics such as pose-downs then tests of strength and athleticism before engaging in a dramatic back-and-forth contest. I remember one particular part of the match, when Davey was caught in a rear chinlock, and I started a chant of, "BULLDOG! BULLDOG! BULLDOG!" as my dad smiled at my sheer enthusiasm. It was not long before others joined, and soon the entire arena was trembling with the sound. Smith powered out of the hold and made his comeback, before hoisting Rude up for the running powerslam. Sensing defeat, the "Ravishing One" got himself disqualified and promptly rushed out of the venue. The sell-out crowd were euphoric at the fact that a fellow Briton had held off the onslaught of one of America's most dastardly pro wrestlers and was standing victorious in the ring.

'The next day, I could not wait to tell all the kids at school about the WCW show the night before, however, there was one small problem. After hours of yelling and screaming, I had lost my voice. Nevertheless, that entire event was my favourite experience as a young wrestling fan, and I will never forget the thrill of seeing the British Bulldog perform at the apex of his fame in my hometown arena.'

* * *

Whilst memories of Davey remain strong and are held with a global fondness due to his popularity in America, Canada, Japan and especially in the UK, his legacy has been secured in the best possible way by his children. Georgia continues to build her platform, where she does public appearances in lieu of her late father, she posts classic clips of him in action online every day and continues to produce and promote new and replica Bulldog merchandise. Harry is now a veteran and champion wrestler himself, appearing under the name 'Davey Boy Smith Jr'. Alongside his best friend TJ Wilson, Harry won the WWE tag team championships as the 'Hart Dynasty', which included Jim Neidhart's daughter Natalya.

'Nattie' and TJ had become childhood sweethearts and eventually married in 2013. She is now widely regarded as one of the greatest and most influential female wrestlers of all time.

Like his father before him, Harry also became a North American heavyweight champion when Stampede Wrestling opened its doors for a third and final time between 1999 and 2008. He and TJ were the stars, TJ becoming known as the 'Stampede Kid' in Calgary due to his in-ring resemblance to Dynamite. As a tag team, they appeared more Bulldog Dynasty than Hart Dynasty.

Harry has travelled the world many times but, fittingly, found his spiritual home both in and out of the ring in Japan, where he wrestled with distinction for New Japan for many years, winning titles both there and in Europe.

It was back in Florida, however, where Harry proudly strode out on to the *WrestleMania* stage, flanked by his sister and his mother, who both beamed with joy, to induct his iconic father into the WWE Hall of Fame. He lifted the leashed canine British Bulldog that accompanied them up on to the podium for the cheering virtual audience to see.

Harry introduced the audience to Buffy, the granddaughter of the legendary Matilda, before waxing lyrical about his legendary father. He spoke of his talent, his power and his athleticism, before speaking emotionally about the Davey he knew, with a huge heart, a wonderful personality and a great sense of humour.

Harry spoke of two of his father's most glorious victories – at Wembley against his uncle Bret and against another uncle of his, Owen, when Davey was crowned the champion of Europe.

He reminisced about the British Bulldogs and the Hart Foundation revolutionizing tag team wrestling into what we know it as today.

He acknowledged the Dynamite Kid and the influence he and Davey had in Japan and on him and his own career, too, before stating that he feels the spirit of both the Bulldogs with him every time he steps foot in the ring.

'Davey was such a great father,' Harry concluded, 'he was a great friend – he'd give you the shirt off his back. He was a great athlete and one heck of a performer.'

THOMAS BILLINGTON
05/12/1958 – 05/12/2018

'I benefitted from his greatness and through our matches in
Stampede, WWE and everywhere in between, I became a
better wrestler because of him. Dynamite truly was the best
wrestler ever, pound-for-pound. Tom was family, my brother-
in-law, and we were very close. In many ways, I felt like one
of the few people who truly knew him, both the good and the
bad. I saw Tom one final time this past June in England, and I
can only hope that he is finally at peace. My thoughts are with
his children, Bronwyne, Marek and Amaris, and the entire
Billington family.'

Bret Hart

IN DECEMBER 2000, the Dynamite Kid finally sat amongst his peers again in a wrestling locker room. Wheeling himself around independently and clad in a trademark black leather jacket, Tom held court as wrestlers old and new listened to his legendary war stories while they got ready for their matches at the *Rebellion* pay-per-view at Sheffield Arena, South Yorkshire.

Tom had chatted jovially to the office staff to whom he had once proved such a scourge, including agents Jerry Brisco and Pat Patterson and even Vince McMahon himself, as those ingrained in the business battled to clap eyes on a happier and healthier version of the man who had given so much to their sport.

Young stars such as Matt and Jeff Hardy, Edge, Christian, Chris Jericho and The Rock listened intently to the man so much of their repertoires were built upon. Dean Malenko and Mick Foley dashed to greet the man they had shared many memorable ring moments with in Japan.

Tom would release a statement on his website regarding his reacquaintance with the current global stars of wrestling: 'I told them to keep doing what they were doing and take care of themselves. But they probably won't. Because when I was wrestling, neither did I.'

Two of the men Tom had been aiming that message at were Chris Benoit and Eddie Guerrero.

***

'The steroids started the drug use,' Michelle Billington told the 2007 CNN documentary *Death Grip*. 'Prescription drugs because of the injuries, which also started the alcohol.'

The mainstream media exposé on the dark side of wrestling had been produced following the most sickening event for the industry yet: the Chris Benoit double-murder-suicide.

The media circled with frenzy around the global scandal, and Benoit's steroid and prescription drug use were soon being reported as a major contributing factor to his deplorable final hours. It hadn't taken much more investigation for them to unearth his desire to be just like the Dynamite Kid.

The interviewer dug deep, quizzing Michelle about those darkest days. 'It became so bad that I just wanted to get out,' said a smartly dressed Michelle. 'And the way I was going to get out was that I was going to put my two children on the bed – the master bed – Bronwyne and Marek; and Tom had a lot of guns, so I went to get his gun and I wanted to shoot Bronwyne and Marek and then myself.' Michelle was now sobbing. 'And the only reason I didn't do it is because I couldn't guarantee that we would all die.'

The interview was interspersed with images of 1980s Tom looking ludicrously muscular, bloody, scarred, toothless and demonic – although it failed to mention that much of that was just the brilliant portrayal of his heel character.

'This,' boomed the voice of the narrator as the screen cut to a shot of a shirtless Tom manoeuvring himself through the narrow space between the kitchen and the living room of his council flat, 'is the Dynamite Kid today.'

Tom wheeled past a door with a large hole in it and up to the table, which was cluttered with his medication, ashtrays and cigarettes. The camera zoomed in on a surgical pin which protruded sharply from the end of one of his toes.

He told the interviewer that he only stopped taking steroids because a doctor diagnosed him with an enlarged heart, otherwise he would've already died like so many others.

'Yeah, I took painkillers,' Tom confirmed. 'My back, my knees – oh Christ, my shoulder, different things.'

'I don't think it was violent,' Tom said about his own domestic behaviour in those hard times, 'I mean, I put a shotgun under her chin once, but it had no shells – I only pretended that.'

On that note, the music took a sinister turn and the camera panned across the scene. 'This,' the narrator chimed, 'is the man Chris Benoit idolised.'

Having sacrificed his whole life for the wrestling business, Tom was suddenly being linked to the scandal which was threatening to destroy it.

Nancy Toffolini had been a wrestling trailblazer herself in the 1980s, as one of the industry's first glamorous valets. Her alluring looks and mannerisms earned her an equally mysterious moniker for her femme fatale character: 'Woman'. She became the on-screen valet and off-screen wife of WCW wrestler and booker Kevin Sullivan.

Sullivan had been in a programme with Brian Pillman when Pillman defected to the WWF in 1996, so Sullivan filled the void opposite him in the ring with Chris Benoit. Benoit was brilliant – the living, breathing clone of the Dynamite Kid. Like Tom, Benoit struggled on the microphone as a babyface, unable to muster the natural charisma required to retain the fans' affection. Therefore, to generate heat into their storyline, Sullivan decided to have flirtations between Chris and Nancy develop into a love affair.

In one of wrestling's most perfect examples of life imitating art, Chris and Nancy began a real-life love affair. Sullivan would never live down that he had 'booked his own divorce'.

In the year 2000, Chris signed for the WWF alongside three of his best friends in Eddie Guerrero, Perry Saturn and Dean Malenko. That same year, Nancy gave birth to their son Daniel, and they got married.

Eddie Guerrero was fired late in 2001 for alcohol and drug abuse. He returned six months later after wowing the independent circuit to prove his recovery was complete. Whilst free of his alcohol and pill reliance, he suddenly appeared much more muscular. His absence had only served to increase his perennial popularity with the fans; now thicker set and apparently clean, and with the road paved for smaller wrestlers, a main-event run began. Chris Benoit was also being pushed right to the top and the fans really got behind the two popular veterans' quests to finally win top honours.

Benoit won the *Royal Rumble* in January 2004, giving himself a shot at Triple H's world heavyweight championship (the former NWA/WCW championship, now part of the WWE). The following month, Guerrero received one of the greatest pops in the history of the sport when he defeated Brock Lesnar for the WWE championship in a shocking upset.

At *WrestleMania XX*, Guerrero successfully defended his belt against Kurt Angle, before Benoit made Triple H submit with the crippler crossface in a classic triple threat match that also included Shawn Michaels. The educated Madison Square Garden audience were overjoyed at the climax of the perfectly told two-part drama.

As confetti rained down from the rafters, Guerrero joined Benoit and the pair hugged and celebrated emotionally. Soon, their families climbed in the ring to share the moment with them too, including Nancy and four-year-old Daniel, as well as Benoit's older son David and daughter Megan from his first marriage.

Chavo Guerrero Jr, Eddie's nephew, had joined the WWE and taken to travelling the roads with his uncle and Benoit. On 13 November 2005, Chavo entered 38-year-old Eddie's hotel room and found him unconscious on the bathroom floor. Chavo attempted CPR as well as calling for Benoit's help. Before they called 911, they reportedly followed a wrestling tradition that had evolved for this type of scenario; a tradition borne out of the age-old mantra: 'protecting the business' – apparently, they flushed Eddie's supply of steroids down the toilet.

Benoit fell into a pit of depression following Eddie's death, which had also caused the spotlight on wrestling to heat up. He had soon added anti-depressant and anti-anxiety medication to his menu.

Distancing himself from a problematic home life, Benoit spent almost all his time on the road or working out. The little time he and Nancy did have together was largely spent yelling at each other.

Guerrero's death had finally forced the WWE to be seen to be doing something about the alarming death rate amongst former and now even current athletes. They introduced a 'Wellness Program', which included such things as regular drug screening and physical health checks. But as with every other time they had brought in such measures, the abusers seemed to be one step ahead of the testers.

Benoit had told WWE officials he was going to be missing some house shows over a weekend in June 2007 because both Nancy and Daniel were suffering from food poisoning. But after the ultra-professional Benoit failed to show up for the Sunday pay-per-view *Night of Champions*, a 'welfare check' was called for. The local authorities found the bodies of Nancy and Daniel strangled, with Bibles placed next to them. They then found Benoit in the basement, slumped by his weight machine with the cable wrapped around his neck.

* * *

After drifting apart from Dot, Tom was left existing alone. He had become more and more reclusive, turning down invitations to social engagements and wrestling conventions and reunions, never wanting his current appearance to be seen by his peers.

Dot still called in to see him and care for him, as did his brother Mark with his daughter Leah and Tom's aptly named nephews, Thomas and Mark. Tom's health continued to deteriorate, albeit slowly, as he carried on existing in his self-imposed purgatory over 4,000 miles away from his children.

There are 151 professional wrestlers named in the main body and timeline of this book who would've reached the age of 60 by its publication day. Of those, 46 (over 30 per cent) died before they saw that birthday; only 104 lived beyond that landmark. Thomas Billington, forever unique, is the missing number. He died *on* his 60th birthday in December 2018.

Shortly after the death of the great Dynamite Kid, Harry Smith and Satoru Sayama led traditional 'ten-bell-salutes' at major shows in Japan, as both New Japan and All Japan paid tribute to one of their finest ever *gaijin*.

Selected championships and accomplishments

- **All Japan Pro Wrestling**
  - All Asia Tag Team Championship – with Johnny Smith
  - NWA International Junior-heavyweight Championship
  - World's Strongest Tag Determination League Fighting Spirit Award (1984, 1985) – with Davey Boy Smith
  - World's Strongest Tag Determination League Skills Award (1989) – with Davey Boy Smith
  - World's Strongest Tag Determination League Fair Play Award (1990, 1991) – with Johnny Smith
- **Atlantic Grand Prix Wrestling**
  - AGPW International Heavyweight Championship
- **Canadian Wrestling Hall of Fame**
  - Class of 2001
- **Joint Promotions**
  - British Welterweight Championship
  - British Lightweight Championship
  - European Welterweight Championship
- **New Japan Pro Wrestling**
  - WWF Junior-heavyweight Championship
  - Greatest *Gaijin* Junior Section (2002)
- **Pacific Northwest Wrestling**
  - NWA Pacific Northwest Heavyweight Championship
  - NWA Pacific Northwest Tag Team Championship – with the Assassin
- **Stampede Wrestling**
  - Stampede British Commonwealth Mid-heavyweight Championship (5 times)
  - Stampede International Tag Team Championship (5 times) – with Loch Ness Monster, Kasavubu, Duke Myers and Davey Boy Smith twice
  - Stampede North American Heavyweight Championship
  - Stampede World Mid-heavyweight Championship (3 times)
  - Stampede Wrestling Hall of Fame (Class of 1995)

- **Tokyo Sports**
  - Lifetime Achievement Award (1991)
- **World Wrestling Federation/Entertainment**
  - WWF Tag Team Championship – with Davey Boy Smith
- **Wrestling Observer Newsletter**
  - Best Flying Wrestler (1984)
  - Best Technical Wrestler (1984) – tied with Masa Saito
  - Best Wrestling Manoeuvre (1984) Power clean dropkick
  - Hardest Worker (1983)
  - Match of the Year (1982) v Tiger Mask on 5 August, Tokyo, Japan
  - Most Underrated (1983)
  - Most Impressive Wrestler (1983–1985)
  - Tag Team of the Year (1985) – with Davey Boy Smith
  - *Wrestling Observer Newsletter* Hall of Fame (Class of 1996)

Legacy

Thomas Billington's legacy within the wrestling business is truly unique. He changed the industry forever, smashing through the global glass ceiling that was holding the naturally smaller men down. He destroyed the assumption that wrestlers less than 6ft and 230lb couldn't compete with the natural heavyweights or draw the same money, crowds or attention. His web of inspiration is as vast and wide-ranging as the Hart family tree. He will, unfortunately, be forever linked with both the brilliant and the horrifying aspects of Chris Benoit, but without his influence, icons such as Bret Hart, Owen Hart, Tiger Mask (Sayama), Chris Jericho, Jushin Liger and Eddie Guerrero would never have reached the extraordinary heights within the business they did, and subsequently inspired further generations themselves. Bret often speaks of Tom. He regularly says that whilst he was in character, the Hitman would claim to be 'the best there is, the best there was and the best there ever will be', but always insists that, in reality, that honour goes to the Dynamite Kid.

The Dynamite Kid versus Tiger Mask matches have become fabled; forever the unachievable yardstick for which all future generations strive. VHS tapes were valuably traded around the world as smaller wrestlers studied and attempted to copy artistic perfection.

The matches told the age-old wrestling story: two fighters so equally matched that they each tried desperately to find a way to break the stalemate – and yet these ground-breaking matches had the acrobatics of a *Cirque du Soleil* show combined with the brutality of a monster truck rally.

In Japan, Tom's place at the deity-like summit of the *gaijin* pyramid, alongside the likes of Stan Hansen, Bruiser Brody, Billy Robinson and Karl Gotch, is forever etched in stone; as is that of him and Davey as a tag team.

But when researching the Dynamite Kid and his legacy, for every one of the countless quotes that wax lyrical about his profound and unmatched in-ring ability, there is a damning negative statement to match, many of which include phrases such as 'masochistic', 'sadistic' and 'sociopathic'. Maybe it needed someone with his at-all-costs mentality to force through the changes that he did, and he truly gave his life to entertain the fans. His naturally aggressive nature combined with the drug and steroid culture into which he fell created a deadly cocktail of excess. But in recent years, a sporting phenomenon has been discovered: Chronic Traumatic Encephalopathy (CTE).

CTE is a form of degenerative brain damage caused by repeated concussions and blows to the head. It is particularly common in sportsmen such as boxers, American football and rugby players, hockey players and professional wrestlers. An abnormally high number of these athletes go on to suffer from mental health issues from dementia to depression but extending all the way to the point where there are multiple recorded cases of suicide and homicide.

When Chris Benoit's brain was analysed after his death, it was so severely damaged it was comparable with that of an 85-year-old Alzheimer's patient, and yet it had been housed in the body of a 40-year-old steroid user.

'I believe the degeneration of his brain changed who he was and what he was capable of,' Chris Nowinski, a former WWE superstar who retired after multiple concussions to become a neuroscientist studying the syndrome, would say of Chris Benoit.

Someone who wrestled with Tom Billington's style and intensity undoubtedly suffered countless concussions; once again the symptoms of which would've been masked by painkillers and the medley of uppers and downers. No one can possibly know what level of CTE may have been at play in Tom's darkest days.

The implication of Tom's influence in the Benoit tragedy by the media, coupled with the recent CTE awareness, has actually served to add sympathy to Tom's legacy rather than the negativity and controversy it was initially designed to create. As well as being one of the ultimate wrestlers to try and emulate, Tom Billington has become one of wrestling's ultimate cautionary tales.

Almost everyone that Tom wronged during that period of destructive behaviour has found their way to forgive him. His redeeming qualities of loyalty and generosity, coupled with the healing of time and his extraordinary talent, which has never aged on screen, means that all those that were close to him (certainly all those interviewed for this book), remember him fondly. The self-imposed purgatory in which he largely lived out his final years is seen by most as punishment above and beyond his misdemeanours.

Gary Portz got audibly emotional during our telephone conversation, particularly as he spoke of Tom and Michelle caring for him after his stroke. I thanked him sincerely for his time and his wonderful memories as we said our goodbyes and asked him if it was okay for me to contact him again if I felt he could add more to the project. 'Anything,' he said. 'Anything at all; anything for Tom.'

Gary began to tell me just how tough Tom was, describing him as 'the big dog in the yard'. This led me to ask him something that I had been curious about for some time; given Tom's legitimate fighting ability and perceived enjoyment of it, combined with his shoot-style training and unique wrestling abilities, did Gary share my thoughts that, if the MMA scene had been around at the time, might that have been a discipline even more suited to Tom? Knowing where my question was heading, Gary cut me off, excitedly saying, 'I think that all the time! That's what he would've done – and he'd have been brilliant at it!'

Despite being widely regarded as one of wrestling's greatest and most influential stars ever, the Dynamite Kid has not yet been inducted into the WWE Hall of Fame.

* * *

Tom's legacy lives on in one of the most direct and yet eerie ways possible back in his home town. His nephew, aptly named Thomas, is the doppelganger of his uncle – both in his appearance and in his wrestling style. At just 21 years old at the time of this writing, he is one half of the 'Billington Bulldogs' alongside his younger brother Mark, who is slightly taller with dark wavy hair and a chiselled jawline. To watch them feels like having stepped out of a time machine to see Dynamite and Davey at the same respective ages.

I visited Mark (senior) and he was extremely hospitable and welcoming. The corridor of the house he shares with his wife Annette, two sons and daughter Leah is clad completely in wrestling posters and memorabilia; some that of his legendary older brother, some from the budding careers of his boys, who are hot property on the UK independent scene and have offers flooding in from Japan and America as news of another incarnation of the Dynamite Kid in Thomas and possibly the British Bulldogs as a tag team travels the world.

Mark speaks of his brother with a level of pride it is difficult to match. Tom was, and always will be, his hero. With Leah joining us for company (and to help her dad navigate, while I drove) Mark took me on a guided tour of the British Bulldogs' home town.

We'd only turned one corner when Mark said, 'That's where David is,' pointing to the church we were passing. Moments later, we were parked outside the house in which he and Tom had been raised and where their parents had seen out their lives.

A left, a right and another left to the end of a cul-de-sac and the house where Davey's dad Sid still lives was pointed out to me – the house where Davey had grown up. I thanked Mark for showing me this (being aware of the wedge that the acrimonious split of the Bulldogs had caused between the two sides of the family, I hadn't asked or expected him to show me the Smith sites of Golborne). Mark then took me to the site of Ted Betley's old gym, which is now a shed at the end of the driveway of a huge house. Apparently, the residents are used to seeing people standing outside their gate taking selfies with their shed in the background.

We drove by Tom's various residences and even the scrapyard he worked at as a security guard. Finally, on the way back to his house, Mark suggested we go and see Davey. The clouds broke and the sun shone down on the graveyard as Davey's grand headstone came into view, alongside his mother's and sister's. Someone clearly tends to it regularly, as there was a British Bulldog action figure and a trading card standing proudly by his picture (and there had been a wild thunderstorm earlier that week).

I gave Mark and Leah my humble thanks for their time and their hospitality, and yet Mark continued to ask me if there was anything else that he could do for me. 'There probably will be,' I told him, 'but you've done more than enough for today.'

As I mowed the back lawn the following afternoon, I received a text from Mark:

'It helped me a lot that yesterday because I have a lot of anger in me with what happened with Tom and David falling out and all the family's falling out … I let it go, it's in the past … It all went beyond just two wrestlers, it was like World War Three between the Billingtons and the Smiths, but it's finished, pal like you say: onwards and upwards.'

* * *

In Canada, the healing process for Michelle, Bronwyne, Marek and Amaris has also spanned three decades. With the additional knowledge of CTE and the understanding of the mental anguish and physical agony Tom was going through at the time, they have found their way to complete forgiveness and they once again love and cherish Tom and the memories they have of him and are actively keeping his legacy as one of the greatest wrestlers of all time alive. They do this with an openness, honesty and dignity that is truly admirable.

'Every year the four of us make plans to be together on Tom's birthday/death-day, which I named "Tommy Day",' Michelle Billington says. 'Only the Dynamite Kid could pull off a December 5th entrance and exit. Everything he did was so spectacular and so was his finishing move, to go home knowing he left the world wanting more!'

AFTERWORD

I WAS six years old when my dad went back to England. He left me with a bottomless hole of grief I dared not delve into too much. I saw him again when I was ten. Out of concern for me acting out at school, my uncle Bret flew me and my brother Marek over to England to spend a few weeks with my dad. It would be another 15 years before I saw him again in the flesh. Those years he was absent from my life held conflicted feelings of yearning for the past, mixed with a great sense of loss and abandonment.

After having my first child, Miami, I began to feel whole. She filled my heart and patched over the abyss of loneliness. Being a new mom and watching all the milestones children go through distracted me for a couple of years, but soon the realisation that my dad would miss out on knowing he was a grandfather started to eat away at me. My heart knew it was time to reconnect with my father.

I reached out to my cousin Craig on Facebook and planned to stay with him while in England. I packed my bags feeling a little anxious because I would be visiting relatives I hadn't seen since I was ten and I really didn't know if my dad even wanted to see me, as cards and letters from him had dwindled to nothing over the years.

Night one I went to the local pub in Golborne with my aunt, uncle and cousins. While talking with them I wasn't sure if I had the guts to see my dad. At that time all his siblings were not on speaking terms with him for various reasons. If I decided to go see him, I was doing it alone.

My aunt Carol reminisced about the time my dad stayed with her when he first arrived back in England. She told me he laid on the couch for days on end and stared at the wall she had covered with our family photos. All this time I wondered if he had missed his children and that right there gave me the answer. It ignited the fire I needed to go knocking on his door.

I was a little hungover and still jet-lagged as I stood knocking on my dad's door the next day. No one answered and when I went back to the car my sense of urgency was deflated. My cousin quickly found out it was the wrong door. I panicked and told him he'd have to come to the door with me the second time as I couldn't muster up the courage to do it alone.

Approaching the correct door with my cousin towered in front of me, I hid behind him. My dad's wife Dot opened the door. Shocked to see Craig, she opened the door wide and I popped out from behind him. Having never met her, she somehow recognised me and excitedly invited us in.

I walked into the living room and for the first time I saw my dad in a wheelchair. Not having seen him in 15 years, I covered my face with my hands and cried.

My dad smiled and asked, 'Why are you crying?'

I pulled myself together and answered, 'Because I haven't seen you in a long time.'

He acted like no time had passed and was beaming with happiness. We easily made up for lost time and I filled him in on all that was going on with me and my siblings. That trip, I went to see him every day and stayed a little longer each time.

Our most memorable visit ended in us crying, holding each other and him saying, 'I'm sorry.' Two powerful words that he didn't need to explain. I knew what they meant, and he didn't need to say any more.

The next few trips to England, I always stayed with him. He was a man of few words and his health seemed to be slowly deteriorating. He never complained and would not leave the house unless it was for doctors' appointments. It broke me to leave him, but I had my daughter and a life in Canada to get back to. Every time I'd leave, he'd shed a tear.

The last time I saw him I had a feeling it would be the last. He was having trouble manoeuvring around his flat and feeding himself, stubbornly refusing to talk about any kind of assisted living. The distance was so hard and costly. I was grateful for his wife and brother

Mark for keeping me updated with his health concerns. I wish I could have been there more in the end after his strokes, which is why I was elated to know he was moved to a full-time care facility. It gave me a sense of relief to know his immediate needs were being met there and he would have medical attention if he required it.

Leaving him and having an ocean between us was so disheartening, but I also left with a sense of accomplishment knowing I helped my dad to reconnect with other family members before his health took a turn for the worse and he could not communicate anymore. My cousins, Harry and Georgia, both visited him at his home in Wigan. I also organised for my uncle Bret to Skype with him. Most importantly, my dad met and saw my sister, Amaris, for the first time on a Skype call. I will never forget how happy he was hearing my brother Marek had gotten married and later seeing the wedding photos. I believe all these reconnections and knowing his kids were doing all right brought him peace and happiness.

I am sure it also made it easier for him to let go when it came time to leave this earth.

When my dad passed, I was in complete shock and newly pregnant with my second daughter, Harlow. It brought me waves of unbearable grief, yet I had some comfort in knowing my dad would always be with me and my siblings. He would finally be able to meet and hang out with my grandkids, too. Whenever lights go out, or we find a dime, or something else happens, we all look around and say, 'Hi, Dad!'

I cannot believe a 25-year-old girl travelled across the ocean to see if the love she shared with her father still existed; thankfully, it did! I'm so grateful we reconnected the last decade he was alive because I don't have to live with regret. Whenever we spent time together, I made sure he knew how much he meant to me. For this I feel blessed.

My dad is forever in my heart. I don't care what anyone has to say about him. He was so gentle and loving towards me and even when he had very little to give, he always gave so much. I wish we could redo this life and have more time together, but one thing is for sure – I will always be a daddy's girl!

Bronwyne Billington

* * *

Dear Dad,

If you were still here, what would I say? I'd tell you how proud I am of your legacy and how proud I am to be your daughter. I'd tell you all about your grandkids: Miami, Taya, Madix and Harlow. They are all little wrestlers in their own way, so unique and strong-spirited. We all have your Dynamite strength. You'd be so proud of your children. We are all kind-hearted, hard-working, family orientated, and loving parents. I think you'd be proud of how our mom held it all together all these years. She always spoke so highly of you and never put you down to us. She makes sure we know everything about you, your relationship with her, where you came from and your career highlights. If it wasn't for the foundational start you gave our family, we wouldn't be where we are today; when you left Canada, you left with nothing and left everything to us. Because of this we had a good upbringing, one my mom had to maintain but the starting point was because of you. Growing up without you was hard. It affected my whole life. I just felt such a strong connection with you.

Daddy's girl Bronwyne, hand-in-hand with Tom, 25 years apart

With you passing away, I think I've finally come to terms with things. I understand now all the sacrifices you made physically, mentally and emotionally. You thought our lives would be better if you went back to England. Although it was painful at times, I see now you made the right choice for us all. The love I have for you is so strong I could never remain mad at you. I want to remember all the good times we shared. I want to keep your legacy alive by sharing your stories to the world. I want your grandkids to know who you were and why being a

Billington is so special. You're hands down the best technical wrestler there ever was. I am blessed to be your daughter and I hope I make you proud. Thank you for being the best daddy to me. I truly cannot wait until we meet again.

Love, your lamb,
Bronwyne

ACKNOWLEDGEMENTS

WE ALL make mistakes; we all make bad choices, but all we can do in this life is to try and bring more happiness than sadness to those we reach; to inspire others and to leave the world having made a positive net contribution. Dynamite and Davey certainly did that.

I would like to thank the following people for their contributions: Martin Bell, Bronwyne Billington, Mark Billington, Michelle Billington, Bradley Craig, Dave Dynasty, Tony Earnshaw, Bret Hart, Bruce Hart, Keith Hart, Ross Hart, Bob Johnson, Pete Knee, Heath McCoy, Dave Meltzer, Gary Portz and the whole team at Pitch Publishing.

And thank you to the following people that have supplied images for the book (apologies if your image wasn't used in the end for whatever reason, but the thought and effort is appreciated all the same): Bronwyne Billington, Leah Billington, Mark Billington, Michelle Billington, Bradley Craig, Tony Earnshaw, Rachel Ling, Richard Olszak, Don Sulatycky, Simon Sonny Williams, Orest Zmyndak.

Finally, I'd like to honour my two main allies and contributors towards this project. They became such a big part of my day-to-day work that I asked them to write the Foreword and Afterword respectively so that their names appeared on the front cover alongside mine, as they deserved to do so. They are Ross Hart and Bronwyne Billington. They both went above and beyond what I could ever have expected of them, even becoming confidantes during times the project struck stormy seas.

From the moment I made contact with Ross he showed he was passionate about the subject, uniquely knowledgeable and supremely conscientious, aiming to help make this book as true, fair, balanced and good as it could be. The constant battle between honesty, dignity and respect whilst attempting to tell the full story was something I needed help and perspective with.

When I asked him if he would read through an early draft as a fact-check, Ross quickly upgraded the service to a proofread as – little did I know that, as well as being the recognised Hart family historian – Ross is also an English teacher! He became a fact-checker, proofreader, my most valued consultant and the Foreword writer.

Ross – I hope you are proud of the final product and the part you played in it. Thank you for the many, many hours you spent on it.

It was Ross who, after our first conversation went so well, contacted Bronwyne to assure her I was genuine.

Bronwyne's friendliness knows no bounds. She has a uniquely good heart and a manner that seems to set everyone at ease around her. She was generous with her time and would even act as my own little researcher in Calgary, contacting family members on my behalf to join the dots I had created for myself. Her attitude towards the reality of her father's flaws and complications is truly admirable. That has led her to a place of acceptance where she can see past those things and love her dad for the complete man he was, because those flaws go hand-in-hand with the qualities of determination, loyalty and dedication that she loves about him and that inspire her too.

Bronwyne is a credit to Tom, but even more so Michelle, with whom she clearly shares those same morals and the same integrity and dignity.

Thank you for your help Bronwyne, it has been a true pleasure getting to know you.

* * *

The Smith family did not contribute towards this book.

SELECTED BIBLIOGRAPHY
AND SOURCES

Note: For clarity, I have omitted 'Contributions by Ross Hart' from the below chapter-by-chapter breakdown. This is because, quite simply, Ross contributed the whole way through.

Introduction
- *I'm Sorry, I Love You: A History of Professional Wrestling*, Jim Smallman
- *Have a Good Week … Till Next Week*, John Lister
- Wrestlingheritage.co.uk

Prologue – Opening quote: *Wrestling Observer Newsletter* archive
- *WWE Network*

Part One – Opening quote: *Straight from the Hart*, Bruce Hart

Chapter 1 – Opening quote: *The Wrestling*, Simon Garfield
- *Pure Dynamite: The Price You Pay for Wrestling Stardom*, Tom Billington (with Alison Coleman)
- *I'm Sorry, I Love You: A History of Professional Wrestling*, Jim Smallman
- *Have a Good Week … Till Next Week*, John Lister
- *Who's the Daddy: The Life and Times of Shirley Crabtree*, Ryan Danes
- Contributions from British wrestling historian Tony Earnshaw

Chapter 2 – Opening quote: *Straight from the Hart*, Bruce Hart
- *Straight from the Hart*, Bruce Hart
- *Pure Dynamite: The Price You Pay for Wrestling Stardom*, Tom Billington
- *Pain and Passion: The History of Stampede Wrestling*, Heath McCoy
- Contributions from British wrestling historian Tony Earnshaw

Chapter 3 – Opening quote: *Pure Dynamite: The Price You Pay for Wrestling Stardom*, Tom Billington (with Alison Coleman)
- *Hitman: My Real Life in the Cartoon World of Wrestling*, Bret Hart
- *Straight from the Hart*, Bruce Hart
- *Pure Dynamite: The Price You Pay for Wrestling Stardom*, Tom Billington (with Alison Coleman)
- *Pain and Passion: The History of Stampede Wrestling*, Heath McCoy
- *Broken Harts: The Life and Death of Owen Hart*, Martha Hart (with Eric Francis)
- *I'm Sorry, I Love You: A History of Professional Wrestling*, Jim Smallman

Chapter 4 – Opening quote: *Pure Dynamite: The Price You Pay for Wrestling Stardom*, **Tom Billington (with Alison Coleman)**
- *Hitman: My Real Life in the Cartoon World of Wrestling*, Bret Hart
- *Pure Dynamite: The Price You Pay for Wrestling Stardom*, Tom Billington (with Alison Coleman)
- Contributions from Keith Hart
- *I'm Sorry, I Love You: A History of Professional Wrestling*, Jim Smallman
- sportsanddrugs.procon.org

Chapter 5 – Opening quote: *Pure Dynamite: The Price You Pay for Wrestling Stardom*, **Tom Billington (with Alison Coleman)**
- *Hitman: My Real Life in the Cartoon World of Wrestling*, Bret Hart
- *Pain and Passion: The History of Stampede Wrestling*, Heath McCoy
- *Pure Dynamite: The Price You Pay for Wrestling Stardom*, Tom Billington (with Alison Coleman)
- *Slobberknocker: My Life in Wrestling*, Jim Ross (with Paul O'Brien) – note: the imagined scene where Jim Neidhart is stretched by Stu was inspired by Jim Ross's own experience
- *Straight from the Hart*, Bruce Hart – note: Bruce tells of the Drumheller dinosaur statue prank and that it was Jake Roberts that first pulled it on a rookie, but I have imagined that rookie to be Jim

Chapter 6 – Opening quote: *Hitman: My Real Life in the Cartoon World of Wrestling*, **Bret Hart**
- *Hitman: My Real Life in the Cartoon World of Wrestling*, Bret Hart
- *Pure Dynamite: The Price You Pay for Wrestling Stardom*, Tom Billington (with Alison Coleman)
- *The Hannibal TV* archive
- *The Eighth Wonder of the World: The True Story of André the Giant*, Bertrand Hébert and Pat Laprade
- *I'm Sorry, I Love You: A History of Professional Wrestling*, Jim Smallman

Chapter 7 – Opening quote: *The Wrestling*, **Simon Garfield**
- daveyboysmith.com
- Contributions from British wrestling historian Tony Earnshaw
- *Hitman: My Real Life in the Cartoon World of Wrestling*, Bret Hart
- *Pure Dynamite: The Price You Pay for Wrestling Stardom*, Tom Billington (with Alison Coleman)
- *The Saturday Afternoon War*, Tony Earnshaw
- CNN: *Death Grip*
- *Chris and Nancy: The True Story of the Benoit Murder-Suicide & Pro Wrestling's Cocktail of Death*, Irvine Muchnik
- *Pain and Passion: The History of Stampede Wrestling*, Heath McCoy
- 'Living with Dynamite', *Fight Spirit Magazine* (issue 88)

Chapter 8 – Opening quote: *Hitman: My Real Life in the Cartoon World of Wrestling*, **Bret Hart**
- *Hitman: My Real Life in the Cartoon World of Wrestling*, Bret Hart
- Contributions from Bruce Hart
- *Straight from the Hart*, Bruce Hart

Chapter 9 – Opening quote: *Wrestling Observer Newsletter* **archive**
- *Pure Dynamite: The Price You Pay for Wrestling Stardom*, Tom Billington (with Alison Coleman)
- *Wrestling Observer Newsletter* archive
- 'Living with Dynamite', *Fight Spirit Magazine* (issue 88)
- *Hitman: My Real Life in the Cartoon World of Wrestling*, Bret Hart

- Contributions from Bruce Hart
- *Straight from the Hart*, Bruce Hart

Chapter 10 – Opening quote: *Wrestling Observer Newsletter* archive
- *Hitman: My Real Life in the Cartoon World of Wrestling*, Bret Hart
- *Pure Dynamite: The Price You Pay for Wrestling Stardom*, Tom Billington (with Alison Coleman)
- Contributions from Bronwyne Billington
- 'Living with Dynamite', *Fight Spirit Magazine* (issue 88)
- *The Saturday Afternoon War*, Tony Earnshaw
- *Dark Side of the Podcast: The Dynamite Kid*

Chapter 11 – Opening quote and scene: *WWE Network*
- *Death of the Territories*, Tim Hornbaker

Chapter 12 – Opening quote: Contribution by Ross Hart
- *Hitman: My Real Life in the Cartoon World of Wrestling*, Bret Hart
- *Wrestling Observer Newsletter* archive
- *Alberta Report*, 26 March 1984
- *Pure Dynamite: The Price You Pay for Wrestling Stardom*, Tom Billington (with Alison Coleman)

Chapter 13 – Opening quote: *Hitman: My Real Life in the Cartoon World of Wrestling*, Bret Hart
- *Wrestling Observer Newsletter* archive
- *Pure Dynamite: The Price You Pay for Wrestling Stardom*, Tom Billington (with Alison Coleman)
- *Death of the Territories,* Tim Hornbaker
- *I'm Sorry, I Love You: A History of Professional Wrestling*, Jim Smallman
- *Hitman: My Real Life in the Cartoon World of Wrestling*, Bret Hart

Part Two – Opening quote: *The Pro Wrestling Hall of Fame: The Tag Teams*, Greg Oliver and Steven Johnson

Chapter 14 – Opening quote: *Pure Dynamite: The Price You Pay for Wrestling Stardom*, Tom Billington (with Alison Coleman)
- *Pure Dynamite: The Price You Pay for Wrestling Stardom*, Tom Billington (with Alison Coleman)
- *Pain and Passion: The History of Stampede Wrestling*, Heath McCoy
- *Hitman: My Real Life in the Cartoon World of Wrestling*, Bret Hart
- *Straight from the Hart*, Bruce Hart
- *Wrestling Observer Newsletter* archive

Chapter 15 – Opening quote: *Hitman: My Real Life in the Cartoon World of Wrestling*, Bret Hart
- *Pure Dynamite: The Price You Pay for Wrestling Stardom*, Tom Billington (with Alison Coleman)
- *Hitman: My Real Life in the Cartoon World of Wrestling*, Bret Hart
- *Straight from the Hart*, Bruce Hart
- *Bad to the Bone: 25 Years of Riots and Wrestling,* 'Rotten' Ron Starr and Rock Rims

Chapter 16 – Opening quote: *Pure Dynamite: The Price You Pay for Wrestling Stardom*, Tom Billington (with Alison Coleman)
- WWE Network
- *Pure Dynamite: The Price You Pay for Wrestling Stardom*, Tom Billington (with Alison Coleman)
- *Hitman: My Real Life in the Cartoon World of Wrestling*, Bret Hart

Chapter 17 – Opening quote: *The Hannibal TV* **archive**
- *Hitman: My Real Life in the Cartoon World of Wrestling*, Bret Hart
- *Jim Cornette's Drive-Thru* podcast archive
- *Pure Dynamite: The Price You Pay for Wrestling Stardom*, Tom Billington (with Alison Coleman)
- *Death of the Territories*, Tim Hornbaker
- *Wrestling Observer Newsletter* archive
- *Dark Side of the Podcast: The Dynamite Kid*
- Contributions from Gary Portz

Chapter 18 – Opening quote and scene: *Have a Nice Day: A Tale of Blood and Sweatsocks*, **Mick Foley**
- *Hitman: My Real Life in the Cartoon World of Wrestling*, Bret Hart
- *Pure Dynamite: The Price You Pay for Wrestling Stardom*, Tom Billington (with Alison Coleman)
- *Something to Wrestle With (Bruce Prichard)* podcast archive (with Conrad Thompson)

Chapter 19 – Opening quote: *Hitman: My Real Life in the Cartoon World of Wrestling*, **Bret Hart**
- *Pure Dynamite: The Price You Pay for Wrestling Stardom*, Tom Billington (with Alison Coleman)
- *Hitman: My Real Life in the Cartoon World of Wrestling*, Bret Hart
- 'Living with Dynamite', *Fight Spirit Magazine* (issue 88)
- Contributions from Gary Portz

Chapter 20 – Opening quote: *Pure Dynamite: The Price You Pay for Wrestling Stardom*, **Tom Billington (with Alison Coleman)**
- *The Eighth Wonder of the World: The True Story of André the Giant*, Bertrand Hébert and Pat Laprade
- 'Living with Dynamite', *Fight Spirit Magazine* (issue 88)
- Contributions by Mark Billington

Chapter 21 – Opening quote: *Pure Dynamite: The Price You Pay for Wrestling Stardom*, **Tom Billington (with Alison Coleman)**
- *Hitman: My Real Life in the Cartoon World of Wrestling*, Bret Hart
- *Pure Dynamite: The Price You Pay for Wrestling Stardom*, Tom Billington (with Alison Coleman)
- *Broken Harts: The Life and Death of Owen Hart*, Martha Hart (with Eric Francis)
- *Heartbreak & Triumph: The Shawn Michaels Story*, Shawn Michaels (with Aaron Feigenbaum)
- 'Living with Dynamite', *Fight Spirit Magazine* (issue 88)
- Contributions from Bronwyne Billington
- *Dark Side of the Podcast: The Dynamite Kid*

Chapter 22 – Opening quote: Contribution by Ross Hart
- *The Hannibal TV* archive
- *Hitman: My Real Life in the Cartoon World of Wrestling*, Bret Hart
- *Straight from the Hart*, Bruce Hart

Chapter 23 – Opening quote: *Something to Wrestle With (Bruce Prichard)* **podcast archive (with Conrad Thompson)**
- WWE Network
- *Pure Dynamite: The Price You Pay for Wrestling Stardom*, Tom Billington (with Alison Coleman)
- *Broken Harts: The Life and Death of Owen Hart*, Martha Hart (with Eric Francis)
- *Death of the Territories*, Tim Hornbaker

Chapter 24 – Opening quote: *Hitman: My Real Life in the Cartoon World of Wrestling*, Bret Hart
- *Pure Dynamite: The Price You Pay for Wrestling Stardom*, Tom Billington (with Alison Coleman)
- *Wrestling Observer Newsletter* archive
- *The Hannibal TV* archive
- *Hitman: My Real Life in the Cartoon World of Wrestling*, Bret Hart
- 'Dark Side of the Ring: The Dynamite Kid', *Vice*
- Contributions by Bret Hart

Chapter 25 – Opening quote: *Pure Dynamite: The Price You Pay for Wrestling Stardom*, Tom Billington (with Alison Coleman)
- *Straight from the Hart*, Bruce Hart
- *Pure Dynamite: The Price You Pay for Wrestling Stardom*, Tom Billington (with Alison Coleman)
- *Wrestling Observer Newsletter* archive
- Contributions by Bruce Hart
- *Pain and Passion: The History of Stampede Wrestling*, Heath McCoy

Chapter 26 – Opening quote: *Pain and Passion: The History of Stampede Wrestling*, Heath McCoy
- *Straight from the Hart*, Bruce Hart
- *Pure Dynamite: The Price You Pay for Wrestling Stardom*, Tom Billington (with Alison Coleman)
- Contributions by Bruce Hart
- *Pain and Passion: The History of Stampede Wrestling*, Heath McCoy

Chapter 27 – Opening quote: *More Than Just Hardcore*, Terry Funk (with Scott E. Williams)
- *Straight from the Hart*, Bruce Hart
- *Pure Dynamite: The Price You Pay for Wrestling Stardom*, Tom Billington (with Alison Coleman)

Part Three – Opening quote: *Wrestling Observer Newsletter* archive

Chapter 28 – Opening quote: *Hitman: My Real Life in the Cartoon World of Wrestling*, Bret Hart
- WWE Network
- *Pain and Passion: The History of Stampede Wrestling*, Heath McCoy
- 'Living with Dynamite', *Fight Spirit Magazine* (issue 88)
- 'Dark Side of the Ring: The Dynamite Kid', *Vice*
- *Hitman: My Real Life in the Cartoon World of Wrestling*, Bret Hart
- Contributions from Gary Portz
- *Wrestling Observer Newsletter* archive
- *Dark Side of the Podcast: The Dynamite Kid*

Chapter 29 – Opening quote: *Hitman: My Real Life in the Cartoon World of Wrestling*, Bret Hart
- *Hitman: My Real Life in the Cartoon World of Wrestling*, Bret Hart
- *I'm Sorry, I Love You: A History of Professional Wrestling*, Jim Smallman
- *Wrestling Observer Newsletter* archive
- 'The Forgotten Steroid Trail that Almost Brought Down Vince McMahon', *Vice*
- *Death of the Territories*, Tim Hornbaker
- *The Eighth Wonder of the World: The True Story of André the Giant*, Bertrand Hébert and Pat Laprade

Chapter 30 – Opening quote: *Wrestling Observer Newsletter* **archive**
- *Hitman: My Real Life in the Cartoon World of Wrestling*, Bret Hart
- WWE Network
- *Wrestling Observer Newsletter* archive

Chapter 31 – Opening quote: *Hitman: My Real Life in the Cartoon World of Wrestling,* **Bret Hart**
- *Hitman: My Real Life in the Cartoon World of Wrestling*, Bret Hart
- *Wrestling Observer Newsletter* archive
- *The Hannibal TV* archive
- *Dark Side of the Podcast: The Dynamite Kid*
- Contributions from Bradley Craig

Chapter 32 – Opening quote: Contribution by Ross Hart
- *Hitman: My Real Life in the Cartoon World of Wrestling*, Bret Hart
- Contributions from Mark Billington
- *Jim Cornette's Drive-Thru* podcast archive
- *Pure Dynamite: The Price You Pay for Wrestling Stardom*, Tom Billington (with Alison Coleman)
- *Something to Wrestle With (Bruce Prichard)* podcast archive (with Conrad Thompson)
- *Wrestling with the Devil: His Reign, Ruin, and Redemption*, Lex Luger (with Johnny Heller)

Chapter 33 – Opening quote: *Jim Cornette's Drive-Thru* **podcast archive**
- *Hitman: My Real Life in the Cartoon World of Wrestling*, Bret Hart
- *Something to Wrestle With (Bruce Prichard)* podcast archive (with Conrad Thompson)
- WWE Network
- *Wrestling Observer Newsletter* archive
- *Heartbreak & Triumph: The Shawn Michaels Story*, Shawn Michaels (with Aaron Feigenbaum)

Chapter 34 – Opening quote: *Wrestling Observer Newsletter* **archive**
- *Wrestling Observer Newsletter* archive
- *Hitman: My Real Life in the Cartoon World of Wrestling*, Bret Hart

Chapter 35 – Opening quote: *Have a Nice Day: A Tale of Blood and Sweatsocks,* **Mick Foley**
- *Hitman: My Real Life in the Cartoon World of Wrestling*, Bret Hart
- *Something to Wrestle With (Bruce Prichard)* podcast archive (with Conrad Thompson)
- WWE Network
- *Wrestling Observer Newsletter* archive
- 'Dark Side of the Ring: Brian Pillman', *Vice*

Chapter 36 – Opening quote: *Pure Dynamite: The Price You Pay for Wrestling Stardom,* **Tom Billington (with Alison Coleman)**
- *Pure Dynamite: The Price You Pay for Wrestling Stardom*, Tom Billington (with Alison Coleman)
- Contributions by Bronwyne Billington
- Contributions from Gary Portz

Chapter 37 – Opening quote: *Wrestling Observer Newsletter* **archive**
- *Hitman: My Real Life in the Cartoon World of Wrestling*, Bret Hart
- WWE Network
- *Heartbreak & Triumph: The Shawn Michaels Story*, Shawn Michaels (with Aaron Feigenbaum)

Chapter 38 – Opening quote: *Wrestling Observer Newsletter* **archive**
- WWE Network
- *Something to Wrestle With (Bruce Prichard)* podcast archive (with Conrad Thompson)

Chapter 39 – Opening quote: *Hitman: My Real Life in the Cartoon World of Wrestling,* **Bret Hart**
- WWE Network
- *Hitman: My Real Life in the Cartoon World of Wrestling,* Bret Hart
- *Something to Wrestle With (Bruce Prichard)* podcast archive (with Conrad Thompson)

Chapter 40 – Opening quote: *Wrestling Observer Newsletter* **archive**
- WWE Network
- *Hitman: My Real Life in the Cartoon World of Wrestling,* Bret Hart
- *Wrestling Observer Newsletter* archive

Chapter 41 – Opening quote: *The Hardcore Diaries,* **Mick Foley**
- *The Hardcore Diaries,* Mick Foley

Chapter 42 – Opening quote: *The Rock Says…: The Most Electrifying Man in Sports-Entertainment,* **The Rock (with Joe Layden)**
- *Broken Harts: The Life and Death of Owen Hart,* Martha Hart (with Eric Francis)
- 'Dark Side of the Ring: The Final Days of Owen Hart', *Vice*
- *Hitman: My Real Life in the Cartoon World of Wrestling,* Bret Hart
- *Wrestling Observer Newsletter* archive
- *Something to Wrestle With (Bruce Prichard)* podcast archive (with Conrad Thompson)
- *Nitro,* Guy Evans
- www.espn.com/magazine/vol5no24davey

Chapter 43 – Opening quote and scene: *Live Audio Wrestling*
- *Wrestling Observer Newsletter* archive
- *Something to Wrestle With (Bruce Prichard)* podcast archive (with Conrad Thompson)
- *Straight from the Hart,* Bruce Hart
- *Pain and Passion: The History of Stampede Wrestling,* Heath McCoy
- www.espn.com/magazine/vol5no24davey

Epilogue – Opening quote: *Pure Dynamite: The Price You Pay for Wrestling Stardom,* **Tom Billington (with Alison Coleman)**

David Smith – Opening quote: *Wrestling Observer Newsletter* **archive**
- WWE Network
- *Hitman: My Real Life in the Cartoon World of Wrestling,* Bret Hart
- *Wrestling Observer Newsletter* archive
- Contribution from Bradley Craig
- *Nitro,* Guy Evans
- 'Dad slams British Bulldog death verdict', *Manchester Evening News*
- 'British Bulldog Davey Boy Smith Set for WWE Hall of Fame Induction Thanks to His Family's Hard Work', *Sports Illustrated*

Thomas Billington – Opening quote: *Wrestling Observer Newsletter* **archive**
- *Pure Dynamite: The Price You Pay for Wrestling Stardom,* Tom Billington (with Alison Coleman)
- CNN: *Death Grip*
- *Chris and Nancy: The True Story of the Benoit Murder-Suicide & Pro Wrestling's Cocktail of Death,* Irvine Muchnik

- *Pain and Passion: The History of Stampede Wrestling*, Heath McCoy
- *Talk is Jericho* podcast archive
- Contributions from Gary Portz
- *Wrestling Observer Newsletter* archive
- 'Dark Side of the Ring: Benoit', *Vice*
- Contributions from Mark Billington
- Contributions from Michelle Billington
- Contributions from Bruce Hart
- Contributions by Bronwyne Billington
- 'British Bulldog Davey Boy Smith Set for WWE Hall of Fame Induction Thanks to His Family's Hard Work', *Sports Illustrated*

INDEX